# Family
# Games

# Family Games

## by Lincoln David Stein

created by
Media Projects
Incorporated

MACMILLAN PUBLISHING CO., INC.
New York
COLLIER MACMILLAN PUBLISHERS
London

*To my family*

*I'd like to thank my cousins
Alix and Claudia for
introducing me to Parcheesi;
my brothers and the kids on my
road for hard knock experience
in many backyard games; my
father, for occasionally losing
at Checkers; the librarians at
Katonah Library for checking
out and checking in seventeen
books at a time; Mara, for
giving me my first experience of
a Scrabble fiend; Rafael, who
gave me the definitive rules for
Touch Football; Brian, who
pointed out half a dozen
mistakes in them; and Carter,
who disagreed with most of the
corrections. And of course my
mother/editor, without whom
neither this book nor its author
would have come to be.*

Copyright © 1979 by Media Projects Incorporated

Macmillan Publishing Co., Inc.
866 Third Avenue, New York, New York 10022
Collier-Macmillan Canada Ltd.

Library of Congress Cataloging in Publication Data

Stein, Lincoln David.
  Family games.
  Includes index.
  1. Games. 2. Family recreation. I. Title
GV1201.S813  1979  794  79-13257
ISBN 0-02-613750-X

Photography by Sally Andersen-Bruce

The author and photographer wish to thank D&G Army Navy, New Milford, Connecticut, for permission to photograph their pin ball machines; The Computer Corner, White Plains, New York, for permission to photograph Video games and Boris; and the Board of Cooperative Educational Services (BOCES), Westchester County, New York, for permission to photograph computers.

Design by Mary Gale Moyes

First Printing 1979

Printed in the United States of America

# Table of Contents

# Family
# Games

# Introduction

The way a family plays is unlike the way the rest of the world plays. We play Gin Rummy for "Gin only" because my youngest brother doesn't appreciate strategy, and my mother refuses to keep score anyway. We don't use the "en passant" move in Chess because it mixes everyone up. We use ghost players on base in Stickball because there aren't enough other kids on our road to make teams of more than two or three. And when we were little, we taught the youngest children to play Hide and Seek by counting to ten, sticking out one finger, counting to ten again, then sticking out another finger, until all their fingers were exposed; they didn't know how to count to a hundred. In our family, and probably in yours, play is idiosyncratic and informal: rules are eased when they are too hard, spiced up when they are too bland.

And this is good. At home, the rules of a game can't be treated like china dolls. Games are to be played with, even battered like rag dolls, until they have taken on a comfortable shape. How else could such an enormous variety of games and variations have come to be? Somebody is always changing something old, inventing something new. Among family and friends, a game is fair so long as everyone shares the same notion of the basic goal and the rules that govern how you get there.

Family Games is written in just that spirit. You'll find here all the best-loved games, whether they were born long before Grandma's childhood or are as new as yesterday. But they are not "according to Hoyle." For each game, you will find the number of players, equipment needed, the object, how to get started and how to proceed, and all the standard regulations. Following this information, however, you may also find ways to make games less competitive to younger children or easier for inexperienced players; ways to increase the challenge for experts or older people; how to make the games longer, or shorter, or quieter, or rowdier; how to adapt a game to crowds of friends; and how to keep kibbitzers away.

Many games, especially those played in streets and backyards, have so many local variations (and even different local names) that it is impossible to give a definitive version. For these we suggest alternate rules, and ways to solve disputes should they arise. In some cases, particularly regulation sports such as Stickball and Football, we have given both a relaxed version, with few rules and fewer penalties, and a more proper set of regulations. Those who play in a backyard with two players on a team (one of whom is not yet out of kindergarten), will probably choose the former. Those who play on a large field with a sufficient number of players of equivalent skills and competitive natures, may choose the latter. In either case, the way to play is clearly explained, and will not be hurt by compulsiveness or compromise. For some of the more complicated games, easy-to-grasp strategies are included to help you get the feel of the game more quickly. Drawings and photographs will help you understand setups and maneuvers, and also introduce you to equipment you may not be familiar with, including computers. Since many people find reading instructions very difficult, there are step-by-step sample games for you to play along with as you learn.

Family Games deals with the real world, where marbles roll under radiators, poor losers throw tantrums, ping-pong balls are used for everything but Ping-Pong, and nearly everybody cheats at Solitaire. This book offers all sorts of sensible advice on how to compare the feats of long-legged teenagers with those of short-legged toddlers, what to do with used paper after an evening of Hangman, how to play Tag after sunset, and how to rig up eerie light for a Halloween party, make homemade prizes, and even discourage an avid games-player when you're just not in the mood.

Families play games of every sort, in every place, in every way imaginable. They may organize a Scavenger Hunt for a family picnic days in advance, but find themselves in an impromptu game of Twenty Questions on the way there. They may insist on the strictest protocol for Poker, but enjoy Badminton without benefit of a net. The same family that harbors a computer game expert may house two vicious Soccer players as well. And while parents may find themselves absorbed in a teenager's Tarot reading one minute, they may have to attend to a toddler game of Wastebasket Toss the next. This book covers a staggering range of games and circumstances, ages and preferences. Beginning with Party Games from Pin the Tail to Charades, the seven chapters go on to include Picnic Games (such as Sack Races and Tug of War), Backyard and Street Games, Anywhere Games that can be played with no more equipment than words or a pencil and paper, Card Games, Board Games (including brand name ones like Monopoly), and Game Room Games, where Ping-Pong tables share space with home computers. You'll find a lot of everything: old-timers like Marbles, newcomers like Frisbees, the elegance of Croquet, the excitement of Roulette, the glamour of Pinball, and dozens of variations of Poker. There are even contests, tournaments, carnivals and fortune-telling games. Each section begins with those games best for the youngest players, continues with intermediate games that can usually be shared among people of disparate ages, and concludes with the most sophisticated games in that category.

But Family Games doesn't have everything. Often the decision to exclude a game was difficult, if not painful. We considered popularity first. If a game has been around for a good long time and is still going strong, it was considered a ''classic'' and included. If a game is new, but its following is increasing rapidly from year to year, it too was included. When we had to choose among several similar games, all popular and all excellent, something had to give. Many games, though not explained in detail, are mentioned in discussion of genres, such as Simulation Games and First Board Games. And, we must admit, personal preference at times colored our choices.

Checkers checked out poorly; many stores don't even stock it any more. But we like it too much to leave it out. And Wari, a game that is rarely for sale because it is hardly known outside its native lands in Africa, was a last-minute choice because it can be played with pebbles in an egg carton, and is so terrific it ought to have publicity. Preference dictated in other ways, too. My family has always enjoyed Tarot, so the section on fortune telling grew rather long. Although we never cared for Dominoes, we love to line the tiles up and knock them over, so the Domino Topple highlights the section on Dominoes.

When neither popularity nor preference came to our aid, we based our decision on how well we felt the game was suited to the family situation. If you've ever tried to round up four—and only four—players in your family, you'll know that a game that can't be played by a flexible number of people is out. Bridge is one of those. Bridge was out on another score too: any attempt to give a bit of leeway here and there on the formalities of the rules would so horrify Bridge players that the heresy did not seem worth it. Age and skill also matter. You may be able to beat your six-year-old sister at Poker, but she can still understand the game. Poker yes, Pinochle no. Regulation Basketball is out because it requires two nets and ten players, items lacking even if you count the neighbors. And finally, for no particular reason, some games, like Ledgeball and King of the Mountain, simply slipped through the cracks.

We are satisfied that Family Games includes almost all the best-loved—and best—games for families. We hope it gives the reader as much pleasure as we have had playing them in our own family and bringing them all together for your enjoyment.

# Party Games

# Chapter 1
# Party Games

The games in this section are those typically played at parties. Many are for children's birthday parties, but there are also some special holiday games and a few parlor games for adults.

If you're unsure of how people will feel about playing games at a party, don't plan them. Instead, have a few games in mind to suggest if the party seems to call for them. Or try an impromptu party: "How about coming over to play Charades tonight?" That way friends are free to say, "No thank you."

Birthday parties, a delight to remember and a dread to give, can hang upon your choice of games. If the games are too competitive for young children, there will be tears, fights and calls to Mommy. If the games are too tame for older children, you'll be left with your Pin-the-Tails in your hand while they troop out the door to play ball. Good sense is needed, too, in deciding the order in which games are presented and how long each should last.

For preschoolers, choose the least competitive games, like Pass the Beanbag; Duck, Duck, Goose; and Fishing. Reduce competition even more by not announcing a winner or offering a prize. When only one child

is left standing in Pass the Beanbag, just announce that's the end of the game. No one will mind.

Avoid games that require blindfolds, unless the children are over six; both Blind Man's Buff and Pin the Tail can confuse and frighten younger children. For older children, Blind Man's Buff is an interesting challenge, Musical Chairs is gratifyingly competitive, and Simon Says tests skill and coordination.

With children of any age, an active, exciting game can end in wildness. When things get out of hand, stop the game short and switch to something quiet and controlled, like Mother May I. When that gets boring, try a game with a concrete reward, such as Pass the Surprise, or Fishing.

The traditional games here are not the only ones that can be included in a birthday party. Picnic games can be used for outdoor birthday parties; and some of them, such as a Potato Race, work fine inside too. To fill up time, adapt Easter Egg Hunt to an indoor game by hiding jelly beans for the children to collect in paper lunch bags. Spider Web, a Halloween game, is another time killer. Both of these games have the additional advantage of providing a prize for each child.

## PASS THE SURPRISE

*Six or more players*

*A small present*
*Tissue paper*
*Tape or string*
*Phonograph or radio music*

*OBJECT: To be holding the unwrapped present when the music stops*

Wrap the present in many layers of tissue paper, each layer secured with tape or string. Different colors of tissue will distinguish one layer from another and make the game easier for young children. Seat the players in a circle, hand one of them the wrapped present, and start the music. Each player passes the present to the neighbor on his right. When the music stops, the player holding the present is allowed to peel off a single layer of tissue. The game continues, and another layer of paper is removed from the present each time the music stops. The player who peels off the last tissue layer gets the present.

Any sensible child will feel conflict between the rules of the game, which require him to pass the present on, and greed, which tells him to hold onto it until the music stops. The distinct rhythm of a waltz or march might encourage steady passing, and perhaps a round of consolation prizes is a good idea for preschoolers.

*EASY BEANBAGS*

*Fill a small child's sock up to the heel with dried navy (pea) beans or other small beans. Tie the top of the sock into a knot above the heel. Cut off the excess with scissors. Or, fill a stray mitten with beans. Stitch up the opening with needle and thread. Either of these makes a small, easy-to-handle bean bag.*

## PASS THE BEANBAG

*Eight or more players*

*Beanbag*

*OBJECT: To pass the beanbag without dropping it*

The players stand in a circle, and one of them starts to pass the beanbag around to his right. The beanbag is passed around and around the circle, as fast as possible, until somebody drops it. Whoever drops the beanbag must sit down outside the circle, and the game continues until only one person, the winner, is left standing.

This easy version is challenging enough to three-year-olds, but must be made harder as children get older. Instead of just passing, try tossing the beanbag from player to player, passing it backwards through spread legs, or handing it around the circle with eyes closed.

# MUSICAL CHAIRS

*Five or more players*

*A set of chairs one less than the number of players*
*Piano, radio or phonograph music*

*OBJECT: To sit down in a chair when the music stops*

Set the chairs up in two rows, back to back, so their seats face outward. The players arrange themselves around the chairs. A nonparticipant starts the music, and the players march or run in time to the rhythm around and around the group of chairs. The instant the music is stopped, everyone must sit down in a chair; lap sitting doesn't count. Since there is one less chair than there are players, one person is left standing. This person is out of the game. Now one chair is removed, and the music starts again. The game continues until only one chair remains, and the player who gets it is the winner.

The faster the music, and the more unpredictable the stops, the wilder the game. But the wilder the game, the more pushing and shoving, and possibly fights and bruises. It's best to have a choice of several tempos at your disposal, like a waltz, a brisk march, and the galloping portions of the William Tell Overture.

## MUSICAL HODGEPODGE

*If you can't get together the chairs needed for Musical Chairs, try this crazy version: Scatter various objects around the room (stuffed animals, pillows, balls) again one less than the number of players. When the music stops, each player must make a dive for an object. The empty-handed player is out.*

## DUCK, DUCK, GOOSE

*Six or more players*

**OBJECT: To remain seated in the ring, and to avoid getting put into the frying pan**

Choose one player to be the first "Goose" (or tapper). The other players sit in a circle. There has to be a good deal of space outside the circle so children can run around it without tripping over furniture.

The Goose walks around the circle, tapping each player on the head and saying, "Duck, duck, duck, duck..." as he taps. When the Goose has lulled the ducks into inattention, he taps one of them and says "goose" instead of "duck." This new Goose must then leap up and chase the tapper around the circle, trying to tag him before he can run completely around the circle and sit down in the vacant spot. The tapper is safely a duck again once he has sat down, and the game continues with the new Goose as tapper. But if the tapper is caught before he can take his seat, his penalty is to sit in the middle of the circle, the "frying pan," until another Goose is caught to take his place.

There is no particular end to the game, and no winner, making it ideal for young players.

## MOTHER MAY I

*Six or more players*

**OBJECT: To reach Mother**

Clear the room of obstacles. Select one boy or girl to be "Mother." Mother stands at one end of the room, and the other players all line up facing her along the opposite wall.

Mother calls out instructions to each child in turn. She may say, "Joey, take two giant steps," or "Mary, take six baby steps." Before making a move, however, the player called must ask, "Mother, may I?" Mother can either give her permission or say, "No, you may not." (If refusals are too frequent, you can also play that Mother always has to give permission.) If a player forgets to ask permission, disobeys, or doesn't take the correct type or number of steps, he must go back to the wall to await his next turn. Anyone caught moving between turns must go back to the wall too. The first player to reach Mother and touch her is the winner, and becomes the next Mother.

This is a game that tests the fairness of players. Mother can, for example, give all the giant steps to her best friend, and a single baby step to everyone else. However, the censure of the group usually prevents such abuses of power, and Mother soon learns to treat her children more or less equally.

### THE STEPS

*Giant step: The longest step a player can take.*

*Baby step: The smallest step a player can take, usually understood to mean the heel of one foot must touch the toe of the other.*

*Umbrella step: A twirl in which the player puts one foot forward, twirls completely around on that foot and lands on the other foot, still facing forward.*

*Kangaroo step: A jump forward on both feet.*

*Pogo step: A hop forward on one foot.*

16

# SIMON SAYS

*Four or more players*

**OBJECT: To carry out Simon's instructions properly**

Select one player to be "Simon." All the other players line up in a row facing Simon.

Simon gives the players simple instructions, such as, "Touch your toes," or "Raise your right hand," which all the players respond to simultaneously. If Simon begins his command with the words "Simon says," the players are to obey. But if Simon does not start his command with those words, players must not follow his instructions. Players are out if they obey when they were supposed to disobey, disobey when they were supposed to obey, or make the wrong movement entirely. The last player left in the game is the winner, and becomes the next Simon.

Simon, of course, tries to trick players into error by giving orders very rapidly, by doing the actions himself, or by giving a set of repetitive orders and then breaking the pattern unexpectedly.

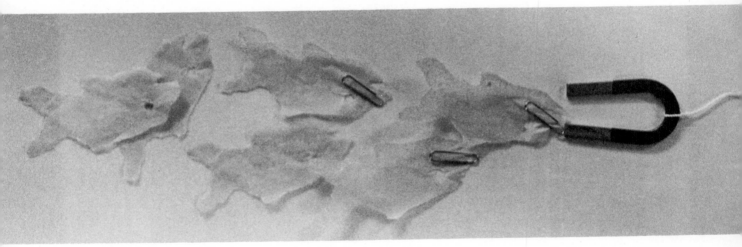

# FISHING

*Two or more players*

*Tissue paper*
*A box of paper clips*
*A carton with high sides*
*A dowel or other stick, about 2 feet long*
*A piece of string, about 2 feet long*
*A horseshoe magnet*

**OBJECT: To catch as many tissue paper fish as you can**

Make the fish by tearing or cutting the tissue paper into pieces about 3 inches long. The fish can be just scraps, or more carefully shaped and decorated with eyes and mouths. Make at least six fish for each player. Fasten a paper clip to the mouth end of each fish. Drop the whole school of fish into the carton, and place the carton on a table. Tie the magnet to the string, and the string to the stick, to make a fishing pole. Seat the players around the table. They shouldn't be able to see into the box.

Players take turns fishing with the pole into the carton. A player is allowed to drop the line in and drag it around the bottom as long as he wishes, but he is not allowed to get up, to peek into the box, or to pull his line part way out to check on his catch. All the fish attached to the magnet when he decides to pull in his line are his to keep. When each player has taken an equal number of turns, the one who caught the most fish is the winner.

## BLIND MAN'S BUFF

*Six or more players*

*Scarf or handkerchief to serve as blindfold*

*OBJECT: To avoid being touched by the Blind Man*

Choose one player to be the first "Blind Man," and blindfold him. All the other players stand in a circle around the Blind Man, join hands and rotate the circle. The Blind Man yells, "Stop" whenever he wishes, and points in any direction. The player he is pointing at quietly enters the circle with the Blind Man, and the other players stand still holding hands in a ring around the two of them. Now the Blind Man gropes with his hands, trying to catch the player, while the player ducks and dodges trying to avoid his touch. Since the player can't leave the ring, the Blind Man sooner or later manages to touch him. The player must then stand still and let the Blind Man feel his face and try to guess who he is. If he doesn't guess correctly, the player can join the ring again, and the game resumes. If he does guess, the player takes the Blind Man's place, blindfolded in the center of the ring, and the game continues. There is neither conclusion nor winner in Blind Man's Buff.

A more raucous version of the game can be played in a room where most of the furniture has been removed or pushed to one side. The players are free to move wherever they wish, while the Blind Man tries to locate and catch one of them. Whoever he catches becomes the next Blind Man, whether he is identified or not.

*HOMEMADE PIN THE TAIL*

*With a marking pen, draw an animal on a large piece of poster paper, brown wrapping paper, or cloth. A donkey is the classic, but a pig, hippo or bunny is fine too. Don't draw the animal's tail. Draw and cut out enough tails for all the players, and mark each with a number, or a child's name or initials. If the material you are using is cloth, you might want to fasten a safety pin to each tail to attach it to the picture when the game is played. Otherwise, use tape.*

*How fancy you want to make the drawing and the tails is up to you. Children might like to do a bang-up job with paints, crayons or markers.*

## PIN THE TAIL

***Three or more players***

***Scarf or handkerchief to use as a blindfold***
***Pin the Tail game, commercial or homemade***
***Freezer tape***

***OBJECT: To pin the tail closest to the right place***

Tape the animal picture to the wall at about the players' eye level. Give a tail to each of the players, and have them line up to take their turns. Each player in turn stands directly in front of the picture, from 5 to 15 feet away. He is blindfolded, and perhaps spun around once or twice to disorient him. He then does his best to walk toward the picture and touch the tail to wherever he thinks is the appropriate spot. The tail is pinned or taped at the spot he has decided on. After all the players have had their turns, the player who pinned his tail closest to the right place is the winner.

## PRIZES

You don't have to offer prizes to winners at a birthday party. An alternative that avoids hurt feelings is a favor for each child from a surprise box. Choose favors that are of various shapes and sizes so they will look intriguing when wrapped. Wrap each in tissue, and tie a string or ribbon to it. Put them all in a box. Each child gets to choose a ribbon and pull out his prize.

Choose the favors wisely. If you give packages of confetti, you'll regret it. Plastic whistles, too. And bubble blowing solution. Balloons aren't too bad, but you will have to stand the pops, the shrill noise of air let out slowly through the stem, and the whoosh of them rocketing through the air. Hand puzzles and magic slates, wind-up toys, costume jewelry, miniatures and crayons are all prizes which seem to lead to the least trouble, but still make kids happy.

# SNAPDRAGON

*Any number of players twelve years old or older*

*Large bowl of seedless raisins*
*Bottle of high-proof cooking brandy*
*Bowl and cover*
*Saucepan*
*Platter*

*OBJECT: To snatch raisins from a flaming platter*

Soak the raisins in the brandy in a covered bowl overnight. Just before the game is to begin, place the bowl over a pot of simmering water to heat the brandy so it will ignite. When the raisins are warm, pour the mixture onto a platter, carry it to the table, and turn all the lights off. Ignite the brandy to turn the platterful of raisins into the Snapdragon. Players grab at the flaming Snapdragon to get raisins to pop into their mouths.

Snapdragon, like any other flaming dessert, burns with an eerie blue light which flickers ghostlike over the raisins. Since alcohol burns with a cool flame, the raisins can be snapped up without injury. Since nearly all the alcohol is consumed in burning, there's no chance of players getting more brandy than is good for them. The taste, of course, is definitely alcoholic. One caution: Players should not wear flowing garments, and should roll up their sleeves before playing. Cool though it is, burning alcohol is still a flame.

---

## HALLOWEEN SPECIAL

Games for a young children's Halloween party should perhaps include no more than the traditional apple ducking, and the less well-known Spider Web. The excitement of masks and makeup, boos and cackles, makes anything more ambitious tend to get out of hand. But for older people, the weird and pseudo-risky game of Snapdragon, and the scary potential of Ghost Story make a better party. Be sure to set the stage for the party. Answer the door in utter darkness, to the moan and shriek of any other guests who have already made their entrance. Glow-in-the-dark paints can be spattered over an old sheet to make a good door-opening costume, even if it's not a costume party. An entrance fee to the party of a Jack O'Lantern—lit with a candle of course—is another idea. Their menacing light can provide the only illumination. If anyone has a strobe light to lend, its stop-action effect is very strange, and the effect of a "black" light (an ultraviolet tube that makes any white object fluoresce) is ghostly too.

# APPLE DUCKING

*Any number of players*

*Large metal tub or other container (you can also use the kitchen sink)*
*Apples*

*OBJECT: To get an apple in your teeth without using your hands*

Clean the tub well and fill it with water. Drop the apples in. Large apples are harder to get a bite on than small apples. Players should be warned ahead of time to wear clothes they don't mind getting wet. Hair will get soaked too.

Each player in turn tries to get an apple in his mouth without using his hands. This proves to be rather hard, and most have to put their heads totally under water, corner an apple against the side of the container, and bite into it. Those who get an apple are winners. Those who don't are losers.

For young children who are frightened of submerging their faces, use only a couple of inches of water so the apples barely float.

*A spiderweb as complicated as this might keep children busy for an hour.*

## SPIDER WEB

***Three or more players***

*Small wrapped favors or bags of treats for each player*
*String, crochet yarn, or a different colored spool of thread for each player*
*Name tag for each player*

***OBJECT: To follow a strand of the spider web to a present hidden at the other end***

To make the web, tie one end of the string or thread to a present, hide the present, and wander with the rest of the string around the house, weaving it around furniture legs, behind pillows, under carpets, and through railings, to form the first strand of the web. When you think the strand is long and complicated enough, cut the end of it, and mark it with a player's name tag. Repeat this until there is a strand of the web for each player to follow to his present. How long and tortuous you make each path, and how much you intertwine the strands with one another, determines the difficulty of the game. The hardest web (and most enjoyable for older children) is made with spools of sewing thread, a different color for each player.

The first task for each player is to locate his tag, so he knows where to start. Then each attempts to follow his strand, unsnarling it from others' strands and winding it up as he goes, until it leads him to his reward. Since everyone finally gets a present, everyone is a winner.

### YUCK

*One way to greet goblins at the door is to make them immediately close their eyes, then put something into their hand, and ask them to identify it before they can enter the house. Naturally, the something should be disgusting. A raw chicken liver, cold cooked spaghetti, or gelatin are awful, but not quite as bad as a live earthworm. Most revolting of all is a raw egg that has been soaked in vinegar until the shell has dissolved, leaving only a thin membrane surrounding the gelatinous innards. Of course if the guest squeezes it, there's another surprise in store.*

23

# GHOST STORY

*Five or more players*

*OBJECT: To invent a portion of a ghost story*

Players sit in a circle, and one is chosen to begin the story. He sets up a spooky atmosphere, and carries the plot to a suspenseful moment, such as, ''Just then the door creaked open, and....'' He stops. The player on his left is now obliged to take up the story at that point, and carry the plot to the next thrilling turn of events. When the story has reached the last player, it is his responsibility to end the tale with a bang. Weak excuses for endings, such as, ''And then he woke up and it was all a bad dream,'' are definitely to be frowned upon.

# PIÑATA

*Four or more players*

*Piñata, filled with candy or favors*
*Stick for bursting the piñata*
*Scarf or handkerchief to serve as a blindfold*

*OBJECT: To burst the piñata*

Hang the piñata from the branch of a tree or in a doorway. It should hang well above the heads of the players. Decide on the order in which players will take turns. The first player is blindfolded,

## HOMEMADE PIÑATA

*A homemade substitute for a store-bought papier mâché piñata can be made from grocery bags. Put one large bag inside another to make a strong container. Put candies or favors inside, and stuff the remaining space loosely with crumpled newspaper. Tie the top of the double bag together tightly with twine, leaving the ends long enough so you can later use them to tie the piñata to a tree limb, or to a nail above the doorway. Decorate the outside with colored markers, or in the traditional manner with crepe paper streamers. The crepe paper can be glued in loops, in short overlapping strips, or left in long streamers. You may either make the bag resemble a face, with paper ears added to the sides and streamers left long to suggest hair, or simply make a gaudy piñata that resembles nothing at all. The best part is always what's inside.*

led to the piñata, and handed the stick. He gets one chance to take a whack at the piñata. If he fails to burst it, the blindfold is put on the next player, and he steps up to take his turn. Players continue taking turns until, at last, one bursts the piñata. Unlike many games, however, everyone wins, because once the piñata spills its treasures all the players are free to grab what they can.

The piñata has religious significance in some areas. It stands for the Devil, tempting mankind with promised sweets, while the blindfolded child stands for the Christian faith, strong in its innocence. Sometimes the "innocents" are presented with three piñatas, one filled with rice, another rags, and the third candy. This is a double blind way to play, since no one knows which piñata to whack at.

## DREIDELS

*A dreidel is a four-sided top used for a relatively innocent gambling game which may be played for pennies. Each side of the top is printed with a Hebrew letter, which together stand for the message, "Nes Gadol hayah sham" (a great miracle happened there). The miracle referred to is the basis of Hanukkah: When the Jews recaptured their temple from the Syrians in 165 B.C., there was only a one-day supply of oil left to keep the temple light burning. Miraculously, the oil held out for eight days—the eight days that are now Hanukkah.*

*To play Dreidel, each player puts an equal number of coins in the "pot" in the center of the group. The first player spins the top. If it comes to rest with the N ( ) uppermost, he wins nothing, and the spin goes to the next player. If the dreidel shows S ( ), he must contribute another coin to the pot before passing the top to the next player. If it shows H ( ), the player wins half the pot; if it comes up G ( ), he wins all the money. When a player wins, the pot must be renewed before the next player takes his spin.*

# CHRISTMAS PARTY

You could call kissing under the mistletoe a holiday game of sorts, but the rules are too well known to discuss. Blind Man's Buff (page 18) can be played as a holiday game, with one rule change that brings it into a class with mistletoe: If the Blind Man catches a player of the opposite sex, the player must forfeit a kiss. Pass the Surprise (p. 14) might be fun on Christmas Eve, when unwrapping is on everyone's mind. Another way to while away the evening is Charades (p. 27), again played with a holiday proviso: that each team enact the name of a carol. The piñata game described here is traditional in the Southwest where piñatas are sold commonly; the dreidel game (in which gambling for money is the point) is played during the Jewish Festival of Lights, which occurs at about the same time of year. A Twelfth Night Cake used to be prepared for the last day of the old English Yule holiday which counted twelve days of Christmas. The rich, fruity cake was baked with a hard bean in the batter. The lucky person who found the bean in his slice of cake became King or Queen of Twelfth Night. There's no reason why you can't make such a cake for Christmas Eve, and instead of the winner being declared King or Queen, the prize could be the role of Santa, who gets to distribute the presents on Christmas morning.

*In this old-fashioned egg-dyeing method, eggs are wrapped in onion skins, then in cheesecloth. The natural pigments in the onion skins dye the eggs as they are boiled.*

# EASTER EGG HUNT

*Three or more players*

*Dyed or decorated hard-boiled eggs*
*Baskets or paper bags*

*OBJECT: To find as many eggs as you can*

After the Easter eggs are hard-boiled and dyed or decorated, hide them—preferably outdoors, under bushes and among roots or stones, over as wide an area as you wish. Then hope for fair weather on Easter morning. Of course there's always a possibility of rain, and cautious families might wish to hide the eggs indoors.

Call the players together and give each a container to gather his eggs into. On the shout of GO! they all scamper off like bunnies after the eggs. The player who gathers the most eggs is the winner.

Since this is such an old-fashioned game, you might enjoy an old-fashioned method of dyeing eggs as well. It is done with onion skins. Cut 6-inch squares of cheesecloth. Line each square with the dried outer skins of red or yellow onions. Skins can best be obtained from the bottom of the bin in markets that still sell unbagged onions. If you can't find an onion bin, the family might enjoy a rousing pre-Easter dinner of onion soup; save the skins of course. Lay a hard-boiled white egg in the middle of each square, bunch the corners together over the egg, and secure the top with a rubber band. Boil the packages for about ten minutes. Run cold water over them to cool them, and unwrap the eggs. They come out with a striking marbelized effect in shades of amber and russet, sometimes streaked surprisingly with green. They are even prettier if rubbed with vegetable oil to give them a sheen. Not only are these eggs more beautiful by far than commercially dyed ones, they are also "natural": no chemicals added.

# CHARADES

*An even number of six or more players, divided into two teams*

*A small pad and pencils*
*A watch with a second hand for keeping time*

*OBJECT: To guess the phrase or sentence acted out in pantomime*

Divide the players into two teams, and choose a captain for each. Decide which team will be the actors. The other team is the audience.

Each member of the audience team writes a phrase or sentence on a slip of paper. Some people allow any phrase or sentence at all, while others limit the choice to a single category, such as names of songs, titles of books, a well-known quote from history, or a proverb, such as, "A rolling stone gathers no moss."

The captain of the audience team distributes one slip of paper to each member of the actor team. Actors are not allowed to show their slips to one another.

The game begins as each actor in turn tries to convey the phrase on his slip to the other players on his team by using pantomime. Neither props nor sounds are allowed. An actor may try to convey the entire sentence in a single action, act it out word by word, or break words into separate syllables (such as "stay" and "pull" for "staple"). His teammates call out their guesses, and rely on signals from the actor to tell them if they are getting close. The captain of the audience team times each try from the moment an actor starts until the moment his teammates guess the entire message. He records the times on a piece of paper.

After all the actors on one team have performed their pantomimes, the two teams switch places, and the game continues with a new set of messages. The team to guess all the messages in the least amount of total time wins the game.

Some common gestures used in Charades are:

Chopping motion—message will be chopped into words (or syllables).

Number of fingers held up—first word, second word, third word, etc., or first syllable, second syllable.

Holding up two fingers, then clenching hand—next two words (or syllables) will be put together.

Arms clasped over chest—entire message will be acted out.

Finger to ear—"sounds like...."

Beckoning—"You're warm."

Pushing away—"You're cold."

Looking foward—future tense.

Looking back—past tense.

Counting on fingers—plural.

Twisting motion of hand—another form of the same word.

Pointing to a teammate—"You're the one who is getting it."

Waving both hands, palm up—"Forget that, I'll try another way."

Finger on tip of nose—"Got it on the nose."

# PARLOR TRICKS

Occasionally, a good trick or two can lift a party out of the doldrums. You might announce to your audience that you intend to break a pencil with a dollar bill. While the snickering is dying out, fold a dollar bill four times lengthwise, being extremely careful to get a good, crisp edge. A few preoccupied remarks about "sharpening" the dollar bill might not be amiss at this time. When the dollar bill is folded, have a volunteer hold a new pencil firmly between his hands, grasping it by its ends. With a firm gesture, raise the folded bill above your head and bring it down quickly on the pencil. It snaps in two.

The secret? While bringing the bill down, you stretch your forefinger out within the folded "V" of the bill, so that your finger, not the bill, snaps the pencil.

And here's another: Set an empty, small-topped beer or soda bottle upright on its base. Place a thin strip of paper on top of its mouth, and the mouth of another bottle on top of the paper. The challenge is to pull the paper out without upsetting the bottles.

Actually, the task is very easily accomplished if the paper is grasped firmly at one end between the thumb and forefinger while the other hand is brought down sharply on the center of the strip. The slicing motion whips the paper out; the bottles don't even jiggle.

And a third: Announce that you will step through a postcard, or other small piece of paper, by pulling it around your body and over your head.

You proceed to do so by first folding the piece of paper in half, cutting it as illustrated, and snipping with scissors first from one side, then the other. When this is finished, make a long cut along the folded edge, from the first snip to the last. Finally, unfold the postcard, open it up into a wide ring, step into it, and pull it up over your head.

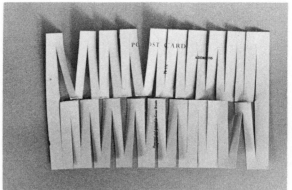

*Cut a postcard as shown.*

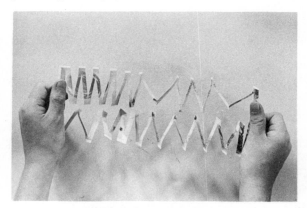

*Pull gently to open it out.*

# ESP

*Two or more players*

*Two pads and pencils*
*Deck of cards*
*A die from a set of dice*
*A glass*

*OBJECT: To test subjects for ESP*

There are three major categories of "ESP" (Extra Sensory Perception) which theoretically can be revealed by tests. These are clairvoyance, the ability to foretell a future event or perceive happenings at a distance; telepathy, the ability to receive messages through impulses from others; and telekinesis, the knack of moving inanimate objects by the power of thought.

Telepathy and clairvoyance are tested for by using an ordinary deck of cards. The testing situation should be quiet and peaceful, with no distracting activity. The tester (ideally a person who has no preconceptions about ESP) and the subject to be tested are seated several yards from one another, facing in opposite directions. Each has a pad of paper and a pencil. The tester holds the shuffled deck of cards.

To test for telepathy, the tester draws a card randomly from the deck. He looks at it, concentrates on its suit, and writes the suit down on his pad. The subject concentrates on receiving the tester's thoughts, and when he thinks he knows the suit of the card held by the tester, he writes it down, and indicates that the tester is to proceed to draw another card. This is repeated at least a dozen times. Then the tester's and subject's pads are compared. Since there are four suits, there is a one in four chance of the subject correctly guessing any suit randomly. So if twelve cards were drawn and guessed at, chances are that twenty-five percent, or three cards, will have been guessed correctly. Any significant departure from this of at least fifteen percentage points can be considered a tentative positive indication of telepathy. Further testing, of course, will tell more.

Clairvoyance is tested for in a similar manner, but the tester does not look at the card he has drawn until the subject has made his guess at the suit and written it down. Only after the subject makes his prediction does the tester glance at the card and record its suit.

Telekinesis can be tested for with a single die. The die is placed within a glass or other container and shaken by the subject while he concentrates on bringing up a particular number (say, 4). The number of times the die lands correctly on 4 is recorded, and divided by the total number of trials. Randomly, 4 should come up only once out of six throws (seventeen per cent). A deviation from this is considered evidence of some telekinetic power.

## OUIJA

*OUIJA (made by Parker Brothers) is a flat tablet of wood used to answer questions about the past, present and future. Printed on the board are the letters of the alphabet, the numerals 0 through 9, and the words YES, and NO. A pointer mounted on three stubby legs comes with the board.*

*For some people, though not for others, OUIJA works with great success. When two or more people place their hands lightly on the pointer and concentrate on a question, they say that their fingertips tingle and the pointer begins to move on its own, pointing out or spelling out the answer to the question. Whether the movement of the pointer is due to unconscious motions in the participants' hands, or to the operation of supernatural forces, no one knows.*

# TAROT

*Two or more players*

*Deck of Tarot cards*

**OBJECT: To divine information about a player's life**

Reading Tarot cards is an intuitive task, requiring imagination and insight. Not only are the meanings of the cards modified by their positions in the spread, but each card is modified by the natures of neighboring cards. If the message from a card seems ambiguous or meaningless when it is first turned over, the diviner should delay reading it until he has turned over a few more cards, to see what light they might shed on the interpretation. Interpretations like, "This means you're about to die," are crude, and may be painful to credulous questioners. Tarot cards speak of subtleties of influence, of trends and potential dangers, of the intricacies of the questioner's personality as it is played against the events of life, rather than simply of the events themselves. Practice helps, but you will find that certain people are by nature more clever diviners than others.

The cards used in the simple, effective spread presented here are the Major Arcana, a special subset of the full Tarot deck. Each of these picture cards—except the one called LE MAT (The Fool)—is numbered from I to XXI. Separate these cards from the deck. The rest of the deck can be used after you have mastered the procedure explained here; there are many books available on the subject.

One player, the person most skilled at reading Tarot, is usually the Diviner for all players. Choose another player to be the first Questioner. The Questioner poses a question aloud to the Diviner. It may be the character of the man she will marry, the course of a business deal, or a vague query that only the Questioner understands the portent of, such as, "Will I get what I am wishing for?" The Questioner is now asked to concentrate on the question, clearing other thoughts from his mind, while he shuffles the Major Arcana. Cards should be randomly inverted by the Questioner as he shuffles, since the presence of upside-down cards adds to the accuracy of the reading. After the Questioner is satisfied that he has imbued the cards with his mental state, he faces the Diviner and sets the cards face down in front of the Diviner.

The Diviner spreads the cards in the pattern shown on page 32, and begins his interpretation. During the reading, the cards are always viewed from the Diviner's point of view.

The Diviner turns one card at a time, starting with the card numbered 1 in the illustration, and proceeds through the cards in the order shown. Each card is turned from side to side rather than from top to bottom, so that the direction in which the card was placed is maintained. If the message from each card is clear to the Diviner, he may read it before the next card is turned. But the Diviner may postpone reading a card until the next several cards are turned to clarify its meaning. All six of the first cards, symbolizing external influences, must be turned and interpreted before the last four, denoting internal factors, are turned and read. After all the cards have been turned and interpreted, the Diviner, using the sum of all the information he has gleaned, should attempt to

## SETTING THE STAGE

The atmosphere for a mystical evening of Tarot reading, OUIJA, or ESP is by far the most important factor in its success. The participants have to be put in a properly receptive mood. Played at high noon, or to the glare of electric lights and the boom of a rock band, OUIJA boards will fail to move and cards won't reveal their secrets.

The best occasion for mystical explorations is when familiar comforts have forsaken you. A power failure is ideal. The house is dark. Messages from the outside world are cut off. Heaven knows when you will be able to cook again, or whether the water supply will hold out.

Since blackouts don't occur on schedule, however, you may have to simulate the atmosphere. You can't summon the smell of ozone, but you can burn incense. You can turn off the evening news, and substitute Indian sitar music. Even better would be a record of wolves howling, perhaps intermixed on your own tape with cracking thunder, moaning wind, drenching rains, and the sad call of the mourning dove. There are all the

wolf howls you'll care to hear on "The Language and Music of the Wolves," Tonsil Records; shrieks and moans are available on sound effect records such as those produced by Thomas J. Valentino, Inc. for Major Records. Quench the lights of course, and conduct your spiritual investigations by candlelight: a single tall taper, a stub stuck in a Chianti bottle, or one of the squat multi-colored candles available during the winter holidays. Firelight would be good too; chemicals that can be added to produce blue and green flames are available at Christmas.

If candlelight is found to be hard on the eyes, a single electric lamp shaded and placed on a table generates a spooky atmosphere. Use a 20-watt bulb. Or maybe you have a dimmer switch. For even better effect, use a colored bulb, available at hardware or lighting stores. Red is good, blue is best. But even a yellow bug light is better than nothing.

Dress appropriately. This is no time for pants suits. If you don't own flowing robes, headbands, feathers and heavy bracelets, at least let your hair down and wear a bathrobe.

answer the Questioner's initial query. Often, however, the Diviner may choose to use the question as a steppingstone to a discussion of other, perhaps more important, aspects of the questioner's life.

When a reading is finished, a second Questioner is chosen from among the remaining players. Players should not have more than one turn as Questioner.

### How to Read Tarot Cards

Each position in the spread has a different significance to which the reading of the card in that position relates. To read Tarot effectively, you must be familiar with the meanings of both the positions and the cards. If the card that falls into position #1, Present Influence, indicates indecisiveness (an upside down L'Imperatrice), that is a different meaning than the same card appearing in position #2, Immediate Obstacles. And since both these positions are in the group of six cards that denote external factors rather than internal ones, the interpretation is likely to relate more to other people or circumstances in the Questioner's life than if the same card showed up in position #7, the internal character of the Questioner himself. Intuition and subtlety enter into the reading too. Should the Diviner take an inverted L'Imperatrice to indicate an indecisive situation, or an indecisive person influencing the Questioner? The accuracy of the Diviner's reading depends on the strength of the feeling he develops for the Questioner as the cards unfold.

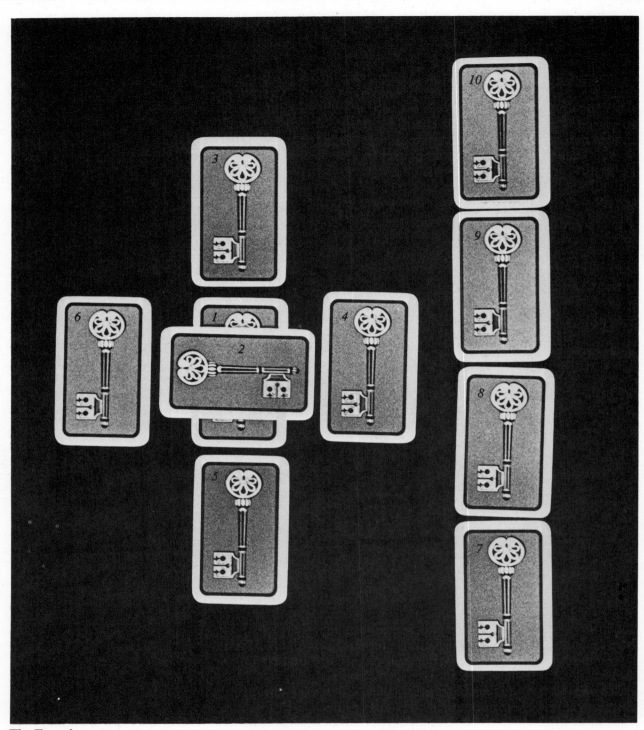

*The Tarot layout.*

To learn Tarot, read the explanations of both positions and cards many times, and refer back to them during practice games until you know them by heart. Study the sample game on pages 37 to 38, to see how your knowledge of the cards and their positions can be put to work in an actual card reading situation.

*The Positions:* Cards in positions #1 through #6 represent factors external to the Questioner which influence the course of his life.

#1: PRESENT INFLUENCES, atmosphere surrounding questioner. Shows the circumstances which influence his current actions.

#2: IMMEDIATE OBSTACLES, indicates the type and nature of the obstacles or preoccupations lying just ahead.

#3: SPECIFIC GOAL, represents either the ultimate or the short-range goal sought by the Questioner. May also indicate the best which can be achieved under the circumstances detailed by the card in position #1.

#4: PAST FOUNDATION, gives the nature of the influences in the far past which may be acting upon the Questioner without his knowledge. Represents the influence of such events on the unconscious mind.

#5: PAST EVENTS, gives the nature of events in the recent past which are affecting the Questioner's current actions.

#6: FUTURE INFLUENCES, shows the general sphere of influences just coming into being. May represent either a concrete event or a train of thought.

Cards in positions #7 through #10 represent the Questioner's inner self and his effect on the outer world:

#7: THE QUESTIONER, represents the Questioner as he now stands in relation to his environment. Often may symbolize the Questioner's personal qualities and traits.

#8: ENVIRONMENTAL FACTORS, shows the Questioner's influence on others. Indicates the Questioner's position in life and his effect on his environment.

#9: INNER EMOTIONS, indicates the Questioner's inner hopes, loves, fears or anxieties. May foreshadow a future train of thought.

#10: FINAL RESULT, indicates the eventual outcome of matters brought about by all the influences, external and internal, revealed by the other cards.

*The Cards:* Each card has its own special meaning, but may be interpreted in a variety of ways depending on the position in which it appears and the proximity of other modifying cards. If a card is inverted to the Diviner, its action is weakened, delayed, or totally reversed.

LE MAT, The Fool: This card signifies folly, extravagance, recklessness, careless happiness, or trusting naivete. May indicate an unwise action, or a denial of reality.

Inverted: A faulty choice in the past, or a mistake ahead. Describes inexperience, apathy or negligence rather than willful folly.

I. LE BATELEUR, The Magician: This card represents masculine creativity, dexterity, craft and skill. It indicates a resolute action carried forward to completion.

Inverted: Weakness of will. Limited interest. Lack of imagination. May signify the misuse of skills or the refusal to put forth effort.

II. JUNON, The Priestess: This card represents wisdom and enlightenment, insight and understanding. The card may portend a farsighted choice of the correct road, or reflect the wise influence of a woman in the Questioner's life.

Inverted: The reverse is short-sightedness and shallowness. An error of omission.

III. L'IMPERATRICE, The Empress: Whether the Questioner is male or female, The Empress is the sign of female accomplishment, of fruitfulness, fertility, comfort and success. The card may symbolize marriage, business or professional fulfillment, a pregnancy, or be read as the good auspice for any creative venture.

Inverted: Indecision and inaction. Sterility in the actual or figurative sense.

IV. L'EMPEREUR, The Emperor: This represents power, wealth and leadership. Indicates conviction, and determination to achieve goals. May signify a man having great effect on the Questioner's life.

Inverted: Immaturity, ineffectiveness or lack of strength.

V. JUPITER, Jupiter: This card reveals mercy and compassion. It may be read as referring to a close friend, or a religious experience.

Inverted: Overkindness, foolish generosity. May indicate the Questioner's vulnerability.

VI. L'AMOUREUX, The Lovers: Represents a coming trial or test of worth, and may advise the careful examination of people and circumstances. Can indicate temptations to be overcome in order to achieve harmony, and often predicts the beginning of a romance.

Inverted: The inverted card is a warning against a hasty decision, or represents fickleness and untrustworthiness in close relationships. Can indicate the onset of difficulties in love and marriage.

VII. LE CHARIOT, The Chariot: This card tells of trouble and conflict in either the past or future. It reveals the need for a solitary battle—external or internal—ending in victory. May represent triumph. If this card appears in the Final Result position, it is read as a firm "yes" to the Questioner's query.

Inverted: Defeat. Collapse of plans. Troubles undealt with.

VIII. LA JUSTICE, Justice: Symbolizes moderation, neutrality, virtue and integrity. It is sometimes associated with honor, chastity or other internal standards of behavior. It may indicate retribution or a bout with the law.

Inverted: The reverse of this card means bias or bigotry, lawlessness, violence, or a corruption of standards.

IX. L'ERMITE, The Hermit: This card is the sign of prudence and discretion. It may represent withdrawal and self-denial, refer to a self-imposed penance, or point to a friend's wise counsel.

Inverted: Rashness or immaturity, similar to the meaning of The Fool. Alternately, the inverted card may indicate over-prudence which results in dangerous delay.

X. LA ROUE DE FORTUNE, The Wheel of Fortune: The wheel represents the changing chances of life. Predicts an opportunity which may be taken advantage of, a stroke of good luck, or an unexpected change in the Questioner's situation.

Inverted: A turn of bad luck, an unfortunate person, or an opportunity not met in time.

XI. LA FORCE, Strength: Power, virility and courage. The card indicates the triumph of spiritual power and purity over worldly obstacles. It may also be the sign of hidden forces at work in the Questioner's environment.

Inverted: Weakness, impotence, pettiness; or the abuse of power.

**XII. LE PENDU, The Hanged Man:** Although ominous sounding, this card indicates nothing worse than a period of transition, of the abandonment of old ways. The card may warn that sacrifices or painful changes are necessary to achieve desired goals.

Inverted: The reverse meaning is a selfishness which is expressed as an unwillingness to sacrifice for the future.

**XIII. LA MORT, Death:** Stands for a drastic alteration or radical change. It indicates the loss of a familiar situation, and in different contexts can refer to death, disaster, illness, the loss of money, or simply an unexpected change of plans.

Inverted: Inverted, this card stands for stagnation or sterility. It may mean death escaped, or an illness recovered from.

**XIV. TEMPERANCE, Temperance:** Indicative of a new-found friendship, or a situation of harmony or trust. When applied to a person's character, the card represents patience, self-control and frugality.

Inverted: The reverse meaning is dissonance. It may indicate a falling out between friends, a lack of patience, or behavior that creates disharmony.

**XV. LE DIABLE, The Devil:** The appearance of this card indicates suffering and downfall, the action of evil forces. The card may refer to the bondage of mind or body by others, or to inner bondage. It can be expressed as chaotic relationships or guilt-ridden self-indulgence.

Inverted: Release from imprisonment, the surmounting of handicaps. Learning the ability to deal with internal evils.

**XVI. LA MAISON DE DIEU, The House of God:** Most commonly, this card portends catastrophe, a disastrous turn of events, or the loss of financial or family stability. It may also foretell a painful experience which upsets old beliefs and assumptions.

Inverted: Entrapment in an unpleasant situation. A period of unrelieved depression.

**XVII. L'ETOILE, The Star:** This card signifies hope and optimism. Its appearance in the pattern is a good omen for the outcome of events, indicating a promising opportunity and a bright future.

Inverted: Futile hope. Bad luck. Disappointment, or only transient good fortune.

**XVIII. LA LUNE, The Moon:** The presence of this card reveals deceit and dishonesty. It may signify false friends and hidden enemies, the presence of a disguised trap, an insincere personal relationship, double-dealing, or the Questioner's own lies and hypocrisy. The appearance of The Moon negates the effects of The Star in close proximity. When found as the first card in the spread, The Moon is occasionally taken to mean a mis-shuffle. (The Questioner may shuffle again to start afresh.)

Inverted: A minor deception, a mistake, or a simple misunderstanding.

**XIX. LE SOLEIL, The Sun:** The Sun outshines The Moon. It symbolizes a happy resolution, a joyous occasion, a time of comfort and satisfaction. Its appearance may tell of an engagement, marriage, or the birth of a child. In describing a person, it may point to a good friend.

Inverted: Separation and unhappiness. A friendship in trouble, an engagement broken, plans disrupted, or happiness delayed.

**XX. LE JUGEMENT, The Judgment:** This card may herald a final test, or indicate an improvement, promotion, or change of position. It can mean rebirth and rejuvenation.

Inverted: Reversed, this card means delay and procrastination, and may refer to a couple's divorce or separation.

**XXI. LE MONDE, The World:** Represents the attainment of all wishes and desires. It symbolizes the beauty of nature and triumph in undertakings, and points to a complete and fulfilled life.

Inverted: Inverted, this card indicates imperfection and failure. It sometimes declares that the Questioner refuses to recognize the meanings revealed by the other cards.

## Sample Tarot Game

The Questioner, fourteen-year-old Dana, asks that age-old question, "Does Michael love me?" She shuffles the cards, concentrating on her query, and gives them to us, the Diviner.

We lay the cards out one at a time, in the proper pattern, face down.

Before turning over the first card, Present Influences, we explain what its position stands for: "Dana, this card represents the present influences on you. It stands for everything in your environment which makes you act as you do." We turn the card over. It's L'ETOILE, The Star.

"This card is a good omen. It means that there is a chance for a bright future for Mike and you. Have you known Mike long?" "I started going out with him about three weeks ago," Dana replies.

Now we turn over the card in position #2, Immediate Obstacles, to see LE BATELEUR, The Magician. Ordinarily, this card refers to intelligence and skill, but in this case it's inverted; the bottom of the card faces left. (In all other positions, an inverted card is upside down to the Diviner.) What can this mean? The inverted interpretation of this card is "weakness of will, lack of imagination, or refusal to put forth effort." In what way is this an obstacle? Who is weak-willed? We decide to postpone the reading of the obstacle card until more cards have been revealed.

Now the next card, Past Foundation. Dana gasps and onlookers pale: it's LA MORT, Death. We quickly reassure Dana that the card doesn't mean "instant death," but merely reflects some occurrence in Dana's past which changed the way her life progressed. Did anything happen to her when she was young which really made a difference? "Gee, I don't know," Dana muses, "except...my family moved here from South Carolina when I was six. Could that be it?" That's it, since if Dana hadn't moved, her whole life afterward would have been different, not to mention the fact that her path and Mike's would never have crossed.

Now card #4, Past Events, is turned over to reveal JUNON, which refers to wisdom, understanding and enlightenment. We think it over. Does Dana share any classes at school with her boyfriend? Dana replies, "Sure, we have French class together. We sit next to each other and pass notes when Mr. Beetlebrow isn't looking." Since JUNON refers to a wise woman, we ask if Dana is good at French. "Sure am," says Dana, "got an A on my last report card! And on my last test I got every question right."

We're still thinking about that Immediate Obstacle card, which refers to will and effort. Perhaps it has something to do with how Mike's doing in class? "Well," admits Dana, "he's not doing so hot. He just doesn't study, and he doesn't like French." With this statement, the cards fall into place: The Immediate Obstacle to Dana's and Mike's relationship is friction between them over Mike's poor grades on the one hand, and Dana's good grades on the other. We offer this interpretation, and Dana nods; she'd felt the problem growing herself.

Now for Dana's Immediate Goal. We turn the card over to reveal L'AMOUREUX, The Lovers. Dana's goal is romance.

The next card, Immediate Future, is helpful. Turned over, an inverted LA LUNE, The Moon, is revealed. This indicates a minor misunderstanding between Mike and Dana. Because of the card's close proximity to Immediate Obstacle, the future card may well portend a quarrel between the friends brought on by Mike's jealousy over Dana's grades.

Moving on to the second, internal half of the spread, we turn over that crucial card, The Questioner, to reveal LA FORCE, Strength. This seems to describe Dana as a strong girl with the courage to speak her mind (which fits in well with our own observations).

The next card, Environmental Factors, is an inverted JUPITER. Jupiter inverted can mean "Overkindness, foolish generosity...or the Questioner's vulnerability." The card's presence in the Environmental Factors position indicates that the card refers to someone or something within Dana's sphere of influence rather than Dana herself—Michael, probably. Does this mean that Michael is easily hurt? Yes, perhaps, especially in consideration of Dana's direct personality, LA FORCE. These last two cards seem to warn Dana that if she isn't too sensitive, she could harm Michael's self-esteem without realizing it.

Card #9, Inner Emotions, refers to Dana's inner hopes or fears. Evidently, the card stands for fears this time. LA MAISON DE DIEU, The House of God, shows that Dana's great fear is that her tentative friendship with Mike will crumble all at once.

The last card, however, should allay Dana's fears. Card #10, Final Result, is LE PENDU, The Hanged Man. A good rather than a bad sign, this card indicates that sacrifice is necessary to achieve desired goals.

With all the cards revealed, we're now in a position to pull all the information together and offer our final interpretation to Dana: In order to achieve Dana's desired goal of romance (L'AMOUREUX), sacrifices are necessary both on Dana's and on Michael's part. They must hold together, despite the friction between them over French class (inverted LA LUNE), and Dana's somewhat strident, occasionally unfeeling manner (LA FORCE). With patience and determination, Dana and Mike may achieve a loving, trusting relationship.

As the cards show, Dana's simple question, "Does Michael love me?" is not simply answered. In the realm of human relationship straight yesses and no's are rare. The only answer we can give is a tentative one: probably not yet, but maybe in the future.

*The sample Tarot game after all
the cards have been turned*

39

# Picnic Games

# Chapter 2
# Picnic Games

Most picnic games are for a large bunch of people, and this is what keeps them fun. Although there is a winner, there are so many losers that they keep each other cheerful.

When you plan on picnic games, be sure to include enough of them so everyone gets to play, but no one feels they have to play them all. The hilarity at the sidelines is half the pleasure. On the other hand, try to get grownups in on the games, as well as the children. If the games are only for the kids, they will rightly feel they have been gotten rid of while the adults go about their more serious business. Adults have no advantage over children in most of these games, and, in something like a Yo-Yo contest, may be sadly out of date. Children have no great advantage either; they are as likely to drop the potato as anyone else. And there is little room for the star pitcher or long distance runner of any age to show off; no one is a champion "wheelbarrow."

Since many of the games are played in teams, keep this egalitarian spirit in mind. Not only should toddlers be equally distributed among teams, but each time a team is formed, it should be reshuffled from whatever bodies are available. Picnics are no time for permanent teams to line up under their own banners and try to win the day.

Suggestions are made throughout this section for handicapping the very young (or the very old), to give them a boost in races or contests. Anyone who shouts, "No fair," has failed to catch the spirit of the day. Some games and contests do require a touch of formality. There are starting and finish lines to lay out, and measurements to make of time and distance. How you mark lines depends on where your picnic is. On the beach, lines scratched in the sand are the easiest. On grass, you could lay out a length of string for a starting or finish line, or mark it with stray socks, sneakers and sticks. Extra markers should be available for marking distances in throwing or jumping contests. Measuring doesn't have to be done to the inch. Anyone who has an even stride can pace out distances, either to set up a course or to measure the distance of a throw or jump. Timing can be done on an ordinary watch that has a second hand. Timekeepers, referees and judges should change as frequently as the makeup of the teams.

Prizes are always a happy ending to a game or contest. For teams, a bag of jellybeans to share around is a good prize. For individuals, we have suggested homemade ribbons, and an occasional "cup" in the form of a mug.

# RED ROVER, RED ROVER

*Six or more players*

*OBJECT: To capture all members of the opposing team by break-ing through their chain*

Divide the players into two teams of equal strength. Each team chooses its own captain, and one team's captain is chosen to be the first caller. The teams face each other, at a distance of about 20 feet, and lock hands, wrists or arms to form a human "chain."

Starting with the first team, the captains take turns calling on a member of the opposing team in this way:

Red rover, red rover
Please send someone over.
Red rover, red rover
Send Roger (or Joshua or Madeline) over.

The person whose name was called dashes toward the opposite chain at top speed, yelling and grimacing to seem more terrible than he really is, and plows into the other team's human chain in an attempt to break through. If you, as a runner, manage to break through the chain, you triumphantly march back to your own team, taking with you as an addition to your team one or the other of the players whose grip was broken under your onslaught.

If you don't manage to break through the opposing chain, you are captured by them and form part of their chain, in the spirit of, "If you can't lick 'em, join 'em."

The team captains take turns calling names until the end of the game. If a captain is captured, a teammate takes over for him. The tide of strength shifts back and forth between the two chains for a while, until finally one team gains enough advantage to tip the scales. Eventually one team has dwindled down to a single player, at which point the game ends, with all those in the intact chain declared the winners.

# RED LIGHT, GREEN LIGHT!

*Four or more players*

*Markers for a starting line*

*OBJECT: To sneak up on the Light and be the first to tag him while his back is turned*

Pick one person to be the first "Light." The Light stands with his back to a convenient tree or wall, while all the others stand behind a starting line about 20 feet away.

When everyone is in position, the Light turns his face to the tree, yells "Green Light! 1—2—3 Red Light! " and snaps back face forward. While the Light is still green, all the other players rush toward him at top speed. But as soon as the Light has turned red and turned around, every player has to stand stock still. If the Light sees anyone moving, he sends him back to the starting line.

After closely scrutinizing all the runners to make sure there isn't a blinking eye among them, the Light turns around again, yells "Green Light! " and the performance is repeated.

The first player to reach the Light and tap him on the back becomes the new Light, and the game continues as before.


# POTATO RACE

*An even number of eight or more players, divided into two teams*

*Raw potatoes, one for each player*
*Two spoons*
*Two large paper bags*
*Markers for a starting line*

*OBJECT: To be the first team to carry all its potatoes to the starting line and drop them into a paper bag*

Indicate a starting line with sticks or other markers. Place two rows of raw potatoes about 30 feet beyond the starting line. Line up each team in a column behind the starting line, place an open paper bag next to the first player on each team, and hand him a spoon.

On GO!, the first player from each team runs out to the nearest available potato in his team's row, and attempts to scoop it up with his spoon and carry it back to the starting line. He is not allowed to touch the potato with his hands, and if he drops it must pick it up on his spoon again, until he gets it safely to his team's paper bag. He drops the potato into the bag, and passes the spoon to the next teammate on line. The process is repeated until all the team's potatoes are in the bag. The first team to get all its potatoes into the bag wins.

Potato races can be made easier for young children by arming them with large kitchen spoons, and using small new potatoes. To make the race harder, use large, uneven potatoes and teaspoons. To play with people of very mixed ages, place the potatoes in columns rather than rows, so that the first potato is only a couple of feet from the starting line, and the others at increasing distances. Line up the players so that the first in line is the youngest. He can scoop up the nearest potato. Older players have to retrieve the farthest potatoes.

## SACK RACE

*Any number of players*

*A burlap sack or worn-out pillowcase for each player*
*Markers for starting and finish lines*

**OBJECT: To be the first to cross the finish line by jumping with both feet in a sack**

Mark the starting and finish lines about 30 feet apart. Distribute the sacks or pillowcases among the players, and line them up at the starting line. Each player must climb into his sack, holding it up about him with his hands.

At the shout of GO!, the players set off jumping or hobbling with both feet inside their sacks toward the finish line. If a player falls, he may get up and continue on, but he can't take his feet out of the sack. The first player to make it over the finish line is the winner.

*These children are practicing for Wheelbarrow, One-legged and Three-legged Races. The boy holding his leg by his pants cuffs is probably not going to finish the race, and the one holding the wheelbarrow handles would do better to hold them in the crooks of his elbows.*

## ONE-LEGGED RACE

*Any number of players*

*Markers for starting and finish lines*

*OBJECT: To be the first to cross the finish line by hopping on one foot*

Mark starting and finish lines about 30 feet apart. Line up the players at the starting line.

On the shout of GO!, players race toward the finish line. The only catch is that they are required to race holding one foot up behind them, and hopping on the other. Some players find it easier to hold up the foot with the hand on the same side; others prefer to use the opposite hand. Also, you will find that you are probably either right- or left-footed. Practice hopping, to find out on which foot you do better. Anyone who releases his foot or stumbles to the ground is disqualified. The first player to pass the finish line is the winner. Alternately, after reaching the finish line, the hoppers can be required to switch feet, and to make the return journey to the starting line in order to win the race.

# THREE-LEGGED RACE

*Any even number of four or more players, playing as partners*

*Rags or large handkerchiefs for binding legs*
*Markers for starting and finish lines*

*OBJECT: To be the first partners to cross the finish line*

Mark the starting and finish lines about 30 feet apart. Players choose partners, and the two are bound together at the ankles with a rag or handkerchief, so that the right leg of one must move in unison with the left leg of the other. This in effect gives them three legs between them. Line up the bound partners along the starting line.

On the shout of GO!, the players stumble off toward the finish line. The first partners to make it, walking or crawling, win the race.


# WHEELBARROW RACE

*Any even number of four or more players, playing as partners*

*Markers for starting and goal lines*

*OBJECT: To be the first partners to get to the goal line and back*

Set up the starting and goal lines about 30 feet apart. Players choose partners, and the pairs line up at the starting line. One is the wheelbarrow, and must walk the race on his hands, while the other is the wheelbarrow driver, and holds his partner's two legs up as though they were the wheelbarrow handles.

On the signal GO!, the players lumber forward, the "wheelbarrows" lurching along on their hands, the drivers clutching their "handles." Ordinary people tend to collapse onto elbows and chests as they near the goal, but collapsing is allowed. Just pick yourself up and keep at it. When the teams reach the goal line they switch positions, the driver becoming the wheelbarrow. The first partners to get back to the starting line win.


# BACK-TO-BACK RACE

*Any even number of four or more players, playing as partners*

*Markers for starting and goal lines*

*OBJECT: To be the first partners to get to the goal line and back*

Set up the starting and goal lines about 30 feet apart. Players choose partners, and the pairs line up along the starting line. Each player must stand back-to-back with his partner, their elbows interlocked, with one partner facing the goal.

On the signal GO!, the partners race toward the goal, one player moving forward, the other being pulled backward. On reaching the goal, the players reverse directions so that the one who was running backward is now moving forward. Any pair breaking the elbow lock is disqualified.

The first partners to get back to the starting line win.

## CUPS AND RIBBONS

You can make your own First, Second and Third Place prizes from lengths of ribbon and paper circles. First is blue, Second is red, and Third is yellow. Cut the appropriate colored ribbon to about 8 inches and notch the ends. Cut two circles about 2 inches across from matching colored paper (or white). The circles can be traced first around the bottom of a juice glass. Fold the ribbon once across itself at an angle in the middle, sandwich it between the two circles, and glue both circles and the ribbon together. If you like, write the event or, later, the name of the winner on one side of the circle. To attach the ribbon to a winner's shirt, make a small ring of tape sticky side out, and stick it to the back of the ribbon.

For the more serious contests, such as the Picnic Pentathlon, the winner of the most events might deserve a more important prize. Gold medals and silver cups are out, but an inexpensive coffee mug (for milk too, of course) is a proud substitute.

## RELAY RACE

*Eight or more players in teams of at least four players each*

*Objects to pass from player to player; one for each team*
*Markers for starting and goal lines*

*OBJECT: To be the first team to complete the relay*

Divide the players evenly into two or more teams. Mark the starting and goal lines 30 feet or more apart, depending on how far you think the players can run. Line up the teams single file at the starting line, and hand the first player on each line a stick, handkerchief or other object.

On the shout of GO!, the first player on each team dashes to the goal line holding his relay stick, touches the line with his foot, and dashes back to his team. He puts the relay stick into the next player's waiting hands, and without a pause the second player rushes out and back, handing the stick to the next player in turn. The dash continues in relays until the last player has run up and back. The first team to complete the relay race wins.

A variation of this classic relay is to whisper a word, sentence or number to the first runner in each team. He has to memorize the message and whisper it to the next player after he has run his course. If a team has completed the relay race, but somehow the phrase has been garbled, it is disqualified from the race, and the next fastest team to have kept the phrase straight becomes the winning team. To avoid argument, it is best for a referee to write down each team's message beforehand.

Still another way to play is to make the relay object the next player in line, who has to be carried piggyback to the goal line and back. After being the rider, a player takes his turn carrying the following player. The last player in the line completes the race by carrying the first player. If adults and small children are playing together, you could allow kids to be riders only, and make the adults do all the carrying.


# TUG OF WAR

*Any number of players, divided into two teams evenly matched for strength*

*Long sturdy rope, made of a natural fiber such as hemp or cotton*
*Markers for center line*

*OBJECT: To pull the opposing team over the center line*

Choose the two teams carefully so they are as evenly matched for strength as you can determine. Mark a center line, and lay the rope down so the middle of it falls on the line.

The two teams take up their positions on either side of the line, each team grasping its half of the rope. There should be a clear space of rope about 3 or 4 feet long between the teams. Sometimes, the last person on the team acts as "anchor," and the rope is tied loosely at his waist. Naturally, an anchor should be the strongest member of the team.

At the shout of GO!, each team begins to pull on the rope, doing its best to pull the opposing team over the center line. If a member of one team crosses the line, if a team releases its end of the rope, or if all the members of a team come crashing down, the opposing team wins.

A traditional method of raising the motivation of tuggers-of-war is to replace the center line with a large mud puddle.

## OBSTACLE COURSE

*Any number of players*

*A watch with a second hand or a stopwatch for timing*
*Markers for starting and finish lines*
*At least four obstacles, which can include:*
   *things to step into, on and onto, such as bricks in a staggered*
      *pattern to step on, tires to hop in and out of, a long log or*
      *beam to walk along;*
   *things to jump over, such as a bale of hay, a big bag of peat*
      *moss or mulch, a heap of pillows;*
   *things to crawl through, such as a barrel with the bottom*
      *punched out, an old plastic garbage pail with the bottom cut*
      *out, a group of tires tied together to form a tunnel*

*OBJECT: To run the course in the least amount of time*

The type of obstacle course you lay out depends entirely on what appeals to you, and what you can easily rig up, so long as it is not likely to cause injuries. The list above gives you just a few ideas; you can add to it such things as a low stepladder to climb up and jump off, or require other physical feats of the obstacle course runners. They can be required to hop on one foot for part of the course, turn somersaults, or walk on hands and knees through a particular area. Just be sure all the players understand what is expected of them by going over the course thoroughly before a game begins.

Once the course has been laid out, complete with starting and finish lines, and you have explained carefully how to move through each obstacle and area of the course, each player gets a turn to race through the course in as little time as he can. If a player louses up on one part of the course (such as stepping off the beam he's supposed to walk along), he must go back to the beginning of that obstacle, start it over, and complete it successfully before continuing on.

As each player goes through the course, time him from start to finish. After everybody has had a chance, the one who made the best time wins the race.

# PICNIC PENTATHLON

*Any number of players*

*Markers for starting and finish lines*
*Markers for recording distances*
*FRISBEE*
*8-foot clothesline and several pillows or old mattress for high jump*
*Tape measure, yardstick or 6-foot rule for measuring (optional)*

*OBJECT: To win as many of the five events as you can*

A Pentathlon is one of those events people tend to get rather serious about, as it involves serious skills. A Sack Race may be comical, but a high jump isn't. Either hold a Pentathlon only for those in a particular age range, or handicap contestants of varying ages as suggested below. A referee, armed with tape or rule for measuring, is optional, but will certainly be helpful.

*FRISBEE Throw:* Set up a shooting line at the edge of any large, open space. Each player in turn throws the FRISBEE forward as far as possible, and the spot where it lands is measured with the tape or by pacing, or is simply marked with a rock or sneaker. The contestant who throws it farthest wins the event. Younger players may be helped by letting them throw from a position in front of the throwing line.

*Long Jump:* Mark out a starting line for the long jump. Contestants take turns making running leaps from the line. After landing, each contestant stays where he is until a marker is placed at the point where his rear heel is touching the ground. Alternately, his jump can be measured with a tape. The contestant who jumps the farthest wins. The starting line can be moved forward to help the younger players.

*High Jump:* Prepare a high jump area by padding it with a mattress or several pillows. Two noncontestants should act as the high jump by holding the ends of an 8-foot clothesline toward the front of the landing area. They should be sure to hold the rope loosely, so that if a player doesn't make the jump, the rope will slip from their hands rather than trip up the jumper. Start at a height of about 2 feet. Those who fail to make it over without touching the rope are eliminated. After everyone has had a try at one height, the rope is raised slightly, and contestants have another go at it. The last contestant left wins the event. To help young people compete,

the jump can be adjusted to relative height. If the rope is waist-high on an adult, it should be lowered to the child's waist before he takes his turn.

*Dash:* Mark the starting and finish lines for the dash at any convenient distance. One hundred yards is classic, but may be too far for some. Line up the players at the starting line. At the shout of GO!, they take off at top speed. The first to cross the finish line wins the event. Little kids with short legs can take part in the race as well, provided they are allowed to start further up the field.

*Hop, Skip and Jump:* This final event of the Picnic Pentathlon uses the same setup as the long jump. After making a running start, each contestant hops up on one foot at the starting line, lands on the same foot farther forward, skips ahead to land on his other foot, and finally jumps as far as possible to land on both feet. His final distance is measured from his rear heel to the starting line, and the farthest distance wins the event.

## TREASURE HUNT

*Any number of players*

*A pad of paper and a pencil*
*Freezer tape*
*Treasure (box of candy, or another prize)*

*OBJECT: To find the treasure*

Hide the "treasure" somewhere in the general area of the game: under or up a tree, covered by a rock, taped to the undersurface of a picnic table, recessed within a stone wall, or buried. Prepare a whole series of clues to lead up to the treasure. Write each clue on a sheet of paper. The first clue might say something mysterious, such as "Around the beast's neck"—a reference to the family dog's collar, on the inside of which is taped the second clue. The second clue leads to a third, and so on, until the last clue directs the seeker to the hidden treasure. All the clues are written down and hidden in their hinted-at locations before the hunt begins.

When all is prepared, the first clue is read aloud to all the players. From then on, it's everyone for himself. The players fan out, each trying to decipher the first clue and find the second one without letting their friends in on its hiding place. A player who thinks he knows the location of a clue sneaks to it unobserved, reads it, and replaces it exactly as it was. He then goes on to find the next instruction. Other good instructions might be, "A cold trail" (in the freezer), "Where the trumpets blow" (behind the trumpet vine in the garden), "Prettily potted" (in a flower pot), or "Watch the time!" (under a clock).

The player who finds the treasure wins it, or, if the prize is intended for all, shares it around.

## TELEPHONE (Rumor)

*Five or more players (the more the merrier)*

*OBJECT: To relay a message without garbling it*

This is a game for when picnickers are exhausted from all the other games and eager for an excuse to rest. It is also a swell way to pass along innocent bits of family gossip.

Just sit in a line, and choose a player at one end of the line to make the first "telephone call." He thinks up a funny message, short or long, and whispers it to the player next to him. He might whisper something like, "I heard Uncle Jack had a little argument with Aunt Vicki, and someone got a faceful of pancake batter." The next player, in turn, whispers the message in his neighbor's ear, and so on, down the line. When the message reaches the last player in line, he says it out loud. Somehow the message always gets so garbled along the way that even the player who made the call can't recognize it. Retracing the message along its route to find out who heard what is the best part of the game.

After placing one call, change places and have another player start a message.

# SCAVENGER HUNT

*Any number of players*

*Pad and pencil*

*OBJECT: To be the first to find objects fitting all the listed descriptions*

Scavenger Hunt is a marvelous affair, which combines excitement and suspense with imagination and humor. It's also a great way to keep children and adults occupied without a moment of boredom.

Make up a list of four or five descriptions which could apply to available objects. The more intriguing the description and the more it leaves to the imagination, the better. Equipment for a Rat Hunt, or Ghostly Trappings, are both excellent categories. They challenge the imagination, and the results can be hilarious. More serious descriptions, but equally ingenuity-stretching, would be Circa 1890 (that could range from an antique to a picture of Great Grandma), or Scientific Specimens (anything from pond water to a moose head). For younger children, make up simpler descriptions, such as A Tool, or Something Old, Something New, Something Borrowed, Something Blue.

Make a copy of the game list for each player, and hand it to him at the start of the game. On the signal GO!, they're off, each trying to find an object to satisfy each of the descriptions on the list. The game can be played as a continuing, day-long affair (you'll need a long or difficult list), or as a shorter, time-limit game.

The first player to round up objects to match all of the descriptions on his list is the winner. Second Prize goes to the one with the most interesting or humorous collection of objects.

*In this Scavenger Hunt, the objects gathered for the category "Equipment for a Rat Hunt" include: decoy rodent, cheese, magnifying lens for following rat footprints, a pleasant new home, basement blueprints for finding rat hiding places, a Pied Piper-type flute, a chart of rat anatomy, a large skewer, and those old standbys, the rat-trap and the family cat.*

# CARNIVAL GAMES

One of the world's terrible injustices is that the local Firemen's Carnival comes only once a year. But you can capture some of the carnival's thrill in your own backyard.

A homemade carnival can be as simple or as deluxe as you want. Your carnival will be a lot of fun, even if you have only a single game booth, or you could go all out with three different games, a lemonade refreshment stand, hot grilled wieners, and maybe one or two sideshows where members of the family give feature performances.

Here are a few easily made carnival games that everybody will get a kick out of. You can run the games for money (five cents or so apiece) and give out prizes, or you can do it just for fun.

Set up game booths by taping large sheets of colored paper (available at art stores), crepe paper (from card stores), or brown wrapping paper around card tables, picnic tables, or picnic benches. Decorate the paper, and write the name of the game with wide marking pens.

*Hit the Can:* This is a simple game, but strangely no one ever gets tired of it.

Place the booth table so that there is a house or garage wall about 10 feet behind it, to stop the balls. Set up three empty soda cans on the booth table, spaced about 2 feet apart. Mark a shooting line about 12 feet in front of the table.

Each person who wants to try gets three softballs (for free or for a nickel), which he throws at each of the cans in turn. If he knocks all three cans over, he wins a prize; but if he misses even one, he loses.

*Ping-Pong Pop:* Gather about a dozen large glasses, or the same number of pint plastic freezer containers. Get a similar number of ping-pong balls. (They are about fifteen cents apiece.) Place the containers on the ground several feet behind the booth table, and arrange them so that there are about 4 inches between each.

Then, for free or for a nickel, give everybody who wants to play three tries at throwing a ping-pong ball from behind the table into a container. Whoever succeeds wins a prize.

To make this game extra special, buy several small goldfish bowls and goldfish from a pet store. Fill the bowls with water, and put a goldfish in each. Whoever gets a ping-pong ball into a bowl wins both the bowl and the fish inside it.

*Penny Pitch:* You can use a standard-size checkerboard for this game, but if you don't have one, draw a grid of vertical and horizontal lines about an inch and a half apart on a sheet of paper about 12 inches square. Lay the board or paper down on the booth table. Tape the edges of the paper down with freezer tape to hold it flat. Mark a throwing line on the ground 2 feet or so in front of the table. The object of the game is to throw a penny onto the grid so that it lands in the center of one of the squares without touching any lines. This sounds easy, but it's not.

Players stand at the throwing line and throw their own pennies one at a time at the paper. Any pennies that land on a line are picked up and collected in a jackpot. Pennies that miss the paper entirely are given back to the thrower.

Any player who wins the game by throwing a penny into the center of a square wins the entire accumulated jackpot.

# YO-YO CONTEST

*Any number of players*

*Watch with second hand or stopwatch for timing*
*One Yo-Yo for each player, or a single Yo-Yo shared in turn*

*OBJECT: To perform a Yo-Yo stunt for longer, or a greater number of times, than your opponent*

Choose a person who is not participating in the contest to act as a timekeeper and referee.

There are all sorts of Yo-Yo stunts that can be used in contests. Before you start, find out from potential contestants what stunts they know how to do. There won't be time during a picnic for anyone to learn and practice a Yo-Yo maneuver that is unfamiliar to him. For novice players, the one who can keep the Yo-Yo going up and down for the longest wins. More experienced players can compete for the greatest number of consecutive loop-the-loops, the longest recoverable rock-the-baby, the greatest number of 'round-the-worlds. If there are not enough players to compete in any one stunt, a competition can be held in front of a panel of impartial judges for the greatest repertoire of stunts.

# FRISBEE TOURNAMENT

*Any number of players, but an even number is needed for*
*The Catch*

*One FRISBEE for each player, or a single one shared in turn*
*Markers for shooting lines and targets*
*Pencil and paper for recording distances*

*OBJECT: To throw the FRISBEE farther, more accurately, or with more finesse than other players*

A picnic on the beach is a perfect opportunity to hold a FRISBEE Tournament. Choose an impartial referee to make measurements, count catches and arbitrate disputes. He should be good at pacing off distances.

*The Distance Throw:* Mark a shooting line in front of a long clear area. The referee stands out in the field, where he can accurately gauge where a FRISBEE lands. Each player takes his turn at throwing the FRISBEE as far as he can. It should be thrown at a moment when the wind isn't interfering with a strong, straight trajectory. As the disc lands, the referee marks the point at which it first touched ground (even if it has rolled further). Each player may be given three throws, only the best of which is counted as his final record, and written down by the referee.

*Target Shooting:* Choose a target a good distance away from the shooting line, say 30-50 feet. The target can be a tree, a shrub, or a large circle scratched on the ground. Each player aims from behind the shooting line, and tries to hit or come as close to the target as possible. The referee should stand near the target, so he can mark where the disc touches ground and record the distance from the target. If no one hits the target, or more than one player does, a play-off is held to determine the winner.

*The Catch:* The players pair off to play this event as partners. Each pair in turn stands a specified distance away from one another (about 30 feet) and throws the FRISBEE back and forth. The partners who throw and catch it the most number of times before missing win the event.

*Specialty Stunts:* Special events may be held for those who are good at FRISBEE stunts. Such stunts might be throwing a FRISBEE into the wind so that it boomerangs and catching it as it comes back, catching it on one finger, throwing it onto the ground in such a way that it skips back up, and so on. If several stunts are performed in this event, each successfully performed stunt can count for one point, and the player with the greatest number of points is the winner.

*There are many types of FRISBEE. The smaller, lighter ones are easier to throw, but the heavier ones have a much longer range.*

## KITE CONTESTS

*Any number of players*

*A kite for each player*
*At least three balls of kite string for each player and a reel or stick to wind the string on*
*A watch with a second hand for timing*

*OBJECT: To fly your kite higher or longer than the other contestants*

Kites shouldn't be flown in areas where there are a lot of trees, near electrical lines, in gale winds, or during thunderstorms. Broad meadows or beaches are ideal locations, and moderate, steady winds are better than gusty, unpredictable breezes. Each type of kite flies best, however, in the breeze for which it was designed. The common diamond kite flies best during light breezes; anything stronger will tear it. Bat and bird kites can withstand higher winds, and are more maneuverable. Box kites are steady under gusty,

strong winds, as are many of the long or multiple-element kites. As for kite strings, the nylon kind can take more stress than cotton, but it gets tangled more easily and knots badly.

To hold a fair height contest, kites should be similar, and the contestants experienced. Each contestant is paired with a "string boy" to help him tie on each new ball of string. Contestants spread themselves a good distance away from one another to launch their kites. They let their kites move out rapidly, careful not to let them dive or become entangled. Their string boys stand near with several extra balls of string. When the first ball of kite string runs out, the string boy ties on a new roll with an overhand knot. The player whose kite goes highest (gauged by the number of balls of string used) is the winner.

Less experienced players can play for time only. A referee records the length of time between launch and fall for each player who competes. The longest time aloft wins.

*Fighting Kites:* In the Orient, fighting kites are preferred for contests. The strings on these small, maneuverable kites are coated near the kite itself with powdered glass or porcelain so that they become cutting edges. Participants try to guide their kites at their opponents' so that the strings cross. Then a quick tug, and snap, the opponent's kite string is severed. The last kite left wins. Whoever is lucky enough to be around when a severed kite comes to the ground gets to keep it. If you want to try this game, crush glass by hammering it between layers of cloth with a hammer. Then run several feet at the top end of your kite string through white glue, then through the powdered glass, to coat it thoroughly. Allow to dry. Discard the remaining glass carefully in the garbage, and handle the coated portion of the kite string with caution.

# CROQUET

*Two to eight players*

*Croquet set*
*Level lawn area, about 60 by 30 feet or similar area*

**OBJECT: *To drive a ball in sequence through all the wickets on the course, and back to the home stake, before the other players***

Croquet sets come with six or eight wooden balls, each with a different stripe color. Each ball is matched to a wooden mallet with the same color stripe. The mallet is used to drive the ball around the course through nine croquet "wickets"—small wire arches which can be pushed into the ground. Two wooden stakes, to mark the beginning and turning point of the course also come with the set.

On a wide grassy area, set up the croquet wickets as shown. Leave about two mallet-head lengths between the two stakes and their nearest wickets. Other than this requirement, the course can be any width or length which fits into your available space, so long as the overall pattern is the same.

Each player chooses a mallet, and takes the ball that goes with it. To decide who takes the first turn, players each take a position 10 feet or so away from the beginning of the course and drive their balls toward the home stake. Whoever gets nearest takes the first turn. Second nearest takes the second turn, and so on.

Each player takes his turn in order, and on each turn uses his mallet to take one whack ("stroke") at his croquet ball, to drive it through the wickets in order, to the mid-point turning stake, and back to the home stake.

Players start their balls midway between the home stake and wicket #1. Then they travel through wickets #1 to #7 in order, as shown by the arrows, and hit the turning stake at the far end. After hitting the turning stake, players reverse direction and continue through the course, trying to knock their balls back to the home stake. The home stake and the last wicket may not be made on the same stroke. If a player hits the home stake after passing through the last wicket, he must use another stroke to hit the stake again.

But this is just the basic idea of the game. Although you ordinarily get only one stroke per turn, every time your ball passes through a wicket, or hits a stake, you're awarded one extra stroke. On your first turn, when it is likely that you'll hit the ball through wickets #1 and #2 in one stroke, you may get two more whacks at your ball before you have to relinquish your turn (one extra stroke for each wicket you passed through). If on one of those two extra strokes your ball passes through another wicket, you are again given an extra stroke.

The rules of croquet also allow you to play aggressively. Whenever your ball hits another player's (either intentionally or by accident), you get to take two extra strokes. Furthermore, since your ball and your opponent's touched, you have several choices for the first of these two extra strokes. You may:
"take croquet" by placing your ball and your opponent's together, putting your foot firmly on your ball, and hitting your

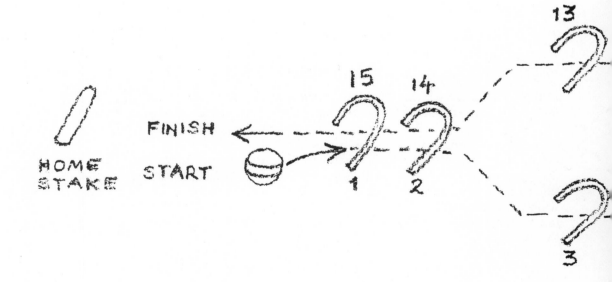

ball so hard that your opponent's is driven away (preferably far away where he'll have to waste several turns just getting back on the course);

make a "split" shot by placing the balls together, and hitting yours so that it is driven forward at the same time your opponent's is knocked somewhere else; or

place your ball a mallet's-head distance from your opponent's ball and take an ordinary stroke.

After any one of these alternatives for the first extra stroke, you get a second, ordinary stroke. But once you've hit another player's ball, you're "dead" on that ball (meaning you can't legally hit it again) until you have passed through a wicket or hit a stake.

Bonus strokes are cumulative only up to a maximum of two. If you hit your opponent's ball on the same stroke in which your ball passes through a wicket, you get only the limit of two extra strokes, not three.

The first player to complete the course and hit the home stake with his ball is the winner. However, the game does not stop just because someone wins. Players still continue through the course to see who will come in second, third, and so on. Players who complete the course don't stop playing either. They continue to take their turns as "rovers," who travel all over the court, hitting other players' balls with their own, and knocking them away. Some play that those who complete the course become "poison." If a player's ball gets hit by a poison ball, he is out of the game.

Croquet can also be played by partners, each with his own ball and mallet. The first pair to complete the entire croquet course wins the game.

# yard & Street Games

# Chapter 3
# Backyard & Street Games

Games for streets and backyards tend to be more beset by rules, regulations and even penalties than the games people play at parties and picnics. The rules aren't official (people from different neighborhoods seldom agree on them), yet to cooperate in these largely team games everyone has to play the same way. Disregard the rules written here if they are not standard in your area.

Whatever set of rules are agreed to by mutual consent will not be perfect, and there will always be cries of "No fair!" Sometimes still another rule—and sometimes one or two less—will solve the problem. What is harder than devising fair regulations ahead of time is monitoring whether they are being followed during the game itself. Impromptu games among friends and family aren't usually supervised by a referee, and it is a great pleasure that they are not. However, lack of an authority with an eagle eye and a loud voice leaves all sorts of dodges open to argument. For the more innocent games in the preceding sections we have suggested protections in the name of justice. No more. Just or unjust, kind or unkind, no advice can soften the way poor players, poor sports, and downright cheats are handled by other street and backyard players. Playing these old favorites is not only a lesson in cooperation, but in conformity.

Some precautions, however, can assure less confusing and more enjoyable games. There is simply no sense in playing the twelve-year-olds against the first graders. The younger ones will be clobbered, and the game will be a bore. Some distribution of players among teams by age and skill is sensible. In a neighborhood, imbalances usually get sorted out over a period of time, and teams become semipermanent. This has the advantage that teammates recognize one another, and don't throw the ball to the enemy. Where strangers are coming together to play, some way of distinguishing one team from another is helpful: Shirts vs. No Shirts, or Socks vs. No Socks.

Bounds, bases and goals become important in many of these games. Garbage cans and rocks may serve for bases, and the perimeter of a backyard often defines the entire playing field. Chalk is the best answer for drawing what is needed on pavement, and a stick can be used to scratch markings in dirt. For grass surfaces, use extra items of clothing, such as sweatshirts, to mark bases, indicate corners of the field, and represent the ends of crucial lines like the center of a football field.

## JACKS

*Two players*

*Set of jacks and jacks ball*

**OBJECT: To finish a series of Jacks games before your opponent**

Jacks may be played with a set of six, ten or even more jacks, depending on the skill of the players. Find a smooth, level spot. Sit facing your opponent with plenty of playing surface between the two of you. To choose who will go first, you and your opponent each in turn put the group of jacks in the plams of your hands, toss the jacks into the air, and try to catch as many on the backs of your hands as possible. Whoever catches the most jacks gets to go first.

Experienced players flip with one hand instead of two to see who goes first, and some play that only the jacks that fall to the ground on the flip must be picked up on the first turn. The one-hand flip may also be used to begin each of the separate Jacks games in a series. If all the jacks are caught on the back of the hand, that flip substitutes for the first step in the game; then the player may flip a second time, and skip the second step in the game if he again catches all the jacks. The player only begins a game on the step at which he misses a flip and lets one or more jacks fall, and only those jacks that fell are picked up in that step. An excellent flipper may bypass a game altogether by successfully flipping through every step of it. Such good flippers need a different method of deciding who goes first: The one who flips successfully the most number of times takes the first turn.

The two players take turns trying to successfully complete a series of Jacks games agreed on beforehand. If a player successfully completes one game, he goes right on to the next. For example, after finishing the Basic Game, he might go on to Eggs in the Basket. If a player misses during a game, he passes the jacks to his opponent. On his next turn, the player starts at the beginning of the game in which he missed on his previous turn.

The first player to complete every game in the series wins the match.

*Basic Game:* This usually begins all Jacks games. After flipping or not as you choose, scatter all the jacks onto the floor with one motion. Then toss the ball into the air, pick up a jack in your right hand, and catch the ball in that same hand after one bounce. (Left-handed players toss and pick up with their left hands.) Put the jack in your other hand, toss the ball again, and pick up another jack. Repeat this process until all jacks have been picked up. The following steps in the game are described for the usual small six-jack set.

After picking up the jacks singly, rescatter them and begin picking them up in the same way, but in groups of two or more. In Twosies, pick up the jacks in pairs; in Threesies, by threes; in Foursies, a group of four and a group of two; in Fivesies, five jacks and the other one. In Sixies, pick up all the jacks at once and catch the ball in the same hand after a single bounce.

*Eggs in the Basket:* After completing the basic game through Sixies, many players go on to this one. Scatter the jacks as before. Then toss the ball, pick up a jack, put the jack in your cupped left hand immediately, and catch the ball in your right hand after one bounce. After all the jacks have been collected, scatter them again, and proceed by twos, threes, fours, fives and sixes, putting the groups into your cupped left hand before catching the ball with your right.

*Crack the Eggs:* After gathering your eggs, the next logical step is to crack them. Scatter the jacks, toss the ball, and pick up the jacks one by one as in the basic game. But before catching the ball, "crack" each jack by tapping it once against the ground. Then catch the ball in your right hand (which is still holding the jack) after one bounce. Scatter the jacks again and repeat, going by twos, then threes, and so on through sixes.

*Pigs in the Pen:* After taking care of the eggs, see to the pigs. Put your left hand, cupped palm down, on the ground, and lift it slightly at the thumb to form a shedlike "pen." After scattering the jacks, toss the ball, and while it bounces push a jack into the pen. Then catch the ball in your right hand. Any jack that doesn't end up in the pen is a miss. After pushing all the jacks into the pen one by one, rescatter them, and proceed by twos, then by threes, and so on.

*Pigs over the Fence:* Place your left hand horizontally on the floor with your pinky down, forming a "fence." Scatter the jacks, and proceed as in Pigs in the Pen. This time, however, instead of pushing the pigs into a pen, carry them over the fence to the far side of your hand. After doing this successfully one by one, repeat it by twos, threes, fours, fives and sixes.

*Sweeps:* Scatter the jacks and toss the ball as in the basic game. But instead of picking up the jacks one at a time, put your fingers on each jack and slide it across the floor until it is near your body. Then pick it up with your right hand, and catch the ball after one bounce. After sweeping the jacks in one at a time, scatter them again and continue sweeping by twos, threes, etc.

*Bounce, No Bounce:* Scatter the jacks. Toss the ball up, pick up a single jack with your right hand, and catch the ball in the same hand after it has bounced once. Then toss the ball again, transfer the jack to your left hand, and catch the ball before it bounces.

After doing this with all the jacks one by one, scatter them again and repeat by twos, threes, and so on.

*Flying Dutchman:* This hardest of all Jacks games requires that you pick the jack up as in the basic game, then toss the ball again, throw the jacks from one hand to the other, and catch the ball before it has bounced more than once. Onesies and Twosies aren't too bad, but completing the sequence through Sixies is a real trial.

## JUMP ROPE

*Three or more players*

*10- to 12-foot length of clothesline, or jump rope*

*OBJECT: To jump the rope as many times as possible*

Two players each hold one end of the jump rope and start it turning away from the other players, the jumpers. The rope should just barely skim the ground at each swing, and maintain an even rhythm. Each jumper in turn times himself to step into the rope just in time to jump over it, and then jumps the rope as many times as possible before missing. When a jumper misses, he steps out; when the swing of the rope is even again, another jumper takes his place. Usually everybody in the game chants out the number of jumps. The one who jumps the most times is the winner.

There are many variations of the game, including those in which:

The jumper skips twice for every turn of the rope, once over the rope and again before it comes back to him.

The rope is rotated towards the players so that as they step in, it comes behind them at their heels.

The rope is lifted so the jumper must jump higher.

Two ropes are turned simultaneously in opposite directions.

The jumper takes a stone or stick with him. On each alternate skip he puts the stone down on the ground or picks it up.

The jumper takes high jumps, and the turners turn at very high speed, so that the rope passes under the jumper twice during each jump.

The jumpers play follow-the-leader. One of the players is chosen as the leader, and the others in their turns mimic his actions. The leader jumps into the rope, skips twice, turns around, jumps on one foot, and so on.

The turners alternately turn the rope very slowly ("salt"), then suddenly speed up to a very high rate ("pepper").

Many chants are traditionally used to keep time, to count jumps, and to demand actions of the jumpers. A few of them follow as examples.

> Mother, Mother, I am sick,
> Call for the doctor, quick, quick, quick.
> *(turners speed up for three jumps)*
> In came the doctor, in came the nurse,
> *(two more players enter)*
> In came the lady with the alligator purse.
> *(and a third enters)*
> Out went the doctor, out went the nurse,
> *(two players leave)*
> Out went the lady with the alligator purse.
> *(the third leaves and only the original jumper is left in)*
>
> Apples, peaches, pears and plums.
> Tell me when your birthday comes.
> *(the jumper chants the months until his birthday, and then the days until his birthdate)*

Had a little girl dressed in blue;
She died last night at half past two.
Did she go up? Did she go down?
*(jumper alternately reaches up on one jump, touches the ground after the next)*
Up. Down. Up. Down.
*(and continue)*

Teddy bear, Teddy bear, turn around.
*(jumper turns)*
Teddy bear, Teddy bear, touch the ground.
*(jumper touches ground)*
Teddy bear, Teddy bear, go upstairs.
*(jumper steps over the rope for a few turns instead of jumping)*
Teddy bear, Teddy bear, say your prayers.
*(praying posture with hands)*
Teddy bear, Teddy bear, turn out the light.
*(This and many other actions can be acted out in pantomime—brushing teeth, combing hair, washing face, etc.)*
Teddy bear, Teddy bear, say goodnight.
*(jumper leaves the game, and the next "Teddy bear" enters)*

*When two jump ropes are used, they are turned in opposite directions. Getting in is trickier than jumping the ropes.*

# HOPSCOTCH

*Any number of players*

*Chalk or stick for drawing hopscotch diagram*
*Stone or other object to toss into the squares*

*OBJECT: To throw the stone into the squares of the diagram and to hop through the diagram in specific patterns without touching lines*

Draw a hopscotch diagram on the ground. There are many kinds, including the one shown in the photograph and the "Snail" shown in the margin. The instructions below are for the classic diagram also shown in the margin.

Choose the order in which players will take their turns hopping through the diagram. At the end of the game, whoever has made the least mistakes in going through the pattern is the winner.

In the basic hopscotch game, the player starts by tossing his stone into the box marked 1. After the throw, the player hops into the diagram. He hops on one foot in boxes 1, 4 and 7, and straddles the diagram with both feet in 2/3 and 5/6. If he touches a line, steps out of the diagram, or lands in a blank spot, he loses his turn. When he reaches the space marked "rest" (or "home"), the hopscotcher lands on two feet, jumps once to turn around, and retraces his steps, picking the stone up on the way back. On the next turn his stone must fall into the space marked 2, and so on in consecutive turns, until he has completed spaces 1 through 7. If at any time the stone lands on a line, outside the diagram, or in a blank area, he loses his turn. For most mis-throws the player may resume again on his next turn at whatever space he missed. But if the stone lands in the end space, he not only loses his turn but must start again from box #1.

Only a few of dozens of variations are given here. Chances are the way the game is played in your neighborhood will differ in some way from all these versions:

After completing the hopscotch diagram for the first time, a player gets to throw the stone into whichever box he chooses. That box becomes his "home," and his initials are written there. From then on he may rest there on both feet, but no one else is allowed to enter that box. As more and more players stake out their homes, the game becomes progressively more difficult. This version is often called Houses.

The diagram is hopped through without throwing the stone, but with both eyes shut. This version is called Sky Blue.

Instead of throwing the stone into each box, the stone is kicked from box to box while hopping on one foot. The whole diagram is hopped through on one foot in numerical order. If the stone comes to rest on a line, it's a miss.

The diagram is hopped and straddled through, but with the stone on the hopscotcher's head.

The diagram is hopped through, but with the stone balanced on one foot held in front of the player.

The diagram is hopped through, and the stone is thrown, but the hopscotcher must stay on tiptoe throughout the game.

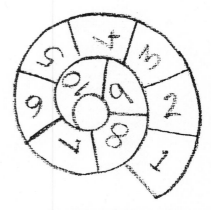

*A spiral Hopscotch diagram.*

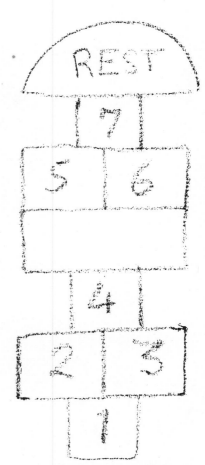

*A classic Hopscotch diagram.*

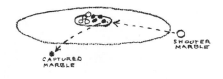

CAPTURED MARBLE

SHOOTER MARBLE

## MARBLES I

*Any number of players*

*Marbles*
*Chalk or stick for marking circle*

*OBJECT: To win other players' marbles by knocking them out of the larger circle with a shooter marble.*

This Marbles game and the two that follow are known by numerous local names and are played in countless variations as well. This version of Marbles is the one Charlie Brown plays.

Scratch or chalk a circle about 3 feet in diameter on the ground, and a smaller circle, about 6 inches in diameter, in the center of the large circle. Each player places an equal number of marbles within the smaller circle. The number might be four or six, depending on how many are playing and what you prefer.

Choose the order in which you will take your turns. In each player's turn, he chooses one of his remaining marbles as his "shooter" and shoots at his opponents' marbles from beyond the edge of the outer circle. If he knocks a marble out of the large circle, he keeps it, and continues shooting from wherever his shooter marble stopped, so long as his shooter remains in the ring. But if his shooter leaves the big circle, he loses his turn, although he still keeps any marbles he has knocked out of the ring. Each player's turn ends when he fails to knock another marble out of the outer circle, or his shooter leaves the ring. If the shooter stays within the circle as his turn ends, it must remain there. Otherwise he may pocket it to use for his next turn.

The game ends when one player has won all (or most) of the marbles; or the game may end by common consent when one player is clearly way ahead, in which case the winner may take any marbles that still remain in the circle.

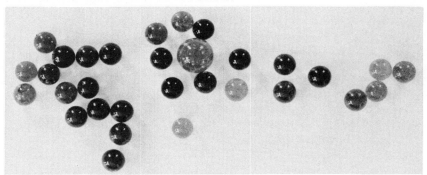

## MARBLES II

*Any number of players*

*Marbles*
*Chalk or stick for marking a shooting line*

*OBJECT: To win other players' marbles by hitting them with your own*

Draw a shooting line on the ground with chalk or a stick. Decide the order in which players will take their turns. The first player shoots his marble out from behind the shooting line. The next player attempts to hit the first player's marble with his own, again shooting from behind the line. If he is successful, he gets both marbles; but if he fails, he loses both his turn and his shooter. At each succeeding turn, all the marbles that have accumulated on the field are fair game, and each player may continue shooting until he misses. When no marbles remain on the field, a player shoots a single marble in, and the game continues as before. When by mutual consent players decide to end the game, the player with the most marbles is the winner.

In a variation of this variation, the first player piles four marbles up to form a pyramid in the field called the "castle." (To do this, lay three marbles on the ground touching each other, and lay the fourth on top in the center of the group.) The next player attempts to knock the castle apart. If he succeeds, he gets all four marbles; but if he fails, the castle's owner confiscates his shooter. At the end of his turn, each player piles up a castle for the next player.

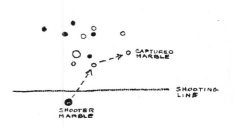

# MARBLES III

*Any number of players*

*Marbles*
*Chalk or stick for marking shooting line*
*Target, such as a spool of thread, large marble, stone or salt shaker; or a hole in the ground*

*OBJECT: To win other players' marbles by first hitting the target and then hitting the marbles*

Each player donates an equal number of marbles, and from these a large ring of at least sixteen widely-spaced marbles is formed. Draw a straight shooting line several feet from the edge of the ring, and place (or dig) the target in the center of the ring.

Decide the order in which players will take their turns. The first player aims for the target in the center from beyond the shooting line. If he fails to hit the target, or if he hits one of the marbles that form the ring, he loses his turn; but if he succeeds in hitting the target without knocking any of the marbles in the ring, he can use the same shooter to shoot at any of the marbles lying in the ring. He shoots with his own marble from wherever it stopped after hitting the target, and keeps any marbles he hits. The first player continues to shoot at the other players' marbles until he misses. He must leave his shooter wherever it last came to rest. The following players do the same, except that after hitting the target, they have the additional option of shooting at any shooter marbles left on the field. The player who captures the most marbles is the winner. When all the marbles have been won, players donate equal numbers of marbles to form a ring as before, and the game resumes.

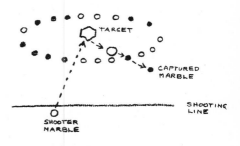

*NOT FOR KEEPS*

*Like all gambling, Marbles games have a way of becoming too serious, and little kids can end up in tears. If someone seems upset that he has "lost his marbles," let him have them back. In these days of mass-produced marbles, it is hard to tell which marbles originally belonged to which kids anyway. When you're not playing for keeps, be sure everyone counts his marbles before the game begins to avoid argument later.*

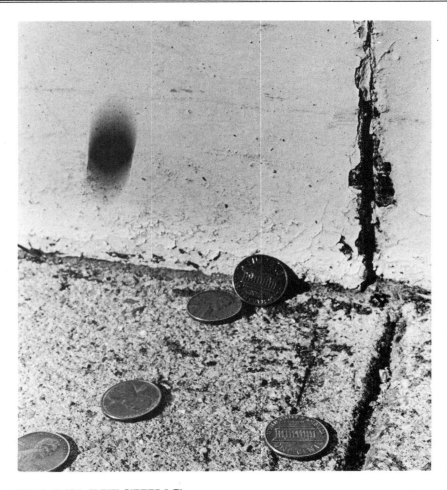

## PENNY-PITCHING

*Any number of players*

*Pennies*
*Wall, curb, or step to pitch pennies against*
*Marker for a pitching line*

**OBJECT: To win other players' pennies by throwing your penny nearest to the wall**

Penny-pitching is a mild gambling game with a skill involved as well. If the game proves to be too expensive or upsetting it can be played for points rather than for keeps.

Draw or mark a pitching line several feet from the wall. You can make it as close as 4 feet, or as far as 10 feet, depending on the skill of the players.

Choose the order in which players will take their turns. They can start with an equal number of pennies, or just what they have on hand. The players stand behind the pitching line and toss their pennies. After each player has taken a turn, the player whose penny comes to rest nearest to the wall, or actually touching it, gets to take all the other coins pitched. The player who accumulates the most pennies is the winner.

A variation of the game requires that the pennies hit the wall and rebound to their final positions. A penny that doesn't hit the wall cannot be a winner.

# HIT THE PENNY

*Two players*

*Small rubber ball*
*Penny*
*Paved surface*

*OBJECT: To hit the penny with the ball without moving the penny, or to flip it over completely*

The two players stand on the paved surface about 8 feet from one another (three sidewalk cracks are about this distance). They place the penny on a crack or imaginary line centered between them.

Decide which player goes first, then take turns throwing the ball at the penny. If a player hits the penny but doesn't move it, he gets one point. If he hits the penny and flips it over completely, he gets five points. If the penny is hit and moves without flipping, there is no score. The trick is to avoid moving the penny closer to your opponent, thereby making it easier for him to hit the penny on his own.

The first to reach 21 points is the winner.


# KICK THE CAN

*Three or more players*

*Tin can (or ball)*
*Marker to indicate home*

*OBJECT: To keep from being captured by It, and to release those already caught*

Choose the player who will be It. Designate a rock, a manhole cover, sweater, or other object to be the can's "home." Place the can on its home.

Any player other than It kicks the can away from its home as far as possible. Everyone runs and hides while It retrieves the can, using only his feet. After It has found the can and placed it on its home, he begins seeking for the other players. (In some versions, It must also count to 100 or run around home several times, to give the other players even more time to hide.)

When It spots someone, he quickly runs to home, bangs the can against the ground, and shouts out the spotted player's name, followed by "Kick the can—1—2—3." The player is then considered captured, and must settle down near home. Free players can release captured players by sneaking up while It is out hunting and kicking the can away from its base. Then all those who were captured are freed, and It must go and retrieve the can again before continuing to search for hiders.

When everyone has been captured by It, the first player captured becomes the new It. Since it is very hard to capture everyone in this game, it's often played that anyone captured a certain number of times (usually three) becomes the new It immediately.

# HIDE AND SEEK

*Three or more players*

*Marker to indicate home base*

*OBJECT: To reach home base without being captured by It, and to release those already caught.*

Select the first player to be It, and choose any area or object to be "home base." This is a safety spot.

It covers his eyes and counts to 100, while the other players spread out and hide in the surrounding area—neither too far out nor too near home base. After reaching 100, It uncovers his eyes, shouts "Ready or not, here I come! " and goes off to look for the hiders. The hiders try to remain hidden until they can dart to home base while It is looking the other way.

If It is off hunting in another direction, you can take a chance and break cover when his back is turned. Rush to home base before It realizes what is happening and shout, "Home free!" This keeps you safe from capture, and frees any players already captured. If It catches sight of you, whether while you are hiding or after you have left your hiding place, you'd better run; if he tags you before you reach home base, you've been captured. Captured players have to sit down near home base for the rest of the game unless another hider releases them by shouting, "Home free."

After everyone in the game has either been captured or has run safely to home, the first hider who was tagged by It and was not later released becomes the new seeker for another game of Hide and Seek. If nobody was captured, It remains the seeker for another round.

Sometimes extra rules are needed to prevent cheating. If It stays so near home base that no one can run in, the first person to come out of hiding shouts, "Base sticking," and It has to move farther away. To prevent hiders from hiding right next to home base, It may sometimes shout at the end of his count, "Anyone within ten feet of base is It!"

*Tap-Tap (I Spy):* The rules to this variation of Hide and Seek are the same as the ordinary version, except that rather than tagging a hider he has found, It runs back to home base and yells, "Tap-tap on Harry, (or I spy Harry) hiding behind the gooseberry bush" (using the name of the hider and the place he is hiding). If a hider is aware he's been spotted before It calls out, he can try to reach the base before It does, and yell, "Home free."

It only captures you if he has gotten both the name and the location correct. Therefore, Tap-Tap is best played at dusk, when both faces and places are hard to make out clearly.

*Sardines:* Sardines is Hide and Seek in reverse. It hides, while the others stay home to count to 100. The players then fan out in all directions to seek the lone hider. Upon finding It, each seeker attempts to join him surreptitiously, without giving the hiding place away to his comrades. This continues until everyone is crammed into one hiding place. The first person who found It becomes the hider for the next round. The game is great to play indoors on rainy days when you can't use the backyard for Hide and Seek.

## NOT IT

*The favored method for choosing who will be It in games like Tag or Hide and Seek goes like this: Somebody yells "Let's play Tag—not it!" The others then yell out, "Not It," and the last to catch on is It. A more time consuming method is the counting-out chant, such as "Eeny meeny miney mo," or "One potato, two potato." Players stand in a circle around the person reciting the rhyme. He taps a foot or hand of each player in time to the rhyme as he recites. The person tapped at the end of the rhyme is out, and the rhyme is repeated without him. The last person remaining in after many eliminations is It.*

*You can see why this variation of Hide and Seek is called Sardines.*

## TAG

*Three or more players*

*OBJECT: To avoid being tagged by It*

Choose one player to be It. It chases the others around until he tags (touches) another player. The tagged player then becomes It, and begins to chase the others. Often the "tagback" is expressly forbidden—tagging the former It immediately after being tagged yourself.

The game ends by mutual consent, usually brought on by exhaustion. There are many variations, only a few of which follow.

*Freeze Tag:* Those tagged by It must stand immobile in whatever position they were in when tagged, until tagged again by a free, unfrozen, ally. It wins the game when all players are frozen. The last player frozen by It becomes It in the next round of tag.

*Floating Tag:* Players are "safe" as long as they remain above the ground—for instance, hanging from a tree limb, or on a shed roof.

*Base Tag:* An area is designated as home. Those who go home are safe, but there is usually a time limit, and It may lie in wait nearby, counting to, say, 25 or 100, when the player will have to leave the safety of home again.

*Chain Tag:* After being tagged, a player joins It by holding on to his hands or clothing. Thus "chained," they continue to chase down players, each of whom must join the rear of the chain when tagged. Eventually only one free player remains. He is the winner and becomes It for the next round.

*Flashlight Tag:* This version is played at night with a flashlight. It tries to zap the other players with a flashlight beam. When all the players have been caught by the light, the first one caught becomes the next It.

## GHOST IN THE GRAVEYARD

*Four or more players*

*Tree or other object to indicate home*

*OBJECT: To sight the Ghost and run home without being tagged*

This game is played at night or at dusk. Choose one player to be the "Ghost." Designate an object or area to be "home." All players but the Ghost cluster around home and count to 100 while the Ghost hides.

Players fan out (often no one is allowed to stay within a certain distance of home) and try to find the Ghost. The Ghost may dash out unexpectedly and try to tag as many players as possible before they reach home, or one player may sight the Ghost and raise the alarm, so the other players can rush home before being tagged. Those tagged by the Ghost become temporarily out until the end of the round, when all players are either tagged or have made it home safely. The game continues in the same way during succeeding rounds, except that all those tagged during the previous round become Ghosts, and try to tag the remaining players. The game ends when only one player remains alive.

# MONKEY IN THE MIDDLE

*Three players*

*Large rubber ball*

**OBJECT: To toss the ball back and forth, keeping it out of the reach of the middle player**

Choose one player to be the "Monkey." The other two players stand about 10 feet apart while the Monkey stands between them.

The two end players toss the ball back and forth, trying to keep it high enough or fast enough so the Monkey can't catch it. If a player fails to catch the ball, the Monkey is free to scramble for it, or he can intercept it as it is thrown back and forth. If the Monkey gets the ball, he takes the place of the player who last threw the ball, and that player becomes the new Monkey. The game continues as before. There is no particular end to this game and no winner. When playing with a much younger Monkey, be sure not to let the teasing element of this game get out of hand. When frustration becomes apparent, a low, slow toss is in order.

# SPUD

*Four or more players*

*Volleyball, soccer ball, or large rubber ball*

**OBJECT: To avoid getting hit by the ball, and to hit opponents**

Choose the player who will start the game. All the players stand in a circle. The starter throws the ball high in the air and yells his own name or the name of one of the other players. Everyone scatters as fast as their legs can take them except the one whose name was called, who runs in to catch the ball.

# WHO GOES FIRST

Unless the rules of the game include a specific way to decide who goes first, you'll have to find a fair way to decide which player or team gets the advantage of the first turn. The fairest way to make the decision is to use one of the following methods.

These methods are designed for use by two players. If two teams are competing, their captains (or two other delegates) represent them. The methods work just as well for choosing the first team to serve in Volleyball as they do in determining the first player to shoot his marble.

*Flipping a Coin:* One player takes a coin from his pocket, makes a fist with his hand, and puts the coin down on his thumb. Then with a snap of his thumb he flips the coin into the air and catches it as it falls. After he has caught the coin, he slaps it onto the back of his free hand and, keeping it covered, asks his opponent, "Heads or tails?" After his opponent makes a guess, the coin flipper uncovers the coin. If the opponent guessed correctly, he goes first. Otherwise, the flipper takes the first turn.

*Even or Odd:* If no coins are to be had, this method works just as well. Each player faces the other with a hand behind his back. One chooses "even," the other chooses "odd." On the count of three, both players flip out their hands, exposing one or two fingers. The player who guessed correctly whether the sum of the fingers held out would be an odd or even number gets to go first.

*Stone, Scissors, Paper:* Two players stand facing one another with one hand behind their backs. On the count of three, each player throws out one of the following: a clenched fist (Stone), a flat palm (Paper), or two out-stretched fingers (Scissors). In every combination of two of these one beats the other: scissors cut paper, stone crushes scissors, paper covers stone. The player whose throw beats the other's takes the first turn. If the two throws are the same (scissors and scissors, for example) the throw is taken over again.

*Climbing the Stick:* This method is favored in Stickball. The two players face each other, and a third player lightly tosses up a bat or broomstick between them. One of the two players catches the stick in one hand anywhere near the bottom or center, and rapidly one by one the two players wrap their fists around the stick going upward so that each fist touches the one below it. When a player has both hands on the stick he lets go with the lower one, and grabs again on top of the upmost fist. Finally there is only room for one more fist at the top of the stick. The player to get this position is the winner.

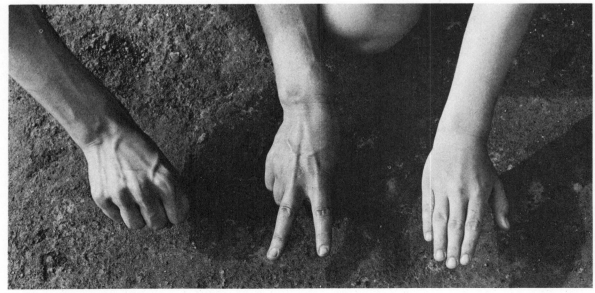

*From left to right the hand positions are: stone, scissors, paper.*

Immediately upon catching the ball, the catcher yells, "Spud," and everyone else must freeze dead in their tracks. The catcher is then allowed to take four steps toward an intended victim before throwing the ball at him. If the ball hits the victim, he gets the letter S. If, however, the ball misses or is caught by the victim, the thrower gets the letter S. The group regathers after the throw, and whoever got the letter is the next name-caller. This continues until some player has accumulated the letters S-P-U-D.

At this point there are several variations of the game. In one version, the player who has gotten all the letters has to crawl through the "mill," a tunnel formed of the other players' spread legs, while the others spank him. In a kinder version, the one to get SPUD is simply out, and the game continues until one winner is left.

To make the game more suspenseful, one player sometimes secretly gives numbers to the others. At the beginning of the game the caller yells out a number, though he does not know which player it signifies. Since the numbers are often forgotten, or two or more players think they have the same number, the game becomes pleasantly confusing.

In taking steps toward the intended Spud target, short-legged young children are at a disadvantage, while long-leggers have too great an edge. To make things fairer, big players can be limited to only one or two steps, while smaller ones can take five or more steps, or be allowed to take four leaps.

# DODGEBALL

*Ten or more players, divided into two teams*

*Volleyball, soccer ball, or large rubber ball*
*Markers for laying out boundaries*

### OBJECT: To put players out by hitting them with the ball, and to avoid being put out yourself

Mark the end bounds of the dodgeball field with two parallel lines about 30 feet apart. Mark a center line between the two endlines, so that the field is split into halves. Depending on the number of players, the field may be quite wide or very narrow, but it usually isn't necessary to mark the sidelines, as the spread of the players themselves indicates the width. Divide the players into two teams, and decide which team goes first. Each team takes half the field and they face each other spread out behind the center line. No team member is allowed to cross over the center line into the other team's side of the field, or to go beyond the end bounds or sidelines to escape the ball.

Players fling the ball as hard as possible at members of the other team, who can either dodge the ball or try to catch it. If someone is hit by the ball and fails to catch it, he is out and leaves the game. If the ball is caught, the thrower of the ball is out instead. The ball is thrown alternately, first by one team, then the other. The team that loses all of its players loses the game.

*BOMBARDMENT*

*This is a variation of Dodgeball. The difference is that players who fail to dodge or catch a ball thrown at them go out by forming a line behind the opposing team's endline. Then, if the opposing team fails to intercept the ball that is thrown at them, it can be caught by one of the out players behind the endline, and he may throw the ball at one of the opposing players. Players are thus subjected to bombardment from both front and rear. If an out player succeeds in getting an opposing player out, he is allowed to come back in on his own side of the field.*

# TOUCH FOOTBALL

*Four or more players, divided into two teams*

*A football*
*Markers for laying out goal lines*

**OBJECT: To score points by breaking through the opposing team's defenses and carrying, passing or kicking the football over their goal line to make a touchdown or a field goal**

Mark two goal lines with chalk on a hard surface or with shirts or other markers on grass. The goal lines of a regulation football field are set 100 yards apart, but the game can be played on a much shorter field provided that the distance between goal lines is greater than the distance any player can throw the ball. A regulation field also has sidelines 53⅓ yards apart, as well as a center, or 50-yard-line, parallel to the goal lines. Whether you want to

*A neighborhood football team is likely to be a motley crew. Team spirit makes up for lack of equipment.*

take the trouble to mark sidelines (and deal with the squabbles that may result) is up to you. Few players will lead a merry chase off the field anyway, when the shortest distance to the goal is straight ahead. If you do opt for sidelines, out of bounds regulations that have to be added to the game are on page 87.

Divide the players into two teams of at least two people each. Usually the teams are of equal size, but two or more smaller players can be considered equal to one larger one. Naturally, you should try to even out skills like passing and running too. Choose the team to make the kickoff. Although there are seldom formal positions such as fullback and halfback, a quarterback, the person who first gets the ball in each play, should be chosen by each team ahead of time.

Touch Football is similar to tackle football, but with fewer regulations and the substitution of a light "touch" or tap for the bone-shattering tackle. The touch may be one-handed and anywhere on the body, or two-handed and only below the belt. In a variation, each player pulls a handkerchief through his belt. Pulling the handkerchief off is equivalent to—but less equivocal than—tagging.

Each team in its turn gets four tries at a time to battle its way past the defending team and get the ball over the opposing goal lines. These tries are called "downs." During a down the ball can be carried by a player as he runs toward the goal or it can be passed from player to player, or, when both these methods have failed to move the ball very far, it can be kicked. Each down ends when the player holding the ball is tagged by a member of the opposing team, or the ball hits the ground. After four downs the ball changes hands, and the opposing team gets its four downs to try to score. If the opposing team's four downs do not result in a touchdown, the first team gets possession of the ball once again for another four downs. This continues until a touchdown or field goal is scored, or the players end the game.

To start the play, line each team up along its goal line in preparation for the first "kickoff." The best kicker on the team chosen to start the game off (let's call them the Foxes) holds the football in his hands and punts it as far as possible down the field away from his own goal line. The receiving team (The Redshirts) rushes to catch the football, and the Foxes surge forward to stop them. If the Redshirts catch the ball, they try to move it down the field as far as possible by running with it or passing it to one another sideways or backward. Forward passes are not allowed during the kickoff. When a player is tagged, or fumbles and drops the ball, all play stops. The spot where the player was tagged or the ball touched the ground is noted or marked, depending on the seriousness of the game. The Redshirts now get ready for their first down. They "huddle" to discuss strategy, and decide on a plan, hopefully rather quickly, so as not to hold up the game. Then both sides line up for the "scrimmage."

In the scrimmage, which begins all downs, the ball is moved to the middle of the field, but on the same imaginary line (parallel to the goal lines) on which it was stopped, and which was noted or marked at the end of the previous down. The opposing teams line up facing each other with the ball between them, like two armies preparing for battle. One player from the Redshirts now grasps the ball where it lies on the ground, and on the word "hike" from

## CREAM THE CARRIER

*If you're holding a football in your hands but you don't feel quite in the mood for the structured rules of football, you can try that kid-tested football standby, "Cream the Carrier." This game is something like Tag in reverse: the player who holds the ball is It and all the other players are out to get him.*

*Cream the Carrier can be played with any size gang of kids—the more the better. One player throws the ball high up into the air and everyone rushes to catch it. The one who catches the ball (or picks it up from the ground) becomes the carrier, and everyone rushes to tackle him. To escape being tackled, the carrier tries to keep ahead of the horde chasing him for as long as possible. Then, if they're gaining on him, he can throw the ball to one or another of his opponents. The one who gets the ball becomes the new carrier, and as his former teammates turn on him like a pack of wolves, he bounds away with all possible speed. If the carrier is tackled before he's able to get rid of the ball, the players pause while he gets his breath. Then he can throw the ball up in the air as in the beginning of the game or, if he's sneaky, make a throwing motion, and while the rest are looking up into the air, put the ball under his arm and race away.*

*The game doesn't have either an end or winner, unless you can say that the last man on his feet after an exhausting game wins.*

## PLAY DIAGRAMS

*These three diagrams are a method of showing football plays. The X's represent the team with possession of the ball. The O's are the defending team. A circle around an X indicates a new position to which the player has run. Solid lines show the path of the ball when it is passed; broken lines show the path of players as they run. The arrows indicate direction of movement.*

*In the first play, the quarterback receives the ball and scoots around the side of the opposing team to run with it. The other players move out from their original positions at the scrimmage to block the opposing team.*

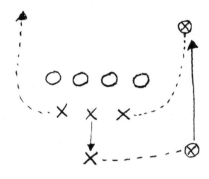

*In the second play, the quarterback moves to one side behind the scrimmage line while a teammate runs down the field to receive a pass.*

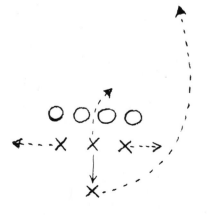

the quarterback standing a few feet behind him, "snaps" the ball back to his teammate's waiting hands. As soon as the ball is snapped, the Redshirts rush down the field to receive a pass, drop back to receive a pass in a less direct but more dangerous sort of play, or stick by the quarterback to protect him from the Foxes—all in accordance with the strategy decided upon in the huddle.

But before the Foxes can step over the scrimmage line to tag the ball carrier, they must shout "One Mississippi, two Mississippi, three Mississippi," or count to ten. This gives the Redshirt quarterback time to step back a bit and take action. Again according to plan (assuming the plan is being followed, which is rare), the quarterback runs with the ball toward the Foxes' goal line or throws it to one of his teammates farther out in the field. The Foxes, on the move by now, try to stop the movement of the ball by tagging the Redshirt carrier. If the carrier is tagged or lets the ball touch the ground, play stops again, the position of the ball is noted, and the two teams get ready for the next scrimmage that starts the second down. If the Redshirts can't make a goal by the end of their fourth down, the Foxes get the ball and form their first scrimmage line from wherever the ball was stopped, but facing of course toward the Redshirt goal line. They now have four downs to make a goal or give up the ball.

There is another way in which the Foxes could gain possession of the ball before the Redshirts have completed their four downs. They could intercept a pass. If a Fox intercepts a Redshirt pass, the ball changes hands automatically and immediately, and the Fox who got it can run or pass toward the Redshirt goal line. If the Redshirts are not taken by surprise, and are able to stop the Fox by tagging him, the Foxes begin their round of four downs at the imaginary line where the Redshirt tagged his Fox.

But what if that Fox runs the ball behind the Redshirt goal line without being tagged? Running the ball, or passing it to a teammate behind the opposing team's goal, is called a "touchdown," and is worth six points in scoring. Or what if the Redshirts, instead of trying that pass that was intercepted, had decided there wasn't much hope of a touchdown on their fourth down, and had kicked the ball over the Foxes' goal line after the fourth scrimmage? Kicking the ball over the opposing team's goal line is called a "field goal," and is worth three points in scoring.

After a successful touchdown or field goal, the teams exchange goal lines. Just as they did at the beginning of the game, the two teams line up along their own goal lines. The team that scored the points kicks off, and the game continues as before.

Ordinarily, football games are played for one hour, divided into four quarters of fifteen minutes each. Play is stopped at the end of each quarter, and the game resumes with a kickoff. At the end of the hour, the team with the higher score wins. It's much simpler to play either until everyone is tired and quits by mutual consent, or until one team reaches a prearranged score, say thirty points.

There are, of course, other regulations that more serious players may wish to add to this informal game. In versions closer to regulation football, teams that act illegally—push or trip another player, continue to run after being tagged, or cross the scrimmage line before the count of "three Mississippi"—are penalized. Penalties may include taking away one down from the offending team, or moving them backward 5, 10 or 15 yards if the ball is in their possession. The defending team may be penalized by giving the equivalent reward to the team that has possession. You may wish to play for a while and see what actions cause trouble in your own style of play before making up regulations to cover them. Your own problem may be more endless huddles or ball hogging than tripping and grabbing. Whatever your regulations are, there is the problem of who is to monitor them. Regulation football leaves it to the referee, but the impartial eye required is hard to come by among family and friends. The fewer rules, of course, the less onerous the role of referee. On the other hand, less competent players may make good referees, or a rotating referee position might strike both sides as fair.

The use of sidelines automatically adds regulations. The rule is, the moment the ball moves beyond the sidelines, whether it is a pass or a run, the ball is considered "dead" and play is stopped. The next down begins with the scrimmage line moved to the point where the ball was last held before going out of bounds. Needless to say, imaginary sidelines don't work at all. Either mark continuous sidelines or forget them entirely.

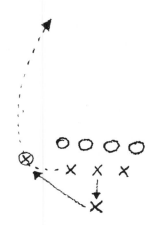

*On the third play, the quarterback tosses the ball to a teammate only a few steps away at the scrimmage line.*

# BACKYARD SOCCER

*Four or more players divided into two teams, but the game is best with four or more per team*

*Soccer ball or large rubber ball*
*Markers for laying out the field*
*Sticks or other tall markers for goal posts*

**OBJECT: To score points by kicking the ball through the opposing team's goal**

Lay out the rectangular soccer field with chalk on a paved surface or with shirts or other markers on grass. The regulation length for the two long sidelines is 110 yards, and the width of the field is 80 yards. This of course may be reduced to suit the size of the teams and space restrictions.

In the middle of the two endlines, place markers for the two goals about 15 feet apart. Sticks several feet high stuck into the ground make the goals easier to judge, but if you are playing on a hard surface or have no stakes, any other tall objects, such as garbage pails, will do.

Divide the players into two teams of equal strength. Decide which team is to have possession of the ball first. Each team chooses the goal they will defend and elects a goalie. The goalies take their positions just forward of their goal markers.

In regulation Soccer, the teams are divided into fullbacks, who stay near the goal in order to defend it; halfbacks, who remain near the center of the field to play both offensively and defensively; and the forwards, who marshal the attack against the opposing goal. But since there usually aren't enough players in Backyard Soccer to take all these positions, players are allowed to move anywhere on the field they wish.

## CAPTAINS AND SIDES

*Small groups of players—five or six—seldom need a captain to run the team. Being the boss of one or two is just silly. When a group is this small, choose sides conversationally by common consent. Best friends object to playing against one another, and sometimes sisters or brothers won't play together no matter what. Two big kids against three small ones may work as well as a big and a small against another big and two smalls. Do the best you can with what you have, and change sides if your first decision doesn't work.*

*For larger groups, the easiest tactic is to choose captains, by a "who goes first" method (p. 82) or by vote. Then the captains take turns selecting their team from among the remaining players. Permanent teams seem at first a good solution. The trouble is that one missing member in a small team can throw the whole thing out of whack. Trading players on such occasions may be helpful.*

At the "face-off," which begins the game, the ball is placed in the center of the field. Two or three members of the team chosen to have possession (let's call them the Bombs) gather around the ball in a loose semicircle, facing the opposing goal. The defending team (the Crackers) stands several feet back to give the attackers plenty of room to start.

When everyone is ready, one of the members of the Bombs kicks the ball to one of his teammates, setting it, and the game, in motion. From then on, until a goal is scored, the team in control of the ball attacks the opposing team's goal, kicking and passing the ball forward into enemy territory until they are close enough to take shots at the goal. The team without control of the ball tries to defend its goal and wrest possession of the ball from the attackers by intercepting it. Once the defenders have control of the ball, they become the attackers and rush toward their opponents' goal.

The ball can be moved by kicking it, or by bouncing it off the head, chest or thighs. One player can dribble it down the field himself by making short forward kicks as he runs, or several players can advance it quickly by passing it among themselves. With the exception of the goalies, who are allowed to use any part of their bodies to defend the goal, no player may touch the ball with his hands, arms or shoulders. Using the shoulders or arms purposely is a "hands" violation and carries a penalty. Soccer is a non-contact sport, so a push or trip between players is also penalized.

When the Bombs move close enough to the Crackers' goal, a member of the team kicks a shot at the goal. The Cracker goalie tries to block or intercept the shot using any part of his body. If the goalie can, he catches the ball, leisurely walks a few feet forward, then kicks the ball out of his hands toward other Crackers, who if they gain possession then become the attacking team and move the ball toward the Bombs' goal. If the goalie fails to intercept the shot at the goal, the goal only counts as a point for the Bombs if the ball goes between the goal markers and flies no higher than the goalie's upstretched arms.

If the Bombs make the goal, and score a point, the ball is picked up and placed in the center of the field for a new face-off, started this time by the Crackers.

If the Bombs and the Crackers each have seven or more people on their teams, they might use the regulation "offsides" rule. In order to prevent a member of the team with possession from stationing himself up close to the opposing goal, where he'd be able to bounce a lucky pass right into the goal without warning, the offsides rule says that an attacking player must have at least two defending players, or one defending player and the ball, between him and the goal at all times. If an attacking player violates this rule, his team suffers an "indirect free kick" penalty. With only a few players on each team, of course, the offsides rule isn't used.

If a member of the Bombs accidentally kicks or bounces the ball out of bounds on one of the sides of the field, the ball is thrown in by a member of the Crackers. This player goes outside the field, picks up the ball, and using his hands, throws the ball forward to a waiting teammate from the point where the ball went out of bounds. The game continues as before.

## SOCCER ON ICE

*Ice Hockey can be played almost exactly like Soccer, except that the ball is replaced by a puck (a real one or a flat stone) and must be hit only with the hockey stick. For safety, no shots that carry the puck up off the surface of the ice are allowed in informal play. The goal lines can be marked by garbage cans instead of sticks. And there is one rule change: Skaters are allowed beyond the end line to retrieve a puck that has overshot the goal. There is one additional bit of cooperation too: if a bunch of you favor Charlie's pond for Ice Hockey, that doesn't mean Charlie gets to clear it every time it snows.*

If a shot kicked by the Bombs misses the goal and goes beyond the Crackers' endline, the Cracker goalie retrieves it, places it about 20 feet in front of the goal, and he or a teammate kicks it forward on the run. If a member of the defending Crackers team accidentally kicks the ball beyond his own endline, his team is penalized with a "corner kick." A member of the Bombs then takes the ball off to a corner on the Crackers' end of the field, and kicks the ball onto the field not far from the goal so that a ready teammate may be able to make a quick score.

Soccer is sometimes played on a time limit basis. A time limit is agreed on at the beginning of the game. At the end of half that time, players take a brief break and resume the game after switching goals. After the expiration of the limit, the team with the highest score wins the game. Timing, however, requires that a bystander be willing to watch the time.

More often, Backyard Soccer is played informally on a score basis, in which the team which first reaches an agreed-upon score wins the game.

# STICKBALL

*Six or more players, divided into two teams*

*A rubber ball or tennis ball*
*Markers for bases*
*Cut-down broomstick or baseball bat*
*Baseball gloves (optional)*

*OBJECT: To accumulate more points than the opposing team by batting the ball out of the other team's reach and running around the bases to score runs*

Stickball, as played in backyards, playgrounds, and streets all over the country, is a simplified version of baseball.

Using whatever markers are handy mark out on the ground the four bases of a baseball "diamond." The four bases should form the corners of a large square. The distances between the bases should be roughly the same, but can be made longer or shorter to suit the area; a good distance is 50 to 75 feet. The base with the least amount of space behind it, from which the batters will hit the ball outward into the field, is "home plate." The other three bases, counting counterclockwise from home plate, are first base, second base, and third base.

Divide the players into two teams of equal strength. Choose one team to be up at bat first. The team at bat congregates behind home plate, and chooses an order in which their own members will go to bat. The other team, the one "in the field," spreads out around the three bases. They try to put at least one man on or near first base, someone to cover second and third, and the rest beyond the bases in the "outfield," where they can catch any balls that are hit far out. If there are enough players on the fielding team, they also choose a pitcher to stand near the center of the baseball diamond and throw the ball to the batter, and a catcher to stand behind home plate and catch throws the batter misses. If there aren't enough players to cover all the bases and provide a pitcher

SOCCER PENALTIES

*DIRECT KICK: This penalty is awarded to the team opposing the one responsible for a violation of hands or of physical contact. Play stops, and the ball is placed at the point where the violation occurred. One good kicker from the opposing team is chosen. As everyone moves out of the way of his kick, he runs toward the ball and boots it as far forward as possible. Then play continues as before. A direct kick is especially dangerous for a defending team if it incurs the penalty within 40 feet of the goal. Then the penalty kick is taken from directly in front of the goal at about 25 feet away, with no one but the goalie to stop the score.*

*INDIRECT KICK: This penalty is awarded to the opposing team for an offsides violation, for charging a player who doesn't have the ball, or for making a dangerous play. It is just the same as the direct kick, except that the kicker must pass the ball to a teammate waiting up ahead, rather than take a direct shot forward.*

and a catcher, the team at bat can provide a stand-in pitcher and
catcher from whoever is unoccupied at the moment, though
someone in the field will still have to race to home base if there's a
chance to put a runner out there. Alternately, the batter can pitch
for himself, just throwing the ball up and hitting it outward, in
which case a catcher will be needed only to put a runner out at
home.

In order, each batter stands up near home plate, takes the bat
(or stick) in his hands, and tries to hit the ball thrown toward him
by the pitcher. The batter can choose to swing at the pitched ball,
or, if he doesn't like the way it was thrown, he can ignore the
throw and wait for another. This is called a "ball." Unlike
regulation baseball, the pitching in Stickball doesn't need to be all
that accurate, since most players swing at anything that comes
close. Therefore the concept of the "strike zone" between a batter's armpits and his knees, in which any pitch must be swung at, is
usually disregarded. For this reason, the rule that the batter can
"walk" to first after four balls may also be ignored.

When the batter hits the ball, the hit is legal only if the ball
flies (or rolls) into the area between an imaginary line extending
from home plate through first base, and another imaginary line
from home plate through third base. Otherwise the ball is "foul"
rather than "fair," and the hit doesn't count.

"strike." If he strikes three times, he's "out," and the next batter
takes his place. Every time a batter hits a foul ball, it also counts as
a strike, unless he already has two strikes racked up; after that,
fouls don't count as strikes. Even if the batter hits a fair ball, he is
still out if the ball is caught on the fly (in either fair or foul

territory) by any member of the opposing team.

If the batter hits the ball into fair territory, he dashes toward first base, and either stays there or, if he thinks it is safe, just touches the base and continues on to second base, third base, or even all the way around the bases and back to home plate, making a "home run." Meanwhile, assuming the ball wasn't caught on the fly, members of the opposing team are scrambling after the ball in an attempt to throw it to a waiting teammate on the base toward which the batter is running. If the runner is tagged with the ball by a member of the opposing team before he reaches the safety of the base, he's out. Runners have to stay on the line between bases; they can't dodge sideways. If the runner makes it to a base safely without being tagged by the ball, he stays there as the next batter on his team comes up to home plate to take his turn. (Batters are, however, allowed to touch first base and overrun it slightly without being tagged, and anyone who has gotten to home plate simply retires to await his next turn at bat.)

A "man on base" (a runner who has made it safely to a base), stays put until another member of his team hits a fair ball. When this happens, he can run as many bases forward as he chooses, or none at all. The moment a man leaves base, he is vulnerable to being tagged with the ball by a member of the opposing team and put out.

Since no more than one runner may be on a base at one time, it often happens that a man is forced to run. For example, if there were a man on first base and another on second base when a batter made a fair hit, the runner on first would have no choice but to make room for the batter, while the runner on second would be forced to run at least to third. If there were one runner on second and no one on first when the batter made his hit, the one on base would have the choice of running or not. Because a forced runner hasn't any choice, a member of the fielding team can put him out just by holding the ball and stepping on the base that the runner is trying to reach; tagging isn't necessary. Since the batter's run to first base is always "forced" (he has no choice in the matter), the fielder on first base never has to do any actual tagging. This "force out" is the basis for the most common "double play," in which two men from the team at bat are put out at the same time. There is a runner on first, and the batter hits a weak ball right to the first baseman's feet; the batter has to run, even though he knows it's useless, and so does the player on first. The first baseman picks up the ball and steps on base, putting the batter out automatically, and then throws the ball to the second baseman, who steps onto the base to force that player out as well.

Whenever a runner reaches home plate safely, his team scores one point, or "run." If there are several players on base when a batter hits a good one, the other players may make it home too, and each add a run to their team's score. When the batting order is run through once, it starts over again at the beginning, and batting continues until the team has had three outs.

When three men are out, the team's turn at bat is finished, marking the end of the first half of the first "inning." The two teams then switch places; the team at bat becomes the new fielding team, and the team in the field comes up to bat. When this new team at bat gets three outs in its turn, the two teams switch again. This marks the end of the first inning, and the second inning

## STICKBALL WITHOUT STICKS

*For a slower game that is easier to play and has no dangerous sticks flailing around, try Kickball. The Kickball diamond is the same as the Stickball diamond, but the distance between bases is shorter, and instead of using a small light-weight ball, Kickball uses a larger rubber ball or beachball.*

*The rules of the game are identical to Stickball. The pitcher throws the ball toward home base, where the "kicker" (rather than batter) attempts to boot the ball into fair territory. If the fielders manage to throw, kick or roll the ball to the first baseman before the kicker reaches the safety of the base, the kicker is out.*

*Three strikes (unsuccessful kicks) is an out, as is a kick caught on the fly. Three outs ends a half-inning, and nine innings ends the game. The team with the most points wins.*

begins. (A full inning ends after each team has been up at bat for three outs.)

At the end of nine innings, or a different number decided in advance, the team that scored the highest total of runs wins the game. If it's a tie, another inning is played and another, if necessary, until the tie is broken.

*Stealing Bases:* If there are enough players on the fielding team (at least six or seven), you can allow runners to "steal" bases between hits. This means that when the pitcher (or whoever has the ball) is looking the other way, a man on base can quickly dash to another base without waiting for a batter to hit the ball. If he makes it to the base without being tagged, he's safe.

With less than six players on each team, it becomes too easy for men to steal bases, and only spoils the game.

*Ghost Men on Base:* If there are three or less players on the batting team, it becomes impossible to have a man on each base and still have one left over to bat. When there are people on all three bases and no one to bat, many players let the teammate whose turn it is to bat leave base and proceed with batting and running as usual. There is said to be a "ghost man" on the vacant base, who runs only when forced to, and can run to home just like ordinary players can. The only difference is that you can't see a "ghost" man, and you can't tag or force him out.

A better way to solve the problem of not having enough players, however, is just to reduce the number of bases to two. The baseball diamond becomes a triangle, with a home plate, first base and second base.

## ONE NET BASKETBALL

*Two or more players, divided into two teams*

*Basketball*
*Basketball net, mounted 8 to 10 feet up on a wall*
*Markers for laying out the court*

*OBJECT: To score points by throwing the ball through the net*

Chalk or mark half a basketball court in front of the net. Set the sidelines perpendicular to the basket and about 20 feet to either side of it. Mark a foul line about 16 feet in front of the net, and a center line another 16 feet beyond that. If you don't have that much space, reduce the dimensions to fit whatever area is available.

Choose two teams of equal strength. The teams spread out on the court in readiness for the "jump ball" which starts the game. Two players—one from each team (your captain, or whoever you think is your best player)—stand facing one another about midway between the foul line and center line. A third player takes the basketball and throws it up between them. The two players jump up, and try to tap the ball to their waiting teammates.

Whichever team gets the ball tries to get it through the basket, while the opposing team attempts to wrest possession of the ball and score its own baskets. The ball can be moved by passing from one player to another, dribbling the ball (bouncing it up and down with one hand), throwing it, or rolling it. The ball may not be kicked or carried. If a player who has been dribbling for a while stops moving and holds the ball, he must pass it to another player or take a throw at the basket; he can't begin dribbling again after a pause.

Almost any means can be used to intercept the ball. It can be grabbed from another player's hands, intercepted as he tries to pass it, caught when he throws it, or picked up as it is rolling along the ground. However, Basketball is a non-contact sport, so players are not allowed to touch one another. Any sort of physical contact constitutes a foul. To simulate a full court, every time a team gains possession of the ball it must be dribbled or passed out beyond the center line before bringing it back in for a shot at the basket.

When a player gets near enough to the basket, he attempts a shot at it. His opponents, of course, try to block his shot with their arms and hands. If the shot misses, he or she or one of his teammates can rush in, catch it "on the rebound" and take another shot. (If a member of the other team gets it instead, the ball must be taken out beyond the center line before it can be shot at the basket.) If the ball goes into the basket, the shooter's team scores two points. The other team then gets possession of the ball, and one member of that team passes the ball to another teammate from behind the center line to continue the game.

When a member of a team carries the ball out of bounds or was the last to touch it before it flew out, the other team gains possession. A member of that team picks up the ball, carries it to the point where it went out of bounds, and passes the ball to one of his teammates.

When a personal foul occurs—one that involves physical contact between two players—the team that was violated is awarded a free shot. If the foul interfered with a player's attempt to shoot a basket, his team may be given two free shots. The best shooter from the team is chosen. He stands at the foul line, takes aim, and throws at the basket. If he misses, all the players run in to try to get possession. If he makes a basket, his team scores one point (in contrast to the two scored by an ordinary shot), and the game proceeds with the scoring team's throw-in from the center line. Other fouls, such as kicking or carrying the ball, or stopping and restarting a dribble, are handled differently. The team that fouled must give up the ball to a member of the opposing team, who takes it out of bounds and tosses it to a teammate to start play again.

If it happens that two players are struggling with each other for the ball, one tugging one way, the other tugging the other way, players can call a "held" ball. The two rivals let go of the ball, face each other, and a third player throws the ball up in the air between them, just as in the first jump ball.

One Net Basketball is sometimes played on a time limit basis. Before the beginning of the game, the two teams agree on a set time to stop, and they elect a timekeeper. At the end of the time limit, the team with the greatest number of points wins the game. More commonly, however, the two teams agree on a scoring goal (such as twenty-one points) at the beginning of the game. The team that reaches the goal first is the winner.

## SMALL TEAM VOLLEYBALL

*Four or more players, divided into two teams*

*Volleyball, large rubber ball, or beachball*
*A volleyball net, or other barrier*
*Markers for boundary lines*

*OBJECT: To score points by hitting the ball to the other side of the net so that the opposing team misses it or fails to return it legally*

Volleyball is best played on an even surface such as a lawn, paving or sand. Set up the net along its full 29-foot length at a height of about 7 feet. If you have no net, a wire fence may do, or even a clothesline strung between two trees and hung with a few rags to make it more visible. Mark out a volleyball court with the net in the center, chalking the bounds lines on pavement, or marking the court with any available objects at the corners. The court should be as wide as the net and about twice as long (regular dimensions are 10 by 20 yards).

Divide the players into two teams, and choose the team that will serve first. Each team chooses one side of the net, and its members spread out within the court bounds more or less in rows, in order to be able to return the ball from any point in the court.

The game begins as the player in the far right corner of the serving side takes the ball in his left hand, tosses it up slightly, and

## SNOWTIME

All the typical backyard and street games come to a halt when the first snowstorm strikes. But the snow itself opens up all sorts of other possibilities for play, most of them quite free of regulations. Snowball fights are a free-for-all, even when played from behind elaborate snow forts. You could of course score each hit, but no one is likely to remember the score when darkness falls and ends the game. There are races and contests that offer better competition. For instance, when the snow has been packed down hard on a good sledding hill or toboggan run, you could hold a race complete with timekeeper and stopwatch. A slalom course for either skis or sleds can be set up with empty plastic garbage pails or thin sticks to swerve around. Good old skating races are terrific, and Ice Tag is fun, too, with or without skates. A more casual contest can be held to judge the best snow sculpture on the block. So much snow is needed for these that they're best built by small groups rather than individuals.

serves by hitting it with his fist or the edge of his palm over the net into the other team's side of the court.

The receiving team tries to return the ball without letting it touch the ground. Each member on the team can use any part of his body above the waist to hit the ball either over the net or to a teammate, but he must not catch, hold or carry it. Each player on the receiving team can touch the ball only once or twice while it is on his side, but not twice in a row, and the team must return the ball within three touches. If the receiving team returns the serve, the ball is volleyed back and forth until one side fails to return the ball; or the ball is hit illegally (more than three times on a side, or the same player hits it twice in a row); or a player catches, holds or carries it; or the ball is hit out of bounds.

If the team which missed the ball is the serving team, it loses the serve. The opposing team gets the ball, serves, and a new volley begins. If the team that missed the ball was the team served to, the serving team scores a point and keeps the serve. Only the team that has the serve can score a point. In order that every member of the team gets a chance to serve, the members of each team rotate their positions whenever the serve switches to their side.

The first team to reach fifteen points (or another scoring limit set beforehand) wins the game.

For informal play, the service rules can be ignored. A team scores a point whenever the opposing team misses, returns illegally, or hits the ball out of bounds. The next team to serve is the one nearest the ball. For very small teams which may have trouble returning the ball, the rules can be altered to allow a team to hit the ball as many times as it needs in order to knock it over the net.

# STREET HANDBALL

*Two players, or four playing as partners*

*A small rubber ball or tennis ball*
*Wall and hard surface for court*
*Markers for laying out court*

**OBJECT: To score points by hitting the ball at the wall in such a way that when it bounces back your opponent will be unable to return it correctly**

Mark out a rectangular court on the ground or paving, using the wall to form one of the rectangle's short sides. The area might be a playground with a backboard, a driveway and garage door, or the paving in front of a building. The regulation court size is 20 feet wide by 34 feet deep but this can be adjusted to suit the amount of wall space and paving available. Mark a serving line parallel to the wall and about 16 feet in front of it. Choose the player (or partners) to serve first.

The players stand in the center of the court, facing the wall. The server takes the ball and drops it. As it bounces back up, he hits the ball with either of his hands so that it flies toward the wall. For the serve to be valid, it must bounce beyond the serving line after it rebounds from the wall. The server gets two tries to serve correctly; if he fails, his opponent gets the serve.

## RACKETBALL

*Racketball is a game with rules similar to Handball. However, the small comfortable racket and the special pudgy rubber ball lend themselves to the most casual sort of play, at times when a relief from scoring and competing is in order. Play either out in the open with two players simply volleying the ball back and forth (no net is necessary), or against a backboard or garage door by yourself or with a partner. The volleying can be liesurely or very fast, to suit your mood. You can also play by just popping the ball into the air as many times as you can without letting it drop; or hitting it onto a sloped roof, letting it roll down, and trying to get it up again repeatedly without letting it touch the ground.*

After the ball has been served, the server's opponent dashes toward the ball as it rebounds from the wall, and attempts to intercept the ball before it has bounced on the court floor more than once. He may hit the ball on the first bounce or before it has hit the ground at all. With a swing of his hand he slaps it back toward the wall. This continues, each player hitting the ball against the wall in turn, until a player fails to return the ball, or hits it improperly, so that it flies over the wall, hits the ground before touching the wall, flies out of bounds on the sides, or bounces beyond the end line. Any of these failures to return the ball correctly constitutes a miss.

After a miss, play stops briefly. If the server's opponent was the one who missed the ball or hit it illegally, the server gets the point, and serves again. If it was the server himself who didn't return the ball correctly, the serve changes hands and the game resumes. You can only score points while you have the serve.

If one player interferes with another at a crucial moment by stepping in his line of sight, batting the ball out of turn, or getting in his way, the player who was interfered with can cry, "Foul!" The entire volley may be invalidated, and taken over again with a new serve by the same player.

The first player to reach twenty-one points wins the game.

The doubles game is played similarly. Whichever partner is nearer the ball when that team is returning it, hits it. During the serve, only the partner who is serving is allowed on the court. The excluded partner can rush back in as soon as the served ball has hit the wall.

A variation of this game can be played with three walls or even four walls enclosing the court. The serve is still bounced off only one (the "front" wall), but during the rest of the game any of the other walls may be used, as long as after hitting a side or back wall the ball ricochets off the front wall before hitting the ground.

# ULTIMATE FRISBEE

*Any even number of players, divided into two teams*

*FRISBEE*
*Markers for bounds and goal lines*

**OBJECT:** *To score points by getting the FRISBEE beyond the opposing team's goal line by passing it from teammate to teammate*

Ultimate FRISBEE is a team game designed especially for the FRISBEE. Mark out a rectangular playing field about 180 feet long and half as wide (it can be made larger or smaller to suit the area). The lines at the ends are goal lines, and the sides are bounds lines.

Divide the players into two teams of equal size, and choose one team to make the "throw-off." Each team picks a goal line to defend, and lines up along it.

To start the game, a member of the chosen team throws the FRISBEE toward the receiving team. If the receivers catch it, or let it fall to the ground without touching it, they get possession of the FRISBEE immediately and start passing it from one teammate to another to advance it down the field. Their opponents, meanwhile, try to intercept it and throw it back the other way. If during the throw-off, however, the FRISBEE touches a receiver who fails to catch it, the throw-off team rushes up, takes possession of it, and tries to move it toward the receivers' goal line.

The FRISBEE can only be moved by passing it from one player to another. You cannot run or walk with it (except for a few excusable lurches after catching a pass), or hand it to another player. But you can pivot with the FRISBEE, in order to pass it in another direction. If a player from one team attempts a pass which isn't successfully caught by a teammate, possession of the FRISBEE passes to the opposing team, and a member of that team throws it from wherever it hit the ground and stopped. Passes can also be intercepted by opposing players, and possession of the FRISBEE often changes in that way.

If one team throws the FRISBEE outside the side bounds, a member of the opposing team throws it in from where it landed.

A team can only score a goal by successfully passing the FRISBEE to a teammate stationed behind the goal line. If it isn't successfully caught by the waiting teammate, the opponents gain possession.

After a successful goal, the two teams switch sides, and the serving team then throws the FRISBEE to the other team, as at the beginning of the game.

The game can be played with a time limit so that the team scoring the greatest number of goals by the end of the agreed limit wins, or by a predetermined score; the first team to reach eleven points (or some other number) wins the game.

*FRISBEE CATCH*

*Like the rubber ball, the games which can be played with a FRISBEE are numberless. The simplest game is two-handed catch, but it can be made more complicated by introducing more players; by playing with two or more FRISBEES simultaneously; or by introducing any rules which might seem fun, such as passing the FRISBEE in patterns, bouncing it off a wall, or keeping it away from a third player.*

# BADMINTON

*Two players, or four playing as partners*

*Badminton net and poles*
*A badminton racket for each player*
*Birdies*
*Markers for boundaries*

**OBJECT:** *To score points by hitting the birdie into your opponent's side of the court in such a way that he fails to hit it back correctly*

On a non-windy day, when the birdie won't be buffeted around unpredictably, stretch the badminton net out between its poles in an open area. Mark the bounds of the badminton court with any available objects, or draw it on pavement with chalk. Two sidelines are marked parallel to each other, split in the center by the net, and two endline bounds are marked at a distance of about 45 feet from the net at each end of the court. Mark two service lines across the court about 3½ feet from the net on both sides.

Each player, or pair of players in the doubles game, takes one side of the net. Decide which player will serve first.

The game begins when one player serves the birdie by hitting it from the rear of his court over the net so that it flies beyond the service line on the opposite side of the court. If he fails, the serve goes to his opponent. If a serve is good, his opponent then tries to hit the birdie back to the server's side, but within the bounds of the court. The birdie can't touch the ground at any point, but it can brush the net, so long as it gets over it. The two players continue volleying the birdie back and forth until one player fails to return the birdie over the net or hits it out of bounds.

# TOURNAMENT

There are two basic ways to set up a tournament, whether the game is Badminton, Jacks, Ping-Pong, or Chess. The first is the kind in which everyone competes in pairs. Every time a match is completed, the loser drops out of the competition. The winners of the first set of matches compete with each other in the semifinals, and the survivors of the semifinals compete in the finals, until one player, the champion, remains. The whole scheme looks like this:

Mom Dad   Suzy Pete   Mike
  Mom        Pete      Mike
     Mom           Pete
          Pete

The larger the family is (or the more friends who get into the act), the more matches it takes to decide the champion.

Unfortunately, this system doesn't make allowances for players who may improve their game during the tournament. Besides, the tournament is over all too quickly. After using this scheme to get a rough idea of who the weakest and strongest players are, you might try setting up the more complicated type of tournament, sometimes called a "ladder."

Make a list of the competing players, with the strongest at the top and the weakest near the bottom. A good way to set this up with the least trouble is to write each contestant's name on a strip of paper and pin the strips in a column on a bulletin board.

Such a list could look like this:

Pete
Mom
Dad
Mike
Suzy

As players improve their game, they can challenge others above them on the ladder. Mike, for example, could challenge Mom to a match. If Mike won, he'd take Mom's place on the ladder while Mom (and everyone below her) would be moved down one:

Pete
Mike
Mom
Dad
Suzy

If Mom succeeded in defending her position by beating Mike (or if the game were a draw), the ladder would stay the same. Shift the strips of paper around to reflect changes in the order.

Using this system, the tournament never really ends. The ladder is dynamic, accurately reflecting people's changing abilities. It also allows new people to come into the competition. When a new player enters the tournament, just put him at the bottom of the ladder and let him work his way up.

What happens at the end of a volley depends on who missed the birdie. If the player who served the birdie at the beginning of the volley missed, he simply loses the serve. His opponent gets the birdie and makes the next serve to begin a new volley. If the server's opponent misses the birdie, however, the server keeps the serve and scores one point. You can only score a point during your serve.

The first player to accumulate twenty-one points (or some other agreed upon score) wins the game.

The regulation doubles game is played in the same way as the singles game, except that each partner on a team gets at least one serve (giving the team a total of two serves) regardless of scoring before the serve passes to the other team. After each successful volley, the players on the serving team switch positions (left to right) on their side of the net.

For informal badminton, the game can be simplified by forgetting the service rules, and playing so that every time someone misses the birdie, or knocks it out of bounds, his opponent scores a point. The next service is performed by whoever the birdie landed nearest. If the birdie is hit into the bushes or very far away, it's the responsibility of the player who hit it last to retrieve it.

The two most effective badminton shots are these:

DROP SHOT: Standing close to the net, lightly tap the birdie in such a way that it just clears the top of the net and drops straight to the ground as your opponent vainly dives for it. This shot is even deadlier when you position it way to one side of the court.

SMASH: With a snap of the wrist, smash the birdie at top speed downward and toward a far corner of your opponent's side of the court. This one takes more practice, as there's a chance you'll hit it out of bounds.

## HORSESHOES

*Two players*

*Four horseshoes and two pegs*
*Markers for throwing lines*

*OBJECT: To score points by throwing your horseshoes nearer to the peg than your opponent's*

You can use a commercial Horseshoes set, or devise your own with real horseshoes and stakes made of 3/4-inch dowels cut into two equal segments each sharpened at one end. On a level area, stick the two pegs firmly into the ground about 40 feet apart (or less, to make the game easier). Mark a throwing line on the ground about 2 feet in front of each peg.

Decide on a scoring goal to reach (twenty-five to fifty points is usual), and choose the player who will throw first. Each player takes a pair of horseshoes—the throwing horseshoes you buy in stores are in colored pairs so that you can tell one player's shoes from the other's.

The first player tosses his horseshoes one at a time from behind the throwing line, trying to land them as near as possible to the opposite peg. Then his opponent tosses his two horseshoes. After both players have tossed, they walk over to the opposite peg, and figure out the score in the following manner.

A player scores one point for each shoe he has thrown that is closer to the peg than his opponent's, providing his shoe is within 6 inches (a man's handbreadth) of the peg. Take your nearest shot and compare it to your opponent's nearest shot. If yours is closer to the peg, you win a point. Now compare your other shot to his other shot. If his is closer this time, he gets a point. Furthermore, each player scores three points for each "ringer" (a horseshoe that encircles the stake and stays there). Distances are measured from where horseshoes come to rest, not where they first hit.

After computing the score, the two players pick up their shoes, and pitch them in turn from behind the throwing line back toward the opposite peg.

The game continues in this way until one player reaches the scoring goal and wins the game.

# Anywhere Games

# Chapter 4
# Anywhere Games

There are games in this section that travel better than any others, because they can be carried in your head. There are no game pieces to lose, no cards to slip, not even a ball to roll off into the bushes. Most of the playing pieces are words and numbers. Adults will be pleased to hear that they also require no leaping, dashing, screaming or throwing—though giggles can't be helped. They do require intelligence, and a store of knowledge helps in some. To complete the neatness, quietness and portability of Anywhere Games, they often lend themselves to play by only two players, although you can add players if they happen to be available.

The joy of such word and number games depends to a degree on wit, but the wit can be appropriate to the players' age. We have suggested games that are excellent for toddlers, for preschoolers and for school-age kids as well as those that provide keen competition for adults. Because of their take-me-along quality, such games can be played in the car during tedious trips, waiting in offices for overdue appointments, or on rainy afternoons when dull minds can use a pick-me-up.

Only slightly less portable are a second category of games included here: pencil and paper games. Besides any bits of scrap paper that are lying around, you can use small pads, and pens or pencils that fit easily into a pocket. The game designs are small enough so several will easily fit on a sheet, with as many on the back. Again, some of these games are for the highly skilled. Sprouts, for instance (page 118), is a mathematician's game, especially when played with more than five dots. But Droodles, Hangman and Boxes can be played by much younger people. It's a pity we can't say the same of calculator games. For many, games that involve long numbers are never easy, although the games included here are not theoretically beyond the grasp of school-age children. You may wonder why games requiring pocket calculators can be considered "anywhere" games. These days, there are people who wouldn't be caught anywhere without their calculators.

There is one inconvenience to this section. Unless you know the games already when you are stuck somewhere with nothing to do, you need the book to tell you how to play. It would be silly to take a book along in order to play games that you're not supposed to have special equipment for (unless you're headed for a vacation, of course), so the only solution is to play plenty of them now and get them by heart. That way you'll be prepared no matter where you find yourself.

# TWENTY QUESTIONS

*Two players*

*OBJECT: To guess the object that your opponent is thinking of by asking no more than twenty questions*

The two players decide who goes first, and what category the object will be in. The category could be An Animal, Something in This Room, A Famous Person, Something You Can Eat, or any other you agree on.

The first player thinks of an item in the category, and the other player begins to ask questions. The questions have to be of the "yes or no" type. You could ask, "Is it red?," "Is it made of paper?" or "Do I use it at dinnertime?" But you could not ask a question requiring a choice, "Does it eat grass or birdseed?," or one that requests a specific answer, "Which side of the room is it nearest?"

When the questioner thinks he has figured out the object, he tells his opponent his guess. If it isn't right, the game continues until he does guess correctly, or until he has used up his twenty questions. Keeping track on fingers of how many questions have been asked may lead to disagreement. Pencil and paper are helpful.

After a player's turn ends, he switches roles with his opponent, who now tries to guess the object.

If you want to keep score and declare a winner, there are two ways to do it. The simplest is to score one point for each object guessed correctly within the twenty question limit. The more complicated, but more telling, way is to score the number of questions required by each player in each round of the game. The player who scores the fewest total questions is the winner.

Good questioning requires strategy. The trick is to make each question count by narrowing down the possibilities as much as possible. If the category is Animals, for instance, the question "Is it brown?" doesn't help you much. A yes answer only narrows the possibilities to zillions of brown animals, including brown birds, reptiles, insects and fish. A no answer offers even less. The question "Is it a mammal?" will tell you more. A no answer at least knocks out a large group of possible animals, and a yes answer narrows the field even more. If the object is a mammal, your next question might relate to size ("Is it smaller than a deer?") or to habitat ("Is it native to this country?"). In only two more questions ("Does it normally live in groups?") and "Am I likely to see it in a zoo?"), you might have discovered that this animal is smaller than a deer, not native to America, communal, and not likely to be seen in a zoo. What next? The sixth question can knock out a lot of possibilities by giving you a clue to diet: "Does it eat vegetation?" The answer is no, but you still don't know enough for wild guessing. Zero in on size again, until you know, say, that it is smaller than a rabbit. Now you're getting somewhere. There really aren't very many small mammals that don't eat vegetable matter—all the rodents, for instance, are now out of the competition. Perhaps the non-native mongoose, not ordinarily seen in zoos, occurs to you—unless you know that they don't live communally. Even ignorance on that score won't defeat the purpose of the next question: "Does it kill its prey in order to eat it?" The answer is no. Now let's see what sort of mental image you can conjure up: a small, clannish sort of creature who eats either carrion (remember, he doesn't kill to eat) or... that's it—blood! Time for a real stab: "Is it a vampire bat?" The answer is yes, and you score well with only seven questions.

However, your good score was the result not only of clever questioning, but of poor strategy on your opponent's part. He chose too special an animal. Had he thought of an antelope—or better yet only one of the dozens of antelope species—you might not have guessed it. The group of larger-than-a-deer, group-living, grass-eating, zoo-inhabiting, non-native animals is enormous. Furthermore, had your opponent thought specifically of the nilgai, which you have probably never heard of, you would have had no chance at all. Needless to say, the player with special knowledge in a category has the advantage in Twenty Questions.

## GUESS THE NUMBER

### Two players

**OBJECT: To guess the number your opponent has in mind in the fewest possible tries**

Agree on who is to go first, and decide on a range within which the number will fall. For instance, it can be any number between 1 and 100, or for experienced players, between 1 and 1000.

The player who goes first thinks of a number within the decided range. The second player can get information about the secret number in only one way: he names a number, and his opponent tells him whether the secret number is higher or lower than the one he guessed (or is the correct number). Questioning continues until the secret number is guessed correctly. Serious players keep track of the number of guesses required to reach the answer; the player who discovers the number in the fewest guesses is the winner.

There is a winning strategy to Guess The Number: Always guess a number that is halfway between the possible limits. At the beginning of a game when you have only the information that the number lies between 1 and 100, guess 50. If your opponent answers "higher," you know the secret number is between 51 and

### QUESTIONS FOR KIDS

*The strategy required for Twenty Questions is too hard for young children, but there are two other questioning games that can be played by children as young as three. I See Something is the easier. One player thinks of an object in sight, and a clue as to its nature—its color, say, or its use. He says, "I see something red", or "I see something to eat." The other player looks around, and either guesses directly or asks questions that will help him guess the object. Animal, Vegetable, Mineral is harder, because the object isn't in sight and the only clue is whether it is made of animal material (a leather shoe or chicken soup), vegetable (a piece of paper or a log) or mineral (a cup or a magnet). There is no limit to the number of questions, but the categories are difficult. A rubber band is vegetable (made of the sap of a tree), and a seashell is not mineral, because it is made by an animal.*

100. Your next guess should be 75. Your opponent answers "lower." Now guess midway between 51 and 75, or about 63. You will soon have his number trapped, say between 63 and 66. You can now guess the only two possibilities singly—either 64 or 65 has to be the answer.

If you think about it, you can see that the strategy for choosing a number that is hardest to guess is to choose a number close to the low or high limit, or close to the midway point. The numbers 2, 99, 49 and 51 require more than the ordinary number of questions.

## GRANDMOTHER'S TRUNK

*Three or more players*

*OBJECT: To remember and recite a growing list of objects in sequence*

Decide on the order in which players will take their turns. The first player thinks of an object—a teapot for example—and starts the game by saying "I put a teapot in Grandmother's trunk." (There is another version of this game called I Went On A Trip. The only difference is that the player says "I went on a trip and took my teapot.") The next player repeats this statement, but adds another item: "I put a teapot and an elephant in Grandmother's trunk." Each player in turn repeats the objects already in the trunk and adds still another to the growing list. When the list has finally grown so long that a player can't remember it all, or mixes up the sequence, the list is started over again by the next player. A person who flubs three times is out, and the last person left in the game is the winner.

Besides the gratification this sort of memory testing offers, the fun of the game comes from the ridiculous contents themselves. Kindergarteners can get hilarious over "a smelly porcupine, sliced worms, maple syrup, cookie crumbs, and mud."

## ALPHABET

*Two or more players*

*Watch or clock with a second hand for timing (optional)*

*OBJECT: To name, within the time limit, a word that begins with a particular letter of the alphabet*

Decide on the order in which players will take their turns, and a time limit for each turn. Fifteen seconds is usual.

The first player names any letter of the alphabet. The rest of the players, in turn, have to name any word beginning with that letter before the time limit expires. If a clock or watch isn't available for keeping time, a player can be chosen to keep time by slowly (and quietly) counting "one-and-two-and-three-and..." until the limit is reached.

## TODDLER GAMES

For those who need much simpler Anywhere Games, to keep a toddler amused during long car rides or while waiting for the doctor, here are two that take advantage of the everyday contents of your pockets or pocketbook.

WHAT'S MISSING is a memory game. Spread out on lap or table a small group of objects such as a key, nickel, comb, and pencil. Help your child name each object and handle them if he wants to. Then tell him to close his eyes while you take something away. When he opens his eyes, he has to tell you which object is missing. Make the game easier with fewer objects, harder with more.

GRAB-BAG can be played using either a coat pocket, pocketbook or a paper bag you have brought along with you. Again, let your child handle and name a group of small objects. Then put them into the bag. This time he has to feel for an object inside the bag, guess what it is, then pull it out to see if he was right.

After the first round, the next player in turn gets to pick a different letter of the alphabet, and the game continues. No one can use a word which has already been spoken, and anyone failing to name a word within his time limit is out of the game. When there are only two players left in the game, one of those previously out takes over as letter-caller. The last player left is the winner.

Alphabet can be made more difficult by making a rule that words must be selected from a specific category, such as Animals or Countries. Or, the game can be played like Ghost, where after losing three times, a player becomes a Ghost, who must make other players into Ghosts by causing them to inadvertantly speak to him.

To make the game easy enough for some preschoolers, play informally and without timing. Say, "Let's think of words that begin with the sound 'buh,'" or "Let's think of the names of animals." Then each of you think up the words without taking turns.

## INITIALS

*Any number of players*

**OBJECT: To answer questions using two words that begin with your own initials**

### LICENSE PLATE POKER

*Though counting telephone poles and competing for who will be the first to see the big bridge may be absorbing games for some, there are car games that appeal to a wider age range in the family. One is trying to complete the alphabet in sequence by finding letters in signs. Even better is License Plate Poker, in which players scan the plates of other cars in search of a "hand" that will beat the other players'. The plate shown here is only a high card hand, which another player might beat in his turn by locating a pair. The letters Q, K, A and J stand for Queen, King, Ace and Jack, but there are no suits in the game. Straights are rare, but three and even four of a kind are remarkably frequent.*

Choose a player to be the first Questioner. The Questioner asks any question at all of each player in turn. The player must answer in two words that begin with his initials.

Players might be asked, "What's your favorite snack?" "Anchovy Hotcakes," might be Ann Higbee's answer, while Ned Walsh might say, "Nutty Waffles." A player who answers incorrectly, or not at all, is out of the game. The last player left in is the winner, and becomes the next Questioner. Naturally, people whose names begin with unusual letters of the alphabet tend to be losers.

To make Initials easier, play with one-word answers beginning with the initial of your first name. There are several ways to make the game harder. You can put a time limit on the answer— five seconds, say, to come up with a correct one. Or you can think up questions that are difficult to answer in two words. "What's the best way to mount a horse?" Ned Walsh might think of "Not Wildly;" but Ann  Higbee might have trouble arriving at "Alternate Hops."

# CATEGORIES I

*Three or more players, but the game is best with at least five*

*OBJECT: To name an object within the chosen category in your turn and in time to the beat*

There is a more sedate version of this game on p. 121, but this one is zany and remarkably hard. Players sit in a circle, and choose the first player to lead the group. The leader thinks up a category, such as Animals, Countries, Colors or Flowers. Then he starts the chant that leads off the game, keeping time by slapping both hands on his knees, then both hands together, and then snapping the fingers of one hand, then the other. All the other players join in, keeping the slap, clap, snap, snap rhythm at a steady pace. The leader chants:

> Let's play
> Categories
> Such as
> Animals

Each line of the chant is in time to the slap-clap of the knee and hands, then there are two snaps of the fingers before the next line of the chant, and so on. In time to the following slap-clap, the player to the left of the leader must say the name of an animal, then there is a two-snap pause, and the next player in turn must chime in with the name of another animal. No names in the category may be repeated, and each player must say his on time with only the two-snap pause between. If players are really good at the game, you can play that whoever misses (is off beat, or can't think of a name, or gives a name not in that category) is out. For un-skilled players it is better to just go back to the beginning and either repeat the category with the same leader for more practice, or go on to the next player and a different category. As you get the hang of Categories, speed up the pace until the group dissolves in hysteria.

## TABOO

*Any number of players*

*OBJECT: To avoid saying a word with the taboo letter*

Choose the player to be the first Questioner. The Questioner selects the "taboo" letter for the round, and announces it to the other players. Then he asks each player in turn any question he wishes. The player asked must respond sensibly, without using the forbidden letter. If he breaks the taboo by saying a word that includes the letter, he is out. Obvious nonsense responses are not fair play. The last player left in the game wins the round and becomes the new Questioner.

Taboo can be applied with equal merriment to ordinary conversation. Decide on the taboo letter, and do your best to get through a minute, an hour, or day without using it. With a little caution, letters like M, X, Z, Q, or L can be avoided, but getting along without E, S, or A is close to impossible.

## GHOST

*Any number of players*

*Pencil and paper for keeping track of letters (optional)*

*OBJECT: To avoid being the one who adds the last letter to a word*

Decide the order in which players will take their turns. Starting with the first, players build up unstated words letter by letter, trying not to complete any word of over three letters. The first player, thinking of the word BARN, might kick the game off with B. The next player could add E, with BEARD in mind. The third player, considering BEND, could name the letter N, making the sequence so far B-E-N. The next player, to avoid finishing the word, says C (with BENCH in mind). The fifth, who can't think of any word but BENCH, would either have to say H and lose that round, or try to bluff the other players by pulling some letter out of the blue (T, for example) and pretending he is actually thinking of a word. If the player following him becomes suspicious, however, the bluffer can be challenged to name the word he is thinking of. If he is unable to meet the challenge by naming a word with that sequence of letters, the bluffer loses the round. If he does have a word in mind that starts with the letters B-E-N-C-T, the challenger loses the round.

Every time a player loses a round, he has taken a step toward becoming a Ghost. He becomes one third of a Ghost after losing his first round, two thirds of a Ghost on his second loss, and a full Ghost on his third loss—at which point he is out of the game. An alternative is to become a G, then a G-H, and so on, until, after five losses, he is a G-H-O-S-T. Full Ghosts are under the obligation to make the remaining players into Ghosts. They do so by trying to trick free players into talking to them. Anyone talking to a Ghost loses the game immediately and joins the other Ghosts.

Last player left alive is the winner.

# BUZZ

*Any number of players*

**OBJECT: To call out numbers, substituting the word BUZZ for any number that is a multiple of five**

Players sit in a circle and one is chosen to start the game. Play proceeds to the left around the circle. The starter calls out, "One!" The next player to his left shouts, "Two!"; the third, "Three!"; and so on around the circle. When the number 5 or a multiple of 5 (such as 15) is reached, the player must substitute BUZZ for the number. If a number contains a 5 but is not a multiple, the 5 must still be replaced by a BUZZ: 53 becomes BUZZ-three. A player who forgets to say BUZZ is out of the game; last one in is the winner. For the most confusing results, play the game at a snapping pace.

If BUZZ alone is not challenging enough, try BUZZ-FIZZ for satisfying chaos. BUZZ still replaces 5 and its multiples, but FIZZ replaces 7 and its multiples as well. The number 21 is FIZZ, 27 is two-FIZZ, while 57 becomes BUZZ-FIZZ. Good luck.

# PERMUTATIONS

*Two or more players*

*Pencil and paper for each player*

**OBJECT: To make as many different words as you can from the letters in a single word**

Players agree between them on one word with which to begin the game. Since the point is to form as many new words as you can from the letters contained within a single word, long words are the most interesting. For instance, from the word TABLE you can form only TAB, TALE, BALE, LATE, ABLE, LET and BET. It is likely any group of decent players will get them all. The number of possible permutations (changes in order) of the various letters in a word like CALISTHENICS is much greater, so there is a chance for the really clever player to show his stuff. You can play that one, two, or three-letter words don't count, or you can let any possible word be scored. Nonsense words, however plausible they sound, are not allowed; a dictionary may be necessary to clear up arguments. A time limit of ten minutes or so may be employed, or you can simply continue until players agree they can't think up any more words. All players begin simultaneously, each working privately on his own piece of paper. At the end of the round, score one point for each word. Each round begins with a new word, and when everyone is tired of the game, the player with the highest total score is the winner.

## WORD TRAPS

*Word traps only work if the person you're trying to trap hasn't already had experience with the trick, otherwise you might as well forget it; he won't let himself be trapped for anything.*

*Go up to your chosen victim and offer to play a game with him. You'll start off by saying, "I one a snake"; he'll say, "I two a snake"; you'll reply, "I three a snake"; and so on. Hopefully, your subject will agree to the game, even if he's not quite sure he understands its purpose. The game will proceed as planned until your victim says, "I eight a snake." Then you pounce. "You ate a snake?! Did it taste good?" Hopefully, your victim will be crushed.*

*The game is also effective with, "I one a garbage pail," or "I one a toothbrush."*

*Here are some others:*

*Say to your victim "They've found snew in the Atlantic Ocean." When he asks, "What's snew?" jump in with, "Nothing much, what's new with you?"*

*After your victim has forgotten that one, and is again unprepared for a trap, tell him, "I saw a henway on TV last night." If he's good enough to ask, "What's a henway?" your punch line is, "About five pounds."*

*If your friend is still gullible enough for more, say, "Pretend there's a rooster sitting at the very top of a peaked roof so that it is half on one side and half on the other. Now if it lays an egg, which way will the egg roll?"*

*He'll puzzle and ponder and tear his hair, trying to find the trick. When he has finally given up, and admits he doesn't know (or makes a guess), mildly say, "The egg won't roll. Roosters don't lay eggs." Get away fast.*

## ON WASTING PAPER

In case anyone complains that pencil and paper games are a waste of good paper, here are alternatives. If both sides of any sort of paper are already scribbled over, by all means take time off from these intellectual games to fold used paper into paper airplaines and throw them about. Of course, you needn't use the pad kept for grocery lists for these games. There are always those discarded homework sheets, the backs of which don't even show the grade you got. And there are envelopes by the dozen accumulating on the hall table daily. Before you use them, be sure there are no bills inside. In restaurants, paper placemats are fine for any of these games, and using them makes the food seem to come more quickly. As a last resort, marking pens work remarkably well on the backs of hands. The games don't wash off well, but they wear off in time for the next Battle of the Boxes.

# DROODLES

*Two or more players*

*Pencil and paper*

*OBJECT: To guess your opponent's Droodle and stump him with yours*

Droodles, like the ones shown here, are funny-looking pictures drawn with just a few simple lines. They can be any subject imaginable: an elephant scratching an ant's back, a sleeping pickle, a dog's tail without the dog. Often the trick of the drawing is an odd perspective, or a partial view. The game is played in turns. Each player draws a Droodle and the others try to guess it. There really is no winner, but you can become known for your cleverness, which is reward enough.

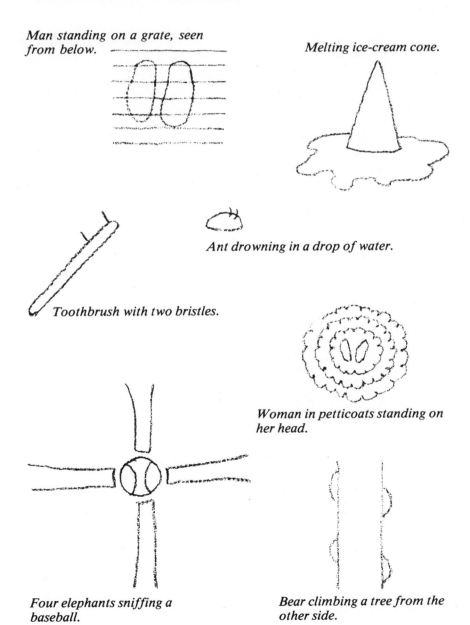

*Man standing on a grate, seen from below.*

*Melting ice-cream cone.*

*Ant drowning in a drop of water.*

*Toothbrush with two bristles.*

*Woman in petticoats standing on her head.*

*Four elephants sniffing a baseball.*

*Bear climbing a tree from the other side.*

## TIC-TAC-TOE

*Two players*

*Pencil and paper*

*OBJECT: To get three of your marks in a row*

Draw a crosshatch of two vertical lines crossing two horizontal lines on a piece of paper. One player chooses O's for his mark, the other X's. Decide which player will go first.

Each player in his turn writes his mark in one of the empty squares of the crosshatch. The first player to write three of his marks in a row is the winner. If neither player manages to get a row of three, and there are no empty squares left, the game is a draw. Players take turns leading off the game.

When two experienced players challenge each other, Tic-Tac-Toe is always a draw unless one makes a mistake. For novice players, the best square to take on your first move is the center. The second player's best move is any one of the four corner squares.

Tic-Tac-Toe can also be played backwards; that is, the first player who gets three in a row is the loser. Oddly enough, this game can always be won by the second player if he knows the strategy. Figure it out.

Try Tic-Tac-Toe on hatches with sixteen or more squares. The game gets more complicated as the board increases in size.

# BOXES

*Two players*

*Pencil and paper*

*OBJECT: To complete more boxes than your opponent*

Decide which player will go first. Draw a grid of pencilled dots, not necessarily square, but at least neatly done. Start with a small grid like the one shown here, and go on to larger ones after you have played a few times. Graph paper, of course, is helpful.

Take turns drawing a line connecting any two dots horizontally or vertically. A box is completed when the fourth side of a square is drawn in, completely enclosing a space. A player who completes a box writes his initial in it, and takes another turn. He can continue taking boxes until there are no more to be completed, and he is forced to draw a line which doesn't complete a box. In the small game below, Benny was forced, at move #14, to connect two dots which would allow Greg to complete a box in the lower right corner. Greg took the box, and put his initial (G) in it. But on Greg's extra turn (#16) he was forced to connect two dots that didn't complete a box. This allowed Benny to complete all the remaining boxes in the grid, taking extra turn after extra turn, and winning with eight boxes to Greg's one.

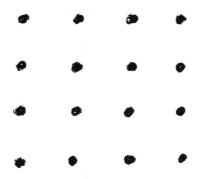

*A grid of 4 by 4 dots for a game of Boxes.*

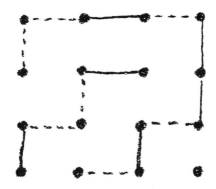

*Turns 1 through 13.*

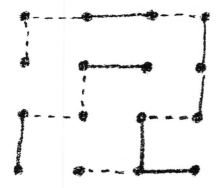

*Benny adds a line in turn #14.*

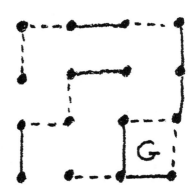

*Greg takes a box in turn #15.*

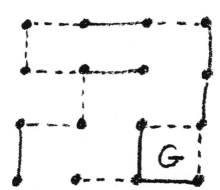

*Greg gets another turn and must add another line because he took a box.*

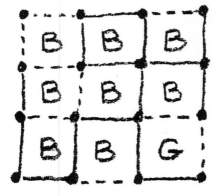

*Now it is Benny's turn, and he takes all the remaining boxes.*

117

## SPROUTS

*Two players*

*Pencil and paper*

*OBJECT: To be the one to take the last turn*

Sprouts is a connect-the-dots game, but it is unusual and absorbing for both adults and children.

Draw three or more dots on a piece of paper and decide who will go first. On his turn, a player draws a curved line connecting two dots, or a closed loop from one dot back to itself. No dot can have more than three lines leading to it or leaving it (a closed loop is considered to be two lines), and no line can cross either itself or any other line. The players take turns drawing curves or loops between the dots. The player who finds he cannot draw any more lines without adding a fourth line to a dot or crossing another line is the loser.

The strategy to this game is to think ahead. Isolate dots from one another with long loops, and count up future moves. Make sure you will be the last one able to add a legal line.

A sample Sprouts game, using three dots, is shown below:

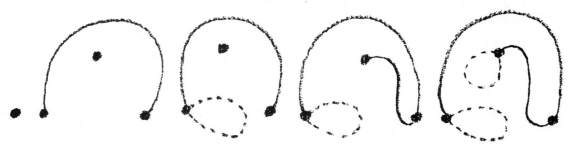

## HANGMAN

*Two players*

*Pencil and paper*

*OBJECT: To guess your opponent's word before he hangs you*

Decide who will be the first "Hangman." The Hangman thinks of a word of any number of letters. He draws a dash for each letter on the paper. Above the dashes, he draws a gallows. The other player then tries to fill in the word by guessing one letter at a time. If the letter he guesses is in the word, the Hangman writes it in above the appropriate dash. If the letter is not in the word, the Hangman writes it off to the side of the paper and begins to hang the player, by adding a feature to the gallows drawing. On the first wrong guess, the Hangman adds the rope; on the second, the victim's head. If the player fails to complete the word before all the parts of his body are drawn, he is hung, and loses. At the end of each round, the players switch places, and the game continues until it becomes tiresome. If scores are kept, the player who has guessed the most words is the winner.

Hangman can be made easier or harder depending on what you count as a feature to be added to the drawing. If you insist on a neck, a bellybutton, and hair, and if you count each limb, hand, foot, ear and eye separately, you would get twenty wrong guesses before you were hung. Since there are only twenty-six letters in the alphabet, you could hardly lose. Counting each pair of parts as a single feature (two eyes, two legs, two hands), you get only fourteen wrong guesses, even if you keep the bellybutton.

Some words that have proven difficult for the guesser to complete before he is hung are: luxury, rhythm, quartz, lyrical, mystical, queasy, doughier, quay, antiprestidigitation and pterodactyl.

# TILLY WILLIAMS

*Three or more players*

*OBJECT: To name things Tilly Williams likes*

This game is best with a group of people, some of whom know the game already and some—the unfortunates—who don't. "Tilly Williams" likes words that have double letters in them, but she dislikes words without double letters. So the word BOOK is among the things Tilly likes, while READING is something she doesn't care for.

As soon as you start the game, others who know it will pick it up, each adding a statement about Tilly Williams, leaving outsiders hopelessly bewildered. Eventually some novices will figure out the rule and join in. If nobody but you knows the game, it's still fun to confuse the others. The game is played with statements about Tilly Williams' likes and dislikes. "Tilly Williams likes kittens, but she doesn't like snow. She doesn't like eating, but she likes her tummy full. Tilly likes books but she doesn't like reading." Other good statements are:

| Tilly likes | But she doesn't like |
|---|---|
| pennies | dimes |
| cabbage | asparagus |
| dollars | cash |
| boots | shoes |
| sleet | rain |
| swimming | water |
| teeth | mouths |
| Pennsylvania | Maine |
| beets | vegetables |
| Beethoven | Bach |
| trees | leaves |
| wood | paper |
| needles | thread |
| winning | games |
| spoons | forks |

See how long you can keep going before you run out of steam or your audience runs out of patience.


# CROSSWORDS

*Any number of players*

*Pencil and paper for each player*

*OBJECT: To form as many valid words as possible*

Each player takes a pencil and a sheet of paper. If there are up to five players taking part, each draws a 5 by 5 box like the one below. If there are more players in the game, boxes 6 by 6 or 7 by 7 should be used. Graph paper is helpful if you are going to play this game often.

Each player in turn names any letter of the alphabet. As a letter is named, the players must put the letter down in any square they choose, in an attempt to form as many words as they can. Letters of the alphabet may be repeated. After all players' boxes have been completely filled, the boxes are collected and scored.

Each horizontal or vertical word formed scores a point for each letter. A four-letter word like GOAT scores four points. Any word that fills an entire row or column also scores one bonus point. Two or more words following each other in a row are allowed, but overlapping words within a single row or column cannot both be scored. For instance, the sequence F-U-N-G-U-S can be scored for FUNGUS, but cannot also be scored for FUN and US.

The player with the highest total score is the winner.

| | | | | | |
|---|---|---|---|---|---|
| W | O | M | A | N | 6 |
| H | A | D | Z | S | 5 |
| I | B | M | L | C | O |
| L | U | L | L | W | 4 |
| E | N | B | A | D | 5 |
| 6 | 3 | 0 | 4 | 3 | + = total 36 |

## CATEGORIES II

*Any number of players*

*Pencil and paper for each player*
*Watch or clock for timing*

**OBJECT: To find words within given categories which also start with a chosen initial letter**

Decide on between six and a dozen different categories of words. For example, choose Animals, Names of Colors, Girls' Names, Musical Instruments, Cities, Sports, Occupations, Trees. Each player writes the chosen categories in a column down the left side of his piece of paper. Decide on a time limit (usually fifteen minutes), and start the game.

To start, one player names any letter of the alphabet, preferably an easy one like A or D for younger children, or a harder one like J or Q for older players. Players write the letter down, and under it list for each category one word which starts with that initial letter. Because of the scoring method, there is an advantage to choosing an unusual word rather than the first one that leaps to mind.

When the time limit is up, or as soon as one player has finished filling in all his categories (whichever comes first), players must all stop writing. Each player then takes his turn reading out his list of words. The scoring is devious. You are given one point for each word on other players' lists that is different from the word you chose. For example, suppose there are five players. Under the initial letter S in the category animal, you wrote SLOTH, while the other four players all wrote SNAKE. You get four points (one for each player's word that was different from your own), while each of the other players scores only one point. If everyone lists the same word, no points are scored in that category. Blank spaces

| | L | S |
|---|---|---|
| Sports | Lacrosse | Soccer |
| Animal | Lion | Snake |
| Flower | Lupine | Sunflower |

don't score, and some play that a player who leaves a blank is penalized one point. A new initial letter is chosen for each succeeding round. Scores are totalled after each round, and the highest scorer after a specified number of rounds is the winner.

*AMAZING MAZES*
*If you keep graph paper around for games like Boxes, try drawing mazes on the same paper. They can be simple, or as complicated as the one shown here. Figuring out how to draw a maze is as challenging as figuring out how to get through it.*

# TAKE A NUMBER

*Two players*

*Two pocket calculators*

*OBJECT: To get the number on your calculator over 999,999*

Each player chooses a six digit number in which no two digits are the same, and enters it on his calculator. Keep your calculators out of each other's sight to preserve secrecy, and decide who will go first. You and your opponent take turns asking each other for digits from 1 to 9 in the same way you would ask for cards in Go Fish (p. 132). When you have a digit your opponent has asked for, you "give" it to him by subtracting it from your own number and letting your opponent add it to his. In order to subtract a single digit from the middle of a number, you have to make allowance for the position it is in by adding on the correct number of zeroes. For example, if your opponent says, "Give me your 7's," and your number is 267923, you respond by saying, "Take 7000." You subtract 7000 from your calculator, leaving you with 260923, and your opponent adds 7000 to his own number. If your number had been 269273, you'd have had to give up only 70, while if it had been 726923, you'd have lost 700,000.

When your opponent asks you for a digit which appears twice in your number, you can give him the lower of the two. If you don't have the digit he asks for, just say, "Sorry, I don't have any."

This continues, you and your opponent alternately robbing each other of the digits between 1 and 9, until one of you passes 999,999. The first one to do this is the winner.

## SECRET NUMBER

*Three or more players*

*A pocket calculator for each player*
*Pencil and paper*

*OBJECT: To order your opponents to add, subtract, multiply and divide numbers on their calculators in such a way that you reach your secret number before your opponents reach theirs*

Players sit next to one another or in a circle. Each player chooses a five digit "secret number," and privately writes it down on his own piece of paper. Then, laying his calculator down so that everyone else can see, each player enters a starting number

between 1 and 10; it doesn't matter if two or more numbers are the same.

Select one player to take the first turn. The other players take their turns after him, going around the group to the left. In his turn, each player gives a command for himself and his opponents to follow on their calculators. The commands involve giving one of the four arithmetic functions ($+ - \times \div$), followed by either a two or a three digit number. For example, a player might say, "Divide by 23"; "Add 640"; or "Multiply by 84." Fractional numbers are rounded out upwards, so that 169.2 becomes 170, and .03197 becomes 1. If an operation results in a negative number, re-enter it as a positive number. After the first player and his opponents have all performed the command operation on their calculators, the turn passes on to the next player.

You should try to give commands that will get you closer to your own number, while foiling your opponents. Although you can always see the numbers on your opponents' calculators, you don't have any idea of what goal numbers they're trying to reach. Therefore, to foil them you've got to look for patterns in their commands. For example, if you notice that one of your opponents always gives a command to add whenever the number on his calculator is below 60,000, and always commands to subtract when his number is above 75,000, you would guess that his goal number is somewhere between those two limits, and try to throw a wrench in somewhere into his plans—even if it takes you a bit out of your way.

Whenever a player's number goes over 999,999, he's out of the game (and if all but one player goes over, the last one in is automatically the winner).

The first player to reach his goal number wins the game, and reveals the number on his paper to confirm his victory.

## DIVIDEND

*Three or more players*

*A calculator for each player*

*OBJECT: To end up with the lowest number on your calculator after taking three turns*

Each player chooses a three digit number, and enters it secretly on his calculator. Until the end of the game, calculators are kept hidden from the opposing players.

Decide which player will go first, and take turns going around to the left. In his turn, each player calls out a number between 1 and 9. After a number has been called, each player (including the caller) looks at the number on his calculator and takes one of the following actions:

If the number called is the same as the last whole number digit on your calculator, divide by the called number.

If the stated number appears on your calculator screen, but not as the last whole number digit, add or subtract by the stated number.

If the stated number doesn't appear on your calculator screen at all, multiply by that number.

Ignore any decimals that appear on your calculator. For example, treat 21.666 as simply 21—1 is the last digit, and the 6's don't "appear" at all.

To give yourself the best chance of winning, on your turn call the last whole number digit on your calculator, so you can divide. If, on another player's call, you have a choice between adding and subtracting, choose the operation that will make the last digit on your calculator as high as possible. Then, when your turn comes around, you will have that high digit to divide by. Avoid getting a zero as your last digit; in that case you would lose a chance to divide on your turn.

Each player gets just three turns. After the turns have gone around three times, each player exposes his calculator screen, and the one with the lowest number is the winner.

As an example of how the game is played, let's say that three players enter the following numbers: Jerry, 287; Suzie, 176; Diane, 346. Jerry, on his first turn, calls the number 7. Since his last digit is 7, he divides, giving him 41. Suzie has the called number, but it isn't her last digit, so she has the choice of adding or subtracting. She decides to subtract, giving her 169. Diane's number doesn't contain a 7, so she must multiply, giving her 2422.

This doesn't mean that Jerry will win, even though his number is now the lowest. Each of the other players must take their turns, and their calls may change everything around. Suzie may make a comeback by calling the number 9. This allows her to divide, giving her 18.777 (read as 18), and forces Jerry to multiply, giving him 369. In the end (after Diane's turn, and two more rounds), there is even a possibility that Diane will win.

*To play calculator games, you need only a calculator that adds, subtracts, multiplies and divides. These simple machines start at about $10; the very small ones, which fit into a shirt pocket, are more expensive.*

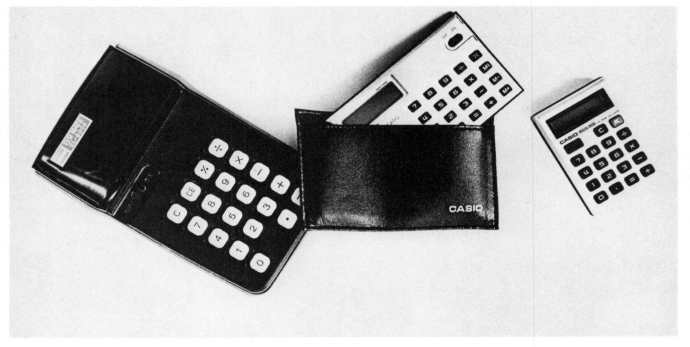

# Card Games

# Chapter 5
# Card Games

The first portion of this section is devoted to card games that are easy enough for children as young as three. If you play often with children under school age, you might keep a permanently doctored deck of cards. You could remove all but the Aces, 2's, 3's, 4's and 5's. Add cards when children are able to recognize names and numbers, to hold more cards in their hands, or their increased skill calls for more complicated games.

As the chapter progresses, games become more complicated in rules and scoring. We have suggested much simpler scoring methods for games where that is possible—for times when the rules alone seem enough for a child to cope with, or when adults are feeling lazy. It is not easy to learn a new card game from written instructions. To help yourself, try playing along as you read instructions step by step. There are also sample games to follow.

New vocabulary may trip you up as you try to understand a game. If someone demonstrates a game of Solitaire to you, he can easily teach you the game without using terms like "foundation," "tableau" or "talon." But if instructions were given here without that terminology, you would have to cope with descriptions like, "the cards in your left hand," "the ones you put above the ones in front of you." That would be more difficult than learning the new vocabulary.

Some card terminology is used interchangeably and is hard to grasp for that reason. Depending on the game, or on the book you read, a round of a game (that starts when the dealer deals the cards and ends when someone has won) may be called a "game," a "hand" or a "deal," as well as a round. Similarly, "deck," "pack" and "stock" are words used to describe the pile of cards from which players may draw to add to their hands. We have aimed for consistency and clarity in our own usage, but it is difficult to clear up the fuzziness completely.

Depending on whom you play with, you may have to deal with protocol as well as rules and terms. Protocol is seldom part of the rules of a game; it is the customary way players treat one another and handle mistakes in dealing or playing. Some people simply will not play Poker with talkative players. In some circles, any mistake in dealing, however slight, is handled by pulling in all the cards, reshuffling, and starting the deal over again. When playing cards off your own turf, it is wise to follow whatever protocol is customary there. Among friends and family, make up the protocol that suits you.

# CONCENTRATION (MEMORY)

*Two to six players, but the game is best with two*

*Standard deck of 52 cards*

*OBJECT: To accumulate the greatest number of pairs*

Shuffle the deck, and spread the cards out on the table or floor face down, making sure that no two cards overlap. The more irregularly the cards are spread, the more difficult the game. For young children, spread the cards in neat rows. Players can sit surrounding the cards, or all to one side of the spread. Choose the order in which players will take their turns.

The first player turns over any two cards. If the cards form a pair (two Jacks, or two 6's), the player removes them from their positions and places the pair in front of him in his private collection. A player can take repeated turns as long as he turns up a pair each time. If the cards don't match, he must turn them back over exactly where he found them, and the next player takes his turn. When all the cards have been collected, the player who has the most pairs is the winner.

The game moves slowly at first, since the chances are slim that any two cards chosen randomly will be of the same rank. However, as the game proceeds, players will begin to remember the positions of certain cards which appeared in other turns, and make matches more easily. It is the player with the best memory who wins the game, rather than the one with luck.

Concentration, played perhaps with a half deck (one pair in each rank removed), is a good game for young children who are just learning to recognize and name the cards. They can play with an assistant (parent or older child) rather than an opponent.

# BEGGAR-YOUR-NEIGHBOR

*Two players*

*Standard deck of 52 cards*

*OBJECT: To capture all of your opponent's cards*

This exciting, fast-moving game has the advantage of a concrete, sensible object which very young players grasp enthusiastically.

Divide the deck in two, so that each player has twenty-six cards. Holding their stacks of cards face down so no one can see them, the players alternately turn over single cards and lay them face up in a pile between the two of them. First one player turns up a card and lays it face up, and then the other puts a card face up on top of the first card. Then the first player puts a card on top, and so on. This continues until one of the players turns over a "battle card"—any face card or an Ace.

When one player turns up a face card or an Ace, the other must pay a penalty of a certain number of cards from his hand. There is a penalty of four cards for an Ace, three cards for a King, two cards for a Queen, and one card for a Jack. If one player pays a penalty and none of the cards he pays are battle cards, his opponent captures the entire center pile, puts it face down underneath his own cards, and leads off with a single card face up to start a new pile. But if a face card or Ace is turned up while paying a penalty, the situation is reversed; the opponent is now obliged to pay the number of cards specified by the turned-up battle card. For example, Jimmy turns up a King; Peggy, his opponent, must pay three cards. First she plays a 6, then a Queen. Jimmy is now on the hot seat: He turns up a 2, then a Jack. Peggy, hoping for a battle card, turns over a 9. Too bad. Jimmy takes the whole stack, including Peggy's Queen, puts it on the bottom of his stack of cards, and leads off with a new card from the top.

Whoever captures all the cards is the winner.

### FIFTY-TWO PICKUP

*This game is good only once with a victim who has never heard of it. You say, "Want to play Fifty-Two Pickup?" Your victim says, "Sure. How do you play?" "Well," you continue, "I toss the fifty-two cards up in the air" (as you toss them), "and you pick them up" (as you exit). This is most satisfying with a younger brother or sister.*

# WAR

*Two players*

*Standard deck of 52 cards*

*OBJECT: To capture all of your opponent's cards*

Divide the deck in two, so that each player has twenty-six cards. Each player puts his cards face down in a neat pile in front of him so they can't be seen. Then the players simultaneously turn up one card each, and place them side by side in the center of the table. The player with the higher card takes them both and puts them underneath his stack. Aces are highest, deuces lowest. Play continues this way.

If both cards are of the same rank, a "war" commences. Each player solemnly and slowly chants, "I declare war," on each word laying a card face up so that it overlaps his first card. The final cards laid down determine the outcome of the war. The player whose third and final card is highest takes all eight cards in the center. If the final cards match, another war ensues, and another, if need be.

Some play in a slightly different manner: Only two additional cards are laid down in the wars, the first face down and the second face up. The second card determines the outcome of the battle.

The player who captures all the cards is the winner. Since this is a game that takes ages to win, many War "veterans" play that the first player to win five battles (or some other number), wins the whole game.

## GO FISH

*Two to six players*

*Standard deck of 52 cards*

*OBJECT: To collect the most sets of four matching cards, or to be the first to get rid of all the cards in your hand*

Players sit in a circle on the floor or around a table. Choose a dealer. The dealer deals out five cards to himself and each of the other players. He places the rest of the deck face down in the center.

Starting with the dealer, each player in turn calls out the name of any other player and asks him to hand over cards he needs. For example, if a player has a 3 in his hand, on his turn he could say to another player, "Martin, give me all your 3's." If Martin has any 3's, he must hand them all over. If Martin doesn't have any 3's, he says "Go Fish!" and the player who asked must pick a card from the pile in the center.

A player can repeat his turn over and over as long as he gets the cards he wants, from another player or the Go Fish pile. When he fails to draw the card he wants, he loses his turn and the play goes to the player on his left.

Any four matching cards of the same rank (such as four 3's or four Jacks) make a "book." Whenever a player gets a book of cards, he immediately takes those cards out of his hand and puts them face up in front of him. There are two versions of how to win Go Fish. In the first, the game ends when there are no more cards in the Go Fish pile. Each player counts his books and the one with the most books wins. In the other version, the first person to get rid of all the cards in his hand is the winner.

## OLD MAID

*Three or more players*

*An Old Maid deck, available at stores, or a standard deck of 52 cards from which three Queens have been removed*

*OBJECT: To pair and put down all the cards in your hand, without getting stuck with the Old Maid*

Sit in a circle on the floor or around a table, and deal out all the cards. It doesn't matter if the cards don't divide evenly. The "Old

Maid'' decks available at book and stationery stores consist of fifty-one cards showing characters like ''chimney sweep,'' ''parson,'' ''milkmaid'' or modern equivalents. There is a pair for each character except one: the Old Maid. A deck that has been prepared by removing three of the Queens is the same; all the cards can be paired by rank (two Jacks, two 4's, etc.), except for the lone Queen. If you can find a really nice Old Maid set, though, it adds to the fun of the game, because the characters themselves may be comical or ominous.

After the cards have been dealt, the players look at their hands and remove any pairs they may have been dealt. Any two matching cards are put together and placed face up in front of the player. When all the players have removed the pairs from their hands, they take turns pulling one card from the hand of the player to their right, without peeking of course. The first player chooses a card from the player on his right. The second player pulls a card from the hand of the first player, and so on. If a player draws a match to one of the cards in his hand, he adds the pair to those already in front of him.

When all the cards have been paired up and discarded, the player left with the unmatched Queen or Old Maid card is the loser.

Since it is bad (or even bad luck) to get stuck with the Old Maid, children usually try to tempt their neighbor to draw it by making the card stick out or look especially inviting. When they have all learned not to fall for this trick, they reverse strategy and fake out the next player by hiding the Old Maid and ostentatiously offering another card. A neighbor is now almost sure to go for the least obvious card, and end up with the Old Maid after all.

A little child loves to play cards as much as anyone, but some aspects of card playing may be beyond his physical or emotional abilities.

Shuffling the deck and fanning cards in the hand are especially difficult. An alternative to the riffle shuffle is laying the cards out face down on the floor, and picking them up in random order. Not only is this easier than the standard shuffle, it is also a better randomizer.

Instead of fanning cards, children can play by leaning their cards against a pillow placed in front of them. Or, they can hold their hand as a deck, and look through it card by card when it is their turn to play.

Many children have difficulty in telling the face cards apart. To overcome this difficulty, the deck for most games can be doctored by removing the Kings and Queens, leaving Jacks the only set of face cards. Decks with large indexes (the numerals in the corners) and bold designs also help in differentiation.

A further problem the young have with card games is one shared by all too many adults. The competition proves too fierce and emotionally distressing to be enjoyable.

Just as you might teach a child a game by exposing all the cards in each player's hand, you can continue for a while to play face up to avoid competition. This may seem to adults to take all the fun from the game, but if you shout, "Hooray! We've used up all the cards," instead of, "Tough luck, you lose," three-year-olds will be delighted. A next step might be to play with the hands held out of other players' sight, but instead of yelling, "I win!" just calmly saying, "I got the most cards, so I have to deal now." Keeping early play relatively pointless will avoid both the bitter repercussions of letting children win on purpose, and the violent

# I DOUBT IT

*Four to twelve players, but the game is best with between six and nine*

*Standard deck of 52 cards (for six or more players, two packs shuffled together make a more interesting game)*

**OBJECT: To get rid of all the cards in your hand**

Sit down together and choose a dealer. The dealer deals out all the cards. It doesn't matter if the cards don't divide evenly. Each player, being careful to keep his cards from being seen, arranges his hand in ascending order, Aces at the left of his hand and Kings at the right.

I Doubt It is a game of bluff and "poker faces," the purpose of which is to win through bald-faced lying. Starting with the dealer, each player in turn puts a number of cards—from one to four (for the single deck) or one to eight (for the double deck game)—face down in the center of the table. As he lays the cards down, he declares aloud what they are: "two Aces," for example.

The order in which the cards are discarded is fixed. The first player must put down Aces (or at least pretend to), the next player 2's, the player after him 3's and so on up to Kings, followed in turn by Aces again. A player is required to state correctly the number of cards he is putting down, but he can lie about their identity. For example, if the required cards are 6's and the player in turn doesn't have any 6's in his hand, he can put down other cards (two Jacks and a 5 perhaps) but say, "Three sixes." If no one doubts his word, the turn moves on to his left. But if someone suspects he is lying, they can challenge him by saying, "I doubt it!" Then the player must turn up the cards he discarded. If they aren't what he declared them to be, he has to take up the entire center pile into his hand as a penalty. If he was telling the truth, then the challenger must take up the entire pile. The game then continues as before.

The first player to discard all his cards successfully wins.

# SLAPJACK

*Two to eight players*

*Standard deck of 52 cards, or for younger players, a deck from which all face cards except the four Jacks have been removed*

**OBJECT: To get all the cards in the deck**

Players sit down in a circle, choose who will go first, and divide the deck evenly among them. If the players are too young to know how to deal, they can take turns pulling single cards from the deck, or the deck can simply be divided into approximately equal-sized stacks.

Players keep their cards in face-down stacks in front of them; no peeking allowed. Starting with the first player, they take turns throwing their top cards onto a face-up pile in the center of the cir-

*feelings that emerge when a
family plays too competitively.
The game this mother is playing
with her son is Slapjack, a good
choice for a preschooler.*

cle. Whenever a Jack is turned over, the players race to slap it with their hands. Whoever hits the Jack first gets the whole pile of cards underneath, and adds them face down to the bottom of his own stack. If a player accidentally slaps a card which isn't a Jack, he has to pay a penalty by giving one of his cards to the player who took the last turn.

A player who loses all his cards has only one chance to get back in the game: by slapping the next Jack that appears. If he manages this successfully, he is back in the game with the pile he slapped; otherwise he is out permanently.

The winner of the game is the one who collects all the cards. Or, to keep the game from taking too long, the game may end the first time a player goes out of the game, with the one who has the most cards at that point declared the winner.

## NOVELTY CARDS

*Giant and round cards are only two of several interesting novelty shapes and sizes you may enjoy playing with. There are also miniatures no more than 2 inches high, and even super-miniatures, measuring a scant half-inch, that are intended for dollhouse card players. For preschoolers, a deck of cards shaped something like hand mirrors has been invented. The cards can be held in a fan more easily because of the narrow handles.*

*Standard decks come in two sizes. There are regular decks and the somewhat smaller bridge decks. The narrower cards are easier for young children to fan in their hands.*

# MILLE BORNES

*Two, three, four, or six players, playing singly or as partners*

*Set of MILLE BORNES cards*
*Pencil and paper for scoring*

*OBJECT: To be the first to accumulate 1000 points by playing Distance Cards*

The game of MILLE BORNES, imported from France by Parker Brothers, is modeled on an automobile trip. Each player attempts to accumulate 1000 miles' worth of "distance" cards. Meanwhile, he also impedes his opponents' progress by slapping them with "hazard" cards, representing some of the many problems that plague a car journey—flat tires, speed limits, and so on.

## The Cards

There are four types of MILLE BORNES cards: distance, hazard, remedy and safety cards.

DISTANCE CARDS: These are cards you play in a row in front of you during your turn. Distance cards score various numbers of miles toward your goal of 1000. There are four 200-mile cards, twelve 100-mile cards, and ten each of 75-, 50-, and 25-mile cards.

HAZARD CARDS: These dusky red cards, which players lay down in front of their opponents, temporarily stop or slow down the playing of distance cards. There are five kinds of hazards: "Stop" cards, representing red lights; "Out of Gas" cards; "Flat Tire" cards; "Accident" cards; and "Speed Limit" cards. The Speed Limit cards don't stop an opponent from playing any distance cards at all, as the other hazards do, but they hamper his progress by keeping him from playing any distance card over 50 miles.

REMEDY CARDS: Once a hazard card has been played on someone's hand, his progress is slowed or stopped until he can find a "remedy" card for the specific hazard. "Roll" cards, the most numerous, counteract the effect of the Stop card (as well as playing another important part in the game, which is described below). "Gasoline" counters Out of Gas; "Spare Tire" remedies Flat Tire; "Repairs" counteracts Accident; while "End of Limit" puts Speed Limit to rights, allowing the play of long distance cards once again.

SAFETY CARDS: The last type, the green "safety" cards, can be played onto your own hand any time during the game. Once played, these cards stop your opponents from playing specific hazard cards on you. There are only four of these cards in the deck: "Extra Tank," which prevents your opponent from playing an Out of Gas card on you; "Puncture Proof," to ward off Flat Tire; "Driving Ace" as a guarantee against Accident; and "Right of Way," which prevents both Speed Limit and Stop.

Safety cards carry bonus points when they are played, and allow you to take an extra turn, as explained below.

Choose one player to be the dealer. The dealer shuffles the deck, and places it face down in the open half of the plastic discard tray which comes with the set. This is the "stock." The dealer gives each player six cards face down. Players hold these cards fanned so other players can't see them.

The player to the dealer's left takes the first turn, and the play continues around the table clockwise until the end of the game. On his turn, each player draws a single card from the stock and adds it to his hand. Then, if possible, he plays a single card down onto his own or one of his opponents' card piles. If the player doesn't have a play (or doesn't wish to make one), he discards any one card from his hand by dropping it face up in the discard half of the tray. Each player should still have six cards left in his hand at the end of every turn.

At the beginning of the game, you and your opponents will probably be primarily concerned with finding Roll cards to play. Without a displayed Roll card, you are not allowed to score points

## PARTNERSHIP

In France, MILLE BORNES was designed as a partnership game for four players. Partners sit opposite one another, but share a common set of speed, distance and battle piles. As in most partnership games, the partners aren't allowed to see one another's hands but each can play distance, remedy and safety cards onto the shared piles, and attack the opposing team's layout with hazard cards. Scoring is figured for each team, rather than for each player.

For two and three individual players, and for six playing in teams of two, the rules may be adapted slightly:

The deck is modified by the removal of a Stop, an Accident, an Out of Gas, and a Speed Limit card.

The trip distance is shortened to 700 miles. The first to reach the goal collects the 400-point bonus usually reserved for 1000-mile journeys.

An extra play is added: the "extension." The first player to reach 700 miles has the option of calling, "Extension!" When an extension is called, the game is played as if the distance goal had always been the standard 1000 miles. Whoever reaches 1000 miles first collects the 400-point bonus for reaching the game limit. In addition, if the extension-caller is the first one to reach the goal, he receives an additional 200-point bonus.

If you find the modification of the deck troublesome, you may play two-, three- and six-handed games in the standard manner.

by playing distance cards. If you have a Roll card, place it face up in front of you, somewhat to your left. This first Roll card begins your "battle" pile. The battle pile shows what condition your "automobile" is in.

When a Roll card is at the top of your battle pile, you can play distance cards. Distance cards are placed in a row to the right of your battle pile, grouped by denomination and overlapped so that you can easily keep track of the number of miles you have accumulated. Only two 200's can be played by any one player during a game.

If you are stuck, unable to play distance cards (either because you have no Roll card, or because an opponent has slapped you with a hazard card you have not yet been able to remedy), you might consider playing a hazard card on an opponent. If you hold a hazard card, on your turn you may play it directly onto the top of an opponent's battle pile, provided that the top card on his battle pile is a Roll card. Once a hazard card is on top of a battle pile, no more distance cards can be played until the hazard is remedied with the appropriate remedy card, and then topped off with a Roll card. Say, for example, that an opponent slaps a Flat Tire down on your battle pile. To get "moving" again, you must first play a Spare Tire card on top of the Flat Tire. But even after you've counteracted the hazard with a remedy, you can't resume playing distance cards until you play a Roll card on top of your battle pile. Stop cards can be instantly remedied by Roll cards, but you are frequently set back two or more turns when an opponent hits you with a hazard.

Speed Limit and End of Limit cards are placed in a separate "speed" pile, to the left of each player's battle pile, because they don't stop you completely. If you hold a Speed Limit card, you can play it onto an opponent's speed pile even while he's struggling to find a remedy or Roll card for his battle pile. Once a speed limit is played, a player can't put down any distance cards greater

*Many children play a simpler version of MILLE BORNES.*

*In this "homegrown" game, as many as four players can take part, each playing for himself. The deck is shuffled, and play proceeds as usual. However, the game doesn't stop at 1000 miles; it goes right on until the stock is exhausted. Then, the discard pile is turned over to form a new stock, and the game continues. This version ends when all the distance cards have been used.*

*The game is scored as before, with points for miles, safeties, all four safeties, Coup Fourrés and safe trip. But since the goal of 1000 miles is ignored, bonuses relating to it don't apply.*

*The player with the highest score at the end of the game is the winner.*

than 50 until he has counteracted the Speed Limit with an End Of Limit card.

It's a good idea to keep at least one Roll card, two remedies, and an End Of Limit card in your hand to cover emergencies. Play distance cards as you draw them (if you can), and either discard or make immediate use of hazard cards.

If you are lucky enough to draw a safety card (one which makes you immune from some sort of hazard), you can keep it in your hand or play it right away. When you play a safety card, put it face up in front of you just above your battle and speed piles. Once it is displayed, your opponents will no longer be able to play the indicated hazard on your battle pile. For example, if you play an Extra Tank card, your opponents can no longer slap you with an Out of Gas card. Playing a safety card cancels a hazard even if it is already in progress; just lift the corresponding hazard off the top of your battle pile, and toss it into the discard pile. Furthermore, playing a safety card entitles you to an extra turn, and gives you a 100-point bonus.

Right of Way, the most sought-after safety, protects you from both Stop and Speed Limit. In addition, the display of Right of Way acts as an automatic Roll card—once you have played a Right of Way, you can accumulate distance cards even if you have no Roll card on top of your battle pile. A Right of Way is no defense against Flat Tires and Accidents, but you need only play the proper remedy card in order to get moving again. Since Right of Way substitutes for Roll cards, note that your opponents may attack by putting down a hazard card directly on top of your previous remedy; this is the only case in which a hazard can go on top of anything but a Roll card. If you have all four safeties displayed you are invulnerable to attack and receive a 700-point bonus.

If you draw a safety near the beginning of the game, keep it concealed in your hand rather than playing it immediately, in the hope that some opponent will hit you with the corresponding hazard card. Immediately after, whether or not it is your turn, put your safety down crosswise above your row of piles, before you or anyone else draws a card. Call out "Coup Fourré" (Koo-Foo-Ray), a fencing term which means a defense that is also an attack. Then remove the hazard that was played on your battle pile, toss it into the discard pile, and draw a card to bring your hand back to six. Each Coup Fourré gives you a bonus of 300 points in addition to the 100 you score for playing a safety. After making a Coup Fourré, you get an extra turn because you played a safety. Following this second turn, the player to your left takes his turn, and the game continues.

To win a game of MILLE BORNES, you must reach 1000 miles exactly. If you have 925 miles to your credit, you can't play anything over 75 miles.

When a player reaches exactly 1000 miles, he cries "STOP," and the game ends. If no player reaches 1000 miles by the time the stock is exhausted, players take turns playing (or discarding) the cards from their hands. The game ends when all cards have been played or discarded.

When the game is finished, each player figures out his score:

Milestones played. . . total of distance cards played

Each safety played. . . . . . . . . . . . . . . . . . . . . . . . .100

Bonus for all four safeties. . . . . . . . . . . . . . . . .700

Each Coup Fourré . . . . . . . . . . . . . . . . . . . . . . .300

Bonus for being the first to complete 1000
miles. . . . . . . . . . . . . . . . . . . . . . . . . . . . . . . . . . .400

Bonus for completing 1000 miles after the
stock is exhausted. . . . . . . . . . . . . . . . . . . . . . .300

Bonus for playing no 200's (safe trip). . . . . . . .300

Bonus for shutout (reaching 1000 before
     opponents have played a single distance
     card). . . . . . . . . . . . . . . . . . . . . . . . . . . . . . . .500

These scores are summarized on a card that comes with each deck.

MILLE BORNES games are often played in cumulatively scored tournaments. After several games, the player with the highest cumulative score wins the match.


# SPIT

*Two players*

*Standard deck of 52 cards*

*OBJECT: To get rid of all your cards*

Spit requires the mental agility to make lightning decisions, and the manual dexterity of a magician. A good player can leave his unfortunate opponent stunned, as a flurry of cards leap into sequence on the table in blinding succession. But Spit is a bad game for two players who aren't well matched in skill, unless the better player is handicapped by being saddled with from five to fifteen more cards than his opponent.

The two players sit facing one another. One shuffles the deck and divides it evenly between them, forming face-down stacks called the "stocks." Holding his stock face down in one hand, each player deals out four of his own cards side by side face up in front of him. These four cards are called his "spread."

The game is played without turns, each opponent playing simultaneously, and as quickly as possible. To start the game, both players simultaneously count "one...two...three...SPIT!" and slap one card each face up in the center of the table between them. These cards start the two center piles.

Each player goes into action instantly, trying to rid himself of cards by slapping cards from his spread onto the top card of either of the growing center piles. A card can be placed on a center pile if its rank is either one above or one below the pile's top card (a possible order for one of the center piles could be 2 3 4 3 4 3 2 A K Q J 10 . . .). When an empty space is left

in a player's spread, he can fill it with a card from his stock. Cards of the same rank appearing in his spread can be placed on top of one another, leaving space for more cards from the stock. Spread cards that have been doubled up, however, can only be taken off one at a time to place on center piles.

If at any time no more plays are possible, the players stop, gasp for breath, and Spit once more, throwing two more cards down on top of the center piles. If this happens when one player has exhausted all the cards in his stock but still has one or more cards left in his spread, only the player still holding cards in his stock Spits. When one player has exhausted all the cards in both his stock and spread, he cries "Stop!" and the round ends. The player without cards then selects the smaller of the two center piles to form his new stock, and his opponent gets the larger pile. The players shuffle their stocks, deal their spreads, and the game resumes with a Spit.

Since having the greater number of cards is a disadvantage, the player losing the first round has an increased chance of losing the second, and an even greater chance of losing the third. Eventually, the game will reach a point where one player will be without cards in his stock after dealing out his spread at the beginning of a round. When this happens, that player is the winner.

Occasionally, two very evenly matched players will have consumed their stocks but will still have cards in their spreads that they cannot place in either center pile. In this case, the player with fewer cards in his spread wins the round. If both players have equal numbers of cards in their spreads, the round is a draw; cards are gathered up, shuffled, and evenly redivided.

There is also a rule for ambidextrous card players, who may be tempted to lay their stock down to leave both hands free for moving cards about. The rule is: only one hand allowed.

# BASEBALL CARDS

*Two players*

*The players' own baseball card collections*

*OBJECT: To win baseball cards*

You can add to a baseball card collection by buying more cards (or buying more bubble gum), by trading, or by playing one of the versions of Baseball Cards explained here. They are games of pure luck.

Baseball cards have a face and a back. The face shows a photograph of the player, the name of his team and its colors, and the position he plays. The back has statistics on the player, and a number that places it within a particular series of cards. The games are played using these various details.

To "flip" for cards, the two players, each holding his stack of baseball cards, stand opposite one another. Players compare their top cards, and the one with the lowest number on the back of his card goes first. The first player calls out, "Match," or "Unmatch." Then, simultaneously, each tosses a card from his stack into the air and lets it fall to the ground. The flip is a "match" if both cards fall face up, or both fall back up. The flip is an "un-match" if one card falls face up, the other back up. If the cards fall the way the first player called them, he gets both cards. If not, the other player gets them. The same player continues to be the caller throughout the game, but there is no advantage, since both players have an equal chance of winning cards. It doesn't matter if players start with uneven numbers of cards, and there is no particular end to the game.

Another way to win baseball cards requires that each player start with an equal number of cards. The two players sit opposite one another, and decide who will go first. The first player slaps down his first card face up, and the second player slaps down his first card on top of that one. This continues, each player in turn placing a card face up on the stack. If a player's card matches the one below it by the ballplayer's position (outfielder on top of out-fielder, pitcher on top of pitcher) he can take the whole stack, and then begin play again with another card. The game ends when one player has won all the cards from his opponent. The matching need not be by position. Some people play that you can take the stack if your card matches the one below it by team (Oriole on top of Oriole, Yankee on top of Yankee).


## CRAZY EIGHTS

*Two, three or four players*

*Standard deck of 52 cards*
*Pencil and paper for scoring*

*OBJECT: To be the first to get rid of all your cards*

Crazy Eights is a great game to play in the back of a car during long trips. It is fast moving, and the cards can be piled up so that they don't slide around easily.

Choose the dealer and deal out the hands: With two players in the game, each gets seven cards; with three or four, give each player five cards. Put the rest of the deck face down in a pile to form the stock, and turn the top card up and place it beside the stock to start the discard pile.

One at a time, beginning with the player to the dealer's left and going around clockwise, players take turns putting single cards from their hands down on the discard pile. A card can be discarded onto the pile if it matches the card on top by suit or rank. A 6 of clubs can go on top of a 3 of clubs, and the 6 of clubs can be followed by a 6 of diamonds.

All 8's are "wild," and can be substituted for any other card. A wild 8 can be discarded on top of any other discard. Furthermore, when you play an 8, you can specify any suit you wish for it.

The next player in turn will have to follow with the suit you specify, or with another 8.

When you can't make a discard that matches the previous one in suit or rank, you must draw cards from the stock until you can, and then discard to complete your turn. You may, if you wish, draw from the stock even if you already have a valid play—perhaps to save an 8 in your hand for an emergency.

The first player to get rid of all his cards is the winner. If the stock is exhausted and no one can make a discard from his hand, the game is "blocked," and the player with the fewest cards in his hand is the winner.

Sometimes a scoring system is used in Crazy Eights. When you win a game by using all your cards, you collect points for the cards remaining in your opponents' hands: fifty points for each 8, ten

*Crazy Eights, like many card games, can be played in crowded places.*

for each face card, one for each Ace, and the spot value of each for all the other cards (seven points for a 7, etc.). When the game is blocked, the player with the lowest total in his hand collects the difference between his total and his opponents' totals. Keep a running score on paper. The first player to reach 100 points (or some other goal) is the winner.

# RUMMY

*Two to six players*

*Standard deck of 52 cards*
*Paper and Pencil for scoring*

*OBJECT: To score the most points by grouping as many cards as possible into combinations of three or more, forming melds*

The Rummy games are a family of fast-moving, straightforward card games, simple enough for children to play and intriguing enough to keep adults in keen competition. You can play the games at a simple level in which only luck determines the winner, or on a plane where skill and strategy make all the difference. This is the standard game from which other Rummies (and the rule variations discussed below) are derived.

Select one player to be the dealer. He shuffles the cards and deals out the hands face down. If there are only two players, each hand contains ten cards. Three to four players get seven cards. With more than four players, the hands are five or six cards each. After the hands are dealt, place the remaining cards in a face-down pile in the center of the table to form the stock. Then pick up the top card and place it beside the stock, face up. This is the first card of the discard pile.

Each player arranges his hand to correspond as closely as possible to the groups of three or more cards called "melds." A meld can be made up of three or four cards of the same rank, such as 7's or Jacks, or a sequence of three or more cards in the same suit, such as the 5, 6, 7 and 8 of hearts. Some play that the "round the corner straight," 2 A K Q, for example, is a legal meld.

Players take their turns in order, starting with the one to the dealer's left. Each player begins his turn by drawing a card, either a potluck card from the top of the stock or the exposed card on the top of the discard pile. Then, if any of his cards form a complete meld, he may lay down his meld(s) face up, spreading it out in front of him so all the cards are visible. He also has the option of "laying off" individual cards from his hand, adding them to his own or other players' melds that are already out on the table. This brings him closer to laying down his entire hand and winning the game. Cunning players will often keep their completed melds to themselves, to prevent their opponents from noting their progress. This has its risks, however, as all cards left in a losing hand, whether complete melds or odd cards, are counted as points for the winner at the end of the game.

If you wish, you may also use an optional rule called "borrowing." This rule allows players to rearrange their own melds already on the table. For example, if a player has already

## BLOCK RUMMY

*In Rummy, when the stock is exhausted, the discard pile is simply shuffled and turned to form the new stock. In Block Rummy, if the pack is exhausted before any of the players has gone out, the game ends, and the player with the lowest count of cards in his hand is the winner. The other players each pay him the difference between their total card points and his.*

## BOATHOUSE RUMMY

*Otherwise the same as standard Rummy, Boathouse requires that a player who wishes to draw a card from the discard pile must also draw an additional card either from the discard pile or the stock. This means that a player will think twice about filling a meld with a card from the discard pile, because in doing so he will be taking the risk of filling his hand with extra cards. Boathouse allows the Ace to be used high, as in A K Q, or low, as in 3 2 A. In scoring, the Ace counts eleven points, reflecting its double use.*

*Laying off a card into another player's meld in Rummy.*

laid out the meld 6, 5, 4 and 3 of spades, and he has a pair of 3's in his hand, he can separate the 3 of spades from his previous meld and combine it with the two 3's from his hand to form a meld of 3's, which he lays down.

If the stock is exhausted before any player wins, the next player can either take the card at the top of the discard pile, or shuffle the discard pile and turn it over to form a new face-down stock. Some people just turn the pile over without reshuffling.

The first player to "go out" (get rid of all his cards by melding or laying off) wins the round. The winning player can make a final discard to get rid of the last odd card in his hand if he wishes, but he doesn't have to; he may prefer instead to include it in a meld. When the round is won, play stops and players all display their hands so the score can be added up.

## Scoring

The winner is awarded a number of points based on the total number of cards left in his opponents' hands. Each face card counts for ten points, Aces are one point, and the rest count at their face value. So, in a three-handed game, if the losers' cards are a Jack, two 6's and a 3, the winner gets a total of twenty-five points.

In a scoring variation, a player who keeps all his melds in his hand until everything is grouped and then lays down his whole hand at once is said to "go Rummy." The player who manages to go out in this fashion rather than piecemeal collects double the usual number of points from each player. Beware, though, of holding on to those melds too long, because they will work against you if someone else goes out first.

Scores can be reckoned on a piece of paper. Often a set of Rummy games are played one after another; the first player to reach 100 points is the Grand Rummy Champion.

# GIN RUMMY

*Two players*

*Standard deck of 52 cards*
*Paper and pencil for scoring*

*OBJECT: To score the most points by grouping as many of your cards as possible in combinations of three or more, forming melds*

Gin, the youngest of the Rummy games, took the country by storm just prior to World War II, and since then has remained a mainstay in the repertoires of card game buffs.

Gin is a two-handed game. The dealer gives himself and his opponent ten cards each, places the rest of the deck face down between them to form the stock, and turns one card face up beside the stock to start the discard pile. The other player takes the first turn. He has the option of taking the up-card from the discard pile and discarding another in its place; or offering his turn to the dealer instead. If the dealer doesn't want the up-card either, he must pass the turn back to the first player, who is then allowed to either take the up-card or draw from the stock.

From then on, each player in his turn draws a card from the stock or the discard pile and discards a card from his hand, keeping ten cards in his hand at all times. As in Rummy, each player tries to form melds of three of more cards of similar rank (such as three Jacks) or in sequence and suit (the Queen, Jack and 10 of diamonds).

The game differs from Rummy in that neither player is allowed to lay down any of his melds until he has reduced the count of his "deadwood" (ungrouped cards) to ten points or less. He can then "knock" by making a final discard face down on top of the discard pile, and spreading his hand out in front of him. His opponent must then spread his hand out in a likewise manner and, if he can, lay out spare cards from his deadwood onto the Knocker's melds. The number of points of deadwood in each player's hand is then tallied up, and the player with the least points wins the difference between his count and his opponent's. There are, in addition, bonuses for tying or "undercutting" the Knocker and for knocking with no deadwood at all, as explained below.

As an example, take this sample endgame:

## SCORING BY FIVES

*If you want to keep track only of rounds won in a card game, rather than the actual point scores, this is the easy way to do it. make a single vertical mark for each win. Continue making the marks in a row until there are four of them. When you win a fifth time, cross the four marks with a diagonal. Then start a new group of five with the next win. When you are finished playing, the number of rounds you won will be easy to figure. Count the groups by fives (five, ten, fifteen, twenty...). Then, if there is an uncompleted group of marks, add those on for your total.*

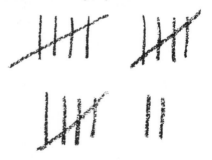

Camilla:

Shi Ming:

148

Camilla, having only four points in unmatched deadwood (4 of hearts), chooses to knock. She makes a face-down discard, says, "Knock with 4," and lays her hand down.

This catches Shi Ming in a bad predicament. He was hoping to draw the 7 of diamonds to complete the sequence 9 8 7 6 and go out with no deadwood at all. Instead, because Camilla knocked first with four, Shi Ming is stuck with twenty-five points in deadwood in his hand. This would pay Camilla twenty-one points—the difference between the deadwood in the two hands. However, Shi Ming is allowed to lay off his deadwood onto Camilla's melds, which changes the situation considerably:

Shi Ming lays down the melds in his hand that are complete and then proceeds to add his 9 and 8 of diamonds to the end of Camilla's Q J 10 and to put his 6 of diamonds with her three 6's. This leaves Shi Ming with only two points in deadwood (his 2 of spades), undercutting Camilla by two points. Not only does Shi Ming receive the two-point difference between his and Camilla's deadwood, but he also gets a 25-point bonus which is awarded to a player when his final deadwood count ties or is below the Knocker's count. The bonus gives him twenty-seven points in all. Note that Camilla, as the Knocker, is not allowed to lay her 4 of hearts with Shi Ming's 4's, even though she looks like she's trying to get away with it.

There is also a special bonus for players who go "Gin"—knock with no deadwood at all. For this, a player receives twenty-five extra points. Since Gin is a "perfect" hand, his opponent is not allowed to lay off any deadwood on his melds, often making this move a crushing blow.

*The end of the sample Gin Rummy game.*

*Camilla "knocks" with four.*

*Shi Ming can lay off his 6 of diamonds onto Camilla's 6's, and his 8 and 9 of diamonds on her 10, Jack and Queen of diamonds, undercutting her by two.*

# CARD RANKS AND VALUES

The difference between the value and the rank of a card has to be understood clearly in order to play and score many games. The "spot" or "face" value of a card is the same as a numeral on the card or its number of spots. A card with the numeral 9 and nine spots has a spot or face value of nine. Face cards do not have a face value, because they lack spots or numerals. Rank refers to the value of a card in relation to other cards (and in such games as Poker to the value of a hand in relation to other hands, as explained on pages 168-169). A 9 ranks above an 8 and below a 10. Face cards rank above a 10 even though they have no spot value. Of the three face cards, King is highest, Jack lowest, and the Queen is in the middle. An Ace, which has a spot value of only one, may rank either below a two or above a King, depending on the rules of the particular game. And it may be valued either as one or as eleven in games where it can assume either rank. The scoring value of a card may relate to spot value, to rank, or to neither.

In Rummy, scoring is based on the spot values of the number cards; the face cards, though they have no spot value, are assigned a scoring value of ten. In Casino, neither spot value nor rank is used for scoring; certain cards are assigned "bonus" values. And sometimes the scoring value of a card depends on the rank assigned to it by the player himself. In Twenty-One, a player can proclaim the score of his A 8 hand to be either nine or nineteen, since he is allowed to rank the Ace high or low.

*Since going out with a Gin is exciting, some families play for Gin only, not allowing any deadwood at all. This tradition is good for those who hate math too, as you can simply score one point for each Gin and forget all the other scoring.*

If it happens that the stock is down to two cards and neither player is able to knock, the game ends without a winner. The hands are gathered in and the deck reshuffled. Gin Rummy is often played to a total score of 100 points.

Because of the nature of the draw and the scoring, Gin is a game of wits and strategy. Players note each other's draws from the discard pile to deduce what sequences an opponent is trying to fill; and just as attentively watch all discards to see what he doesn't want. When he thinks he's got his opponent figured out, the Gin Rummy fanatic carefully retains all the cards his opponent has appeared eager to get, and casually throws him cards of the rank or suit he has been rejecting.

Often the player who can knock with a low score refrains from doing so, hoping to undercut his opponent, only to find that his opponent adopted the same strategy and has been able to Gin. Just as frequently, the player going for Gin is foiled when his opponent knocks with an Ace or deuce.

## HEARTS

*Three to six players*

*Standard deck of 52 cards*

*OBJECT: To score the least points by avoiding taking hearts or the Queen of Spades*

Choose the dealer and divide the cards evenly among the players. If any spare cards are left over after dealing an equal number to each player, place the spare(s) face down in the center of the table.

This is the "widow," which is taken by the player who takes the first "trick."

Each player organizes his hand so that cards of like suit are placed together in sequence. Aces rank high, deuces low. Each player chooses the three cards in his hand that he feels will do him the least good, and places them face down in front of the player on his left. Players then pick up the cards that were passed to them, and once again organize their hands.

The player on the dealer's left "leads" first, placing any card he chooses face up in the center of the table. One at a time, the other players around the table put down cards of the same suit on top of that card. The player who puts down the highest ranking card of the suit that was led takes all the cards played. He places these cards, his trick, in a stack in front of him. The player who won the trick now leads off the next round with any card he

*A player "shooting the moon" in Hearts.*

## THE ONE-HAND CUT

*These photographs show step by step how to cut a deck using only one hand. It takes a lot of practice, but when you have the one-hand cut perfected, it's a swell show-off.*

chooses. When a player has no cards of the suit that was led, he can play a card of a different suit, but he can't take the trick. This continues until players' hands are depleted.

When there are no more cards left to play, each player looks at the tricks he took and counts up the number of hearts he has. For each heart, a player scores one point. This might seem good, but in fact the player with the least points wins the round.

To give the basic game more suspense, two cards, the Queen of Spades and the Jack of Diamonds, are given special values. The Queen of Spades, known as the "Black Lady," has the same value as thirteen hearts, and adds that number of points to the score of the player unlucky enough to get her. The Jack of Diamonds, on the other hand, is eagerly sought after because the person who captures it in a trick has his score *reduced* by ten points. Hearts is usually played in tournaments. The first player to get fifty or one hundred points at the end of several rounds is the loser, and the player with the least points is the winner.

Some also play with the option known as "shooting the moon." To shoot the moon, a player has to take all the hearts and the Queen of Spades. If successful, he has twenty-six points taken off his score. (Some play that he has an option to add the twenty-six points to an opponent's score instead.) But the procedure is risky, for if the other players realize that one player is trying to shoot the moon, they will step in and take a single heart trick of their own, and the foiled player will receive the full load of all the hearts he has accumulated.

Most players dispose of the hearts in their hands by throwing them off when they are out of the suit that has been led. This means that if you lead a high card, such as the King of clubs, and one of the players is out of that suit, he may dispose of a spare heart, which will wind up in your trick. The best strategy is to lead with low cards and to save your high cards for taking innocuous tricks.

Of prime importance in Hearts is the initial passing of three cards to the player on your left. The cards you don't want to get stuck with are the highest spades—Ace and King—either of which will take the Queen of Spades; and the high hearts, which are fatal when someone leads a low heart and you have nothing lower. The Ace, King and Queen of Diamonds, on the other hand, give you the chance of catching the Jack and are good to hold onto.

If you hold the Black Lady, try to hang onto her so that you can keep track of what she's doing! You should be able to get rid of her by throwing her down as an out-of-suit spare, but if you give her to an opponent on a pass, chances are she'll wind up in a trick you are forced to take. Then again, if you have the Queen of Spades but no more than three other spades, it's a good idea to get rid of her since you might otherwise be forced to play her and take the trick in following suit.

To capture the Jack, keep track of all the diamonds taken until it looks as if most of the lower ones are gone. Then lead a high diamond (the Ace, King or Queen) in the hopes of flushing out the Jack. If you hold the Jack yourself, the only way to keep it is to eliminate the three high diamonds from the game by leading low until they have all been forced out. Then lead with your Jack when you are sure to win the trick.

# CASINO

*Two to four players*

*Standard deck of 52 cards*

**OBJECT: To score the most points by capturing as many tricks as possible, especially ones that contain cards of special value.**

Choose one player to be dealer. He deals four cards to each player and another four cards face up in the center of the table.

The immediate goal in Casino is to take cards on the table by matching them up with a card in your hand, in one of several ways. A player may play only one card from his hand in a turn. Cards won are removed from the center of the table and placed together with the card that won them in a "trick" pile in front of the player who took them. As you will see in scoring, certain cards and certain suits will add to your score. When a player isn't able to take a trick (or perhaps doesn't wish to), he "trails" a card by taking it from his hand and placing it face up on the table alongside the other cards. The trailed card can then be won by other players.

There are several ways in which cards on the table can be taken:

PAIRING: A card on the table can be paired with a card of the same rank from your hand and taken from the board. If there is an 8 on the table, you can match it with an 8 from your hand and take it. Or, you may trail a 6 on one turn, and take it with a 6 from your hand on your next turn. Face cards can only be taken by pairing.

COMBINING: Two or more cards from the table can be combined and taken by a card in your hand if they add up numerically to the card you hold. For example, if there are a 5 and a 3 on the table, you can put them together, declare them to add up to eight, and take them both with an 8 from your hand. In the same way, two Aces can be combined and taken with a deuce, and a 2, 4 and 3 can all be taken together with a 9 from your hand. Face cards cannot be used in combining, as they have no numerical value. All other cards are valued by the number of their spots from one to ten.

BUILDING: One card from your hand can be added to (built onto) one or more cards on the table to form a sum which can be taken on your next turn. If there is a 2 on the table, but you hold only a 6 and a 4, you can add your 4 to the 2 at one turn and say, "Building six." On your next turn, you can take the build with your 6. But beware! Your build can be taken in the meantime by an opponent who also holds a 6, or an opponent can add to your build, perhaps putting a 2 down on it to make it an 8 so that he'll be able to take it on his next turn. If you make a build, you are required to take it on your next turn, unless there is some other valid trick you can take (or another build you can make). You are not allowed to trail on a move following the creation of a build.

DOUBLING: To prevent your opponents from adding to your builds, you can double up cards or builds by putting them together

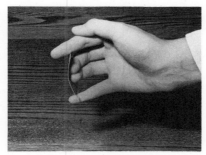

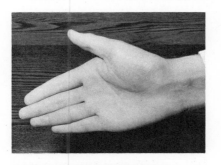

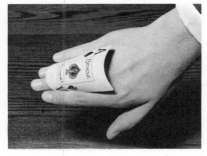

### DISAPPEARING CARD

*Hold the card as shown in the first photograph. Bring your middle two fingers up under the card as shown in the second photo, and use them to pivot the card around to the back of your hand. The result should look like photo #3: an empty hand. To see what has really happened, look at the last picture. You can make the card reappear by reversing the movement of your two middle fingers.*

153

*Though unusual, it sometimes happens that a player in Casino can pick up all the major points in a single turn.*

without adding. For example, say there are a 4, 5 and Ace on the table, while you hold a 6 and a 2. In your move, you can combine the 5 and the Ace, forming 6; and also build the deuce in your hand on the 4, making a 6 build. You then put the two stacks of 6 together, and declare it to be a pile of 6's. Your opponent cannot now add an Ace to the pile to form a 7, because the pile contains more than one group of six.

Similarly, if you hold two 7's and there is a third 7 on the table, you can put one of your 7's onto the table's 7, declare it to be a pile of 7's, and take the pile on your next turn. If there are two 6's on the table and you hold the third 6, you might put both of the table's 6's together and take them with your 6.

The play in Casino is very simple: At his turn, each player uses one card from his hand either to take a trick or to trail a card by placing it on the table with the other cards. When all players' hands are exhausted, the dealer deals out four more cards to each. If the cards on the table are used up in the course of the play, the next player has no choice but to trail a card. The game ends when hands are depleted and there are no more cards to be dealt. Whoever takes the last trick of the game also wins whatever odd cards are left on the table.

## Scoring

At the end of the game, players examine their tricks to figure their score. Points are scored in this way:

| CAPTURE | POINTS |
|---|---|
| The most cards | 3 |
| The most spades | 1 |
| Big Casino (the 10 of diamonds) | 2 |
| Little Casino (the 2 of spades) | 1 |
| Each Ace one point for a total of | 4 |
| Total | 11 |

In addition, each time a player manages to clear the table of all the cards, he scores one bonus point for a "sweep." Sweeps are kept track of by turning up the top card of that trick.

Very often Casino is played in several rounds, the first player to reach twenty-one or some other number of points winning the tournament. Needless to say, because of both the way tricks are taken and the way points are scored, Casino is terrific for teaching the facts of arithmetic to six- and seven-year-olds.


# TWENTY-ONE

*Any number of players, but the game is best with between five and nine.*

*Standard deck of 52 cards*
*Chips for betting*

**OBJECT: To win chips by getting cards which total as close as possible to twenty-one points without going over**

This game, known in casinos as Blackjack, is a snappy gambling game which rivals Poker in popularity. It is unusually fast-moving and zesty, and sports a feature not often found in multi-player games: All players are pitted against one common enemy, the dealer, who pays out bets and takes them in.

Several features of regulation Twenty-One are omitted in this family version because they are complicated, or they slow the rhythm of the game. One is the dealer's option to "double" players' bets, and the players' opportunity of "redoubling." This rule is complicated, and unnecessary in a game where the tokens used for betting are gathered up at the end of the game and put away. Another omitted rule is the one which allows players to "split" a pair of cards and play each one separately; this may make the game confusing for many people. Also, the custom of "burning" a card by showing the top card of the deck and placing it face up at the bottom of the pack when the game begins, is unimportant in a game where the dealer isn't likely to be crooked.

## ROYAL CASINO

*In ordinary Casino, a Jack, Queen or King can only be taken by a matching face card; face cards can't be built onto. In Royal Casino, Jacks are given the numerical value 11, Queens 12, Kings 13, and Aces 1 or 14. Therefore, a 9 and a 3 on the table can be combined and taken with a Queen from your hand, or a King (value 13) and an Ace (value 1) can be combined and taken with another Ace (this time valued at 14).*

## PARTNERSHIP CASINO

*With four people in the game, Casino is best played in teams of two. Partners sit across from one another. The game is played as usual, except that the partners cooperate in building or trailing to provide tricks for one another during the game, and combine their tricks to collect points at the end.*

## MARKED DECKS

*Just so you will recognize a marked deck of cards if a pal springs it on you, examine this picture. At first glance the cards may look like any of those ordinary ones with the complicated geometric patterns on the backs. But examine the dots within the various circles carefully. Some are dark, some are light, and the pattern is different on each card in the deck. The changing pattern is actually a code that tells a player both the suit and rank of every card—merely by glimpsing the back. That means a player who knows the code (there are many of them) can tell what is in your hand, as well as what card will come up next on the draw. Luckily, marked cards aren't hard to spot once you know what to look for.*

Select a player to be the first dealer. This can be done, in traditional Blackjack style, by dealing the cards out to each player in turn: The first to get an Ace is the dealer. Another way to make the selection is to give a card to each player, and the player with the highest card gets the deal. Distribute chips among the players, thirty or more to each.

Starting with the player to his left, the dealer deals himself and each of the other players one card face down. After looking at his down-card, each player places a bet on his card by putting one or more chips in front of him. Players each bet individually against the dealer, so there is no requirement that two or more players bet the same amount. When you lose a hand of Twenty-One, you pay your bet directly to the dealer; when your hand beats the dealer's, he pays you.

Following betting, the dealer proceeds to deal out a round of face-up cards. Before going on with the game, the dealer and his opponents all check their first two cards to see if they form a "natural"—add up to twenty-one exactly. All the cards are given numerical values. Aces count as 1 or 11 (as the player desires), face cards count as 10, and the rest of the cards have the value of their spots (tens count as 10, nines as 9, and so on). A player lucky enough to get a natural announces the fact immediately, shows his cards, and is paid double his bet by the dealer. If the dealer gets a natural, he collects double the amount of their bets from each player, and the hands are passed back in for the next deal. In the rare circumstance that both the dealer and another player get a natural, the dealer still collects from each player, but only the actual amounts of their bets, and hands are passed in.

After settling up accounts with players who got naturals, if any, the game proceeds to its next phase, in which the dealer gives players extra cards if they want them. Starting with the player on the dealer's left, a player who wants to be dealt an additional up-card says, "Hit me," and the dealer gives him another card. If that player wants more cards, he can say, "Hit me again," as many times as he wishes—until he either decides to "stand" with a total of twenty-one or less, or "busts" by going over twenty-one. If he busts, he hands his bet over to the dealer and leaves the game until the next hand. When a player wants no more cards, the dealer moves on to the next player to the left, and serves him in the same way.

After all the players have been served, the dealer serves himself. He turns over his down-card so that everyone can see it, and deals himself additional up-cards until he wishes to stop, or goes bust with over twenty-one. When the dealer is satisfied, each player who hasn't previously busted reveals his cards, and the bets are settled.

Each player with a total greater than the dealer's is paid the amount of his bet from the dealer's chips. If a player's count is the same or lower than the dealer's, he loses his bet and must hand his chips over to the dealer. If the dealer goes over twenty-one, he pays the players left in the game the amounts of their bets, from his own chips.

After each round of Twenty-One, the dealer gathers in the cards that were dealt, places them face up at the bottom of the

*It's easy to see that the dealer in Twenty-One has a tremendous advantage over the other players in the game—an advantage used to its utmost in gambling casinos. In the family game, there has to be a way in which the deal rotates from person to person.*

*There are several ways of accomplishing this. The simplest way is to let each player be the dealer for a specified number of rounds, and then for the deal to pass to the left. Another method is to let the deal pass to any player who gets a natural during a round. This has the advantage of adding an element of uncertainty to the game. A third possible method—recommended for kids who feel cheated if the deal passes out of their hands before they've won a bundle—is to set a rule at the beginning of the game that the deal passes to the next player after the dealer has won a specified number of chips.*

*Champion card sailers claim they can boomerang a card—sail it across the room and get it to return right to their waiting hand. Less skilled players can still drive grownups nuts by sailing cards in the living room. We suggest outdoors as a good practice area, and an old, incomplete deck instead of a nice new one. The motion is a quick horizontal flip of the wrist, which sends the card in a fast flat spin along a low trajectory. When competing, card sailers should try to win for distance. But the boomerang is the ultimate sailing skill.*

deck, and deals out another round. When the dealer gets to the end of the face-down cards, he turns the cards over, shuffles them, and resumes dealing.

## Strategy

The agonizing moment in Twenty-One comes when you must decide whether to be hit or stand pat. If you are super-observant, particularly good at math, and armed with a speedy pocket calculator so the tedious figuring won't irritate other players, you can make a rational decision based on the odds. Or at least expert Twenty-One players say you can.

Perhaps you hold a total of sixteen, and wonder what your chances are of getting a 5, for a perfect Twenty-One. Well, that depends. If no cards had been dealt, the chances of getting one of the four 5's would be four in fifty-two, or one in thirteen. But cards have been dealt, and possibly some of those 5's have been dealt too, only you don't necessarily know how many, because they might not all be among the up-cards you can observe. Besides, twenty-one shouldn't be your goal anyhow. You should be wondering what your odds are for increasing your sixteen without going over twenty-one. There are twenty cards that would help you: all of the Aces, 2's, 3's, 4's and 5's. The experts who are bright enough to rapidly figure out their chances with scant information and complex calculation are certainly amazing. For the rest of us, here is some meager advice: Ask to be hit if your total is eleven or less; stand pat if your total is seventeen or higher. And if you hold between eleven and seventeen? That depends on the dealer's up-card. If the dealer's up-card is 7 or higher, there is a good chance he already has a high enough hand to stand, and therefore will not risk going bust. What's more, he may well be higher than you already. So ask for another card, and take the risk of going over. But if the dealer's up-card is low (not an Ace, which he can use high if he wishes, but a 2, 3, 4, 5 or 6) he will most likely take another card, and risk going bust himself. In that case, stand pat and hope he busts.

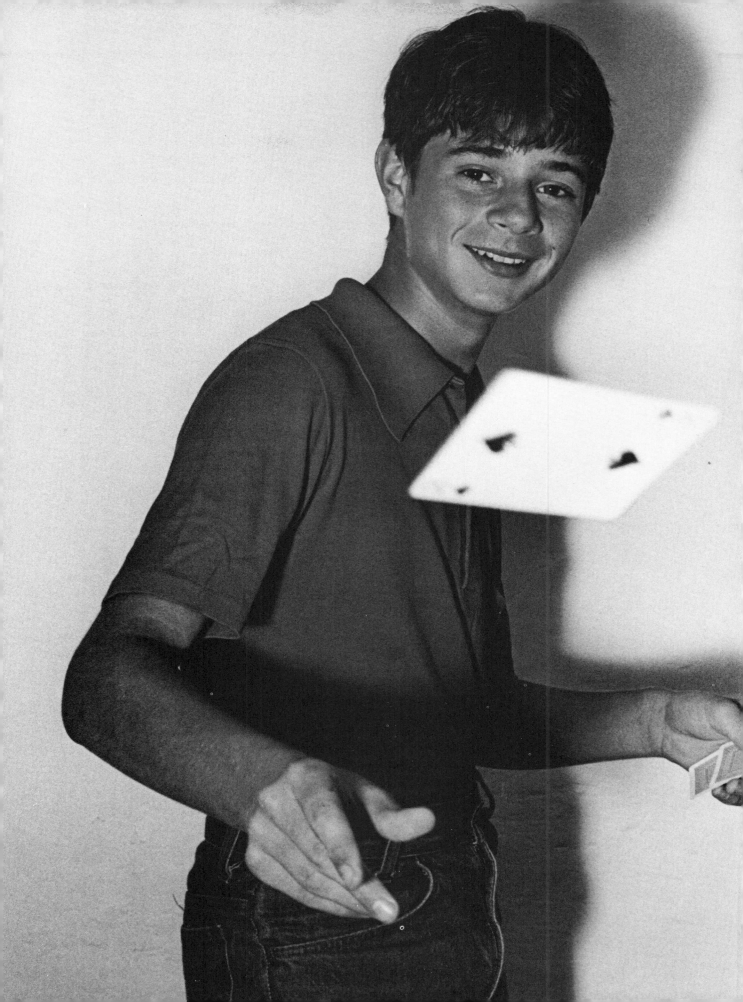

# FANCY SHUFFLES

Before you even try any fancy stuff with cards, arm yourself with several brand-new decks. Old cards get too soft and sticky for tricks. All of the following manipulations can be worked into an impressive shuffling routine.

### The Bridge

This makes an ordinary riffle shuffle look more elaborate. Shuffle the deck using even halves, keeping the edges parallel so the entire top edges mesh. Try to mesh the cards evenly (so there are no bunches of unmeshed cards). Before you push the meshed cards together into a single pack again, bend them firmly into an upside down "U," then push against the top of the curve with both thumbs. With a little practice, the cards should slide against one another, collapsing with a pleasant riffling noise into a single pack.

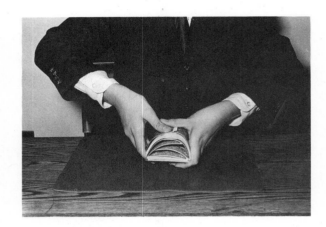

### The Wave

To add this maneuver to a shuffling routine you will need a piece of cloth with a nappy surface. The surface provided by velveteen, felt or flocked paper is about right; special flocked mats are sold in magic stores. Fan the deck into either a straight line or a curve along the surface as evenly as possible. The best way to do this is to lay the deck down, and sweep it out into a fan with one swooshing motion of your flattened fingers. This takes more practice than the trick itself, yet the rest will only work if the cards are evenly overlapped for the entire length of the fan. Now put one finger under the bottom card and lift it gently. As you lift it, it will push up the other cards overlapping it until, when you have it almost upright, the fan will crest. As you continue to push, the crest will move along the fan, leaving face-up cards in its wake. By the time the Wave has moved the full length of the fan, all the cards will have fallen face up. When the crest first forms, you can take a single card, lay it edgewise on the crest as shown, and by moving it to one side then the other push the crest of the Wave back and forth along the fan—a pretty sight when done by an experienced hand.

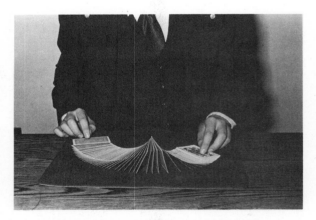

### The Fan

This can be used as a prelude to a shuffle act. Start with less than a whole deck of cards until you get the knack. Hold the deck firmly between your thumb and fingers, with your thumb held way over toward your pinky and resting on the very edge of the deck. With one smooth motion, rotate your thumb as far as it will go in the other direction and at the same time curl your other four fingers away from it. The total sliding movement of thumb against fingers should fan the cards out nicely. To get the almost perfect circular fan shown here with a full deck requires a good deal of practice.

### The Toss

This whiz of a trick can be interspersed with shuffles. There is no big secret to it—just a lot of work and even more picking up of fallen cards. The hand that tosses the cards must make a fast and powerful slicing motion toward the other hand, which is waiting to catch the deck. If the motion is jerky, the cards won't fan out through the air; if it is too slow, the cards will drop to the floor immediately instead of fanning. Try the toss first onto a couch rather than into your other hand. Graduate to doing the toss downward toward your waiting hand. Finally, see if you can toss the cards more or less horizontally.

# DRAW POKER

*Two to seven players, but the game is best with four to six*

*Standard deck of 52 cards*
*Chips for betting*

*OBJECT: To win chips by holding the best hand or by making other players think you do*

Bluffing aside, chips or money are gained in Poker and all its variations by holding the better ranking hand, so the names and ranks of cards should be learned before you begin to play. (See pages 168 and 169.)

Divide the chips evenly among the players. Each player should start with at least fifty chips. Select one player to be the first dealer.

Each hand of Draw Poker is played in five parts: the deal, the first round of betting, the draw, the second round of betting, and the showdown. After each hand, the cards are collected and the player to the dealer's left becomes the new dealer.

Before the deal, the players "ante up"—throw in one chip apiece into a common pile in the center of the table to start the "pot." The dealer then deals five cards face down to each player. The player to the dealer's left has the first opportunity to "open" the pot by throwing one or more additional chips into it. If, after

he views his hand, he doesn't wish to place a bet on it, he may "pass," and the next player now has a chance to open the pot or pass. If all the players pass without placing bets, cards are collected. Each player adds another chip to the pot, and a new hand is dealt from the reshuffled deck.

After the pot has been opened, play continues to the left. Each player in his turn has three options:

He may decide his hand is too weak to bet on and "fold," by placing his cards face down in front of him. A player who folds forfeits any chips he may have placed in the pot previously, and is out of the game during the rest of that hand.

He may "stay" or "call" the bet, by placing into the pot the number of chips that will make his bet equal to the last player's bet.

He may "raise" or "bump" the bet by placing into the pot the number of chips that will make his bet equal to the last player's plus one or more additional chips.

The round of betting ends after everyone still in calls the bets and no one makes a further raise. Everyone who hasn't folded must at this point have placed an equal number of chips in the pot.

A typical round of betting by five players might be as follows: Uncle Henry, sitting to the dealer's left, passes. Susie opens the pot with one chip. Charlie calls Susie's bet, and raises her two chips, putting a total of three into the pot. Aunt Betsy feels the game is getting too hot for her, and folds. John stays, by throwing in three chips to match Charlie's bet. Uncle Henry, who is still in the game because he passed before the pot was opened, matches the current bet of three, and then raises by two chips, throwing in a total of five. To remain in the game, Susie must now put in four chips to raise her total commitment to five, and Charlie and John must each throw in two to stay in the game.

Betting can continue in this manner so long as any players remain. In the basic game the only restriction on betting is that no player may raise twice in a row unless another player has made an intervening raise. This prevents one player from repeatedly raising the pot until the other players are forced to fold. The first round of betting comes to an end when all remaining players have called the last raise, and no further raises are offered.

After the first round of betting, players still in the game are allowed to draw up to five new cards in the hope of strengthening their hands. Each player who wants new cards selects those he wishes to discard and spreads them out face down in front of him. The dealer counts out for him from the deck the desired number of new cards, serving players in order starting to the left and ending with himself. A player may "stand pat" with his cards if he wishes, neither discarding nor drawing. In games played with six or more players, the draw may be limited to three cards, since otherwise the deck could be depleted before all players have been served.

When the draw is completed, and each player has looked at his cards and evaluated his chances, the second round of betting begins with each player putting his ante into the pot. As with the first round, the player to the dealer's left may opt to open the pot or to pass. If all players pass, the final phase of the game, the showdown, follows immediately.

## JACK POT

*To prevent uninteresting showdowns, serious Poker players introduce a rule called Jack Pot, in which the pot can only be opened by a player who holds a pair of Jacks or higher. If no one holds a high pair (or a better hand) the cards are passed back to the dealer, a second ante is added to the previous one, and a new hand is dealt by the same dealer. Jack Pot is played so commonly that many consider it standard, but among children and in informal groups it is often considered an unnecessary complication, and wild cards (p. 174) are used to keep the game exciting.*

At the showdown, each player still in the game turns his cards face up and calls out his hand. The player who holds the strongest hand wins the pot. He removes the chips from the center of the table and places them with the rest of his own chips. Hands which are of equal strength split the pot equally. If there is a leftover chip, it is left in the pot for the next game.

Often, all players but one have folded by the end of the game. When this occurs, the lone better automatically wins the pot. There is no requirement that he display his hand and perhaps reveal an infuriatingly bold bluff.

### Strategy

The essense of Draw Poker is to seem weak when your hand is strong, and to bluff strong when your hand is weak. In serious games, where the stakes are high and the competition sharp, few players would take a risk on a fair to middling hand, or on one which has little chance of being improved by a lucky draw. In informal games, however, where it isn't too expensive to stay "just to see what will happen," it can pay off to try to bluff your way to the pot with a low pair or a high card. Of course a bluff only works if everyone is scared off and folds, leaving you to take the pot; or if the remaining players were also bluffing. When an opponent with a mediocre hand nevertheless sees through you and stays in the game, he is "calling your bluff."

The draw you choose to make depends on the number of players, their skill and the amount of your stake. The draws preferred by most poker players are given below. They are in order from lowest to highest hand.

HIGH CARD: A four- or five-card draw gives you a fifty percent chance of bettering your hand. However, so large a draw is a sure signal to experienced players that you don't even hold a pair. A better idea, if you don't wish to fold immediately, is to replace only your two or three lowest cards. This can have some bluffing power, as it gives the impression that you are holding a pair, but your chances of improving the hand are lowered. If you dare risk it, you can always try the "big bluff": Stand pat (don't draw any cards) and look cool. When it is your turn to bet, raise with a show of assurance. There's a chance the other players will take fright and fold, leaving the pot to you. On the other hand, you might draw one card, giving the impression that you are only one card short of a full house, flush or straight. This performance can be

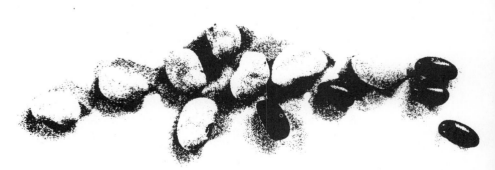

more convincing than trying to pretend you were dealt a "natural"—a perfect hand.

ONE PAIR: One pair is a good hand, if the pair is relatively high. A three-card draw gives you one chance in six of adding another pair, and one chance in nine of forming a triplet. There's a long shot of getting a full house or four of a kind, but too long to count on. Unfortunately, the three-card draw is tagged for what it is, and has no bluffing power. Though you decrease the chances of bettering your hand, a slyer strategy is to replace only your two lowest cards. The other players may then come to the conclusion that you are holding a triplet and get scared out of the game, especially if you bet confidently.

TWO PAIRS: If you hold a low two-pair hand, 8's and 6's say, it is advisable to discard the odd card and make a one-card draw. Chances of getting a full house—almost a sure winner—are one in twelve. If both pairs are high, Aces and Kings for example, you could stand pat (draw no cards). A high two-pair is a strong hand, and the effect that standing pat has on the other players is electric; suddenly they become extremely reluctant to bet even strong hands against what they fear may be a straight or a flush.

THREE OF A KIND: The best idea is to discard the lowest of the two odd cards, and take a one-card draw. This gives you one chance in fifteen of getting a full house, and one in forty-eight of getting four of a kind. It also gives you tremendous bluffing potential. An opponent is free to think you hold two pairs, and imagines his high two-pair or low triplet will beat you. Even better, an opponent can assume you almost had a straight or flush, and couldn't fill it. That's called a double bluff.

FOUR STRAIGHT: Groups of four cards that almost make a straight are of two kinds: "open-ended," in which the sequence could be filled out by either the next lowest or the next highest card in the sequence; and "inside," in which the missing card is somewhere in the middle of the sequence. A one-card draw for an open-ended straight has a one in six chance of success, whereas the chance of filling the spot in an inside straight are one in twelve. The chance should be taken for an open-ended straight, but many players prefer to pass on the inside straight.

FOUR FLUSH: There's a one in five chance that a discard of the one out-of-suit card followed by a one-card draw will give you a flush—among the most valuable hands. If the draw doesn't work, you can either fold, or try to bluff it out.

### HOMESTYLE BETTING

*In friendly circles it's a good idea to set up restrictions on betting to prevent the bad feelings that emerge when enormous bets are won or lost. The usual way to do this is to set limits on the ante, the opening bet, and subsequent raises. In the "one-two" limit, the ante is a single chip, and subsequent raises can be either one or two chips. In a "five-ten" game, ante and opening bet may be as low as one chip or as high as five chips. Each raise can be as high as ten chips. Sometimes the ante is set high and the betting limit low. This encourages players who are running short of chips to stay in the game in the hope of winning a big pot.*

*Another way to control betting is to limit the number of raises per player. This prevents two players from wildly raising each other in an endless contest of bravado.*

*Cheating at Poker was once considered cause for justifiable murder, and though that wouldn't do today, getting thrown out of the game is the least punishment deserved. Children most often cheat by peeking at others' hands—a habit that can usually be controlled by seating players far enough apart from one another that the cheater would have to ostentatiously lean to get a glimpse of his neighbor's cards. Marked decks, in which subtle differences in the design on the tops of the cards declare their face value for those who know the system, are still available, but we won't tell you where. Of course the dealer has the best chance of cheating by "stacking" the deck (and then only pretending to shuffle), dealing himself extra cards, or stuffing an Ace or two up his sleeve. Luckily, the skill required of the card sharp is beyond ordinary deftness, and peeking is still the most common crime. If a member of your family seems to be cheating, give him the benefit of the doubt the first couple of times by simply declaring a misdeal and playing the hand over again. But if the peeking continues, substitute*
*I Doubt It (page 134), where cheating is the essence of the game, and ban the player from Poker.*

**STRAIGHT, FLUSH OR FULL HOUSE:** If you are fortunate enough to be dealt a perfect hand, stand pat; you can't do better. Just be sure not to seem smug during the first round of betting, because other players might catch the scent and bet cautiously. Standing pat is sure to tip them off before the second round of betting, but if they've bet high on the first round the pot will be large enough.

**FOUR OF A KIND:** A one-card draw is the best strategy. Discard the odd card, even though you don't need to, and draw a new one to bluff the other players. Because of the rarity of four of a kind in any deal, the one-card draw will lead them to the assumption of a four straight, four flush, two-pair or triplet. Instead, what you are holding is a practically unbeatable hand.

**PARTIAL STRAIGHT FLUSH:** Discard the one that is out of suit, and take a one-card draw. Your chances are one in three of getting any one of the following hands: a straight, a flush, or a straight flush. Your circumstances are excellent because a card in sequence, of the same suit, or both in sequence and in suit, all give you betting hands.

**COMPLETE STRAIGHT FLUSH:** Stand pat; you've got it made. Just put on your best poker face. The chances of two straight flushes appearing in the same round of Poker are only one in 170 million!

# HOUSE OF CARDS

People have been known to build structures as high as eight floors using this technique for building card houses. Perhaps some have gone even higher. You can build horizontally too, carefully leaning walls against the stronger "tents," and against the edges of other walls. A carpet is definitely the best surface to build on.

Sets of cards are sold specifically designed for building card houses, and they are absolutely lovely. But they demand little skill, as they are put together by interlocking notches. Much more skill, and much more fun, is involved when you use plain old playing cards for your House of Cards.

# RANKING POKER HANDS

The five-card combination a player bets on is called the "hand." Each hand is ranked in value from the highest (most scarce combination) to the lowest (the easiest to come by). Higher-ranking hands "beat" ones made up of more common combinations of cards. In order of rank from the least valuable, or weakest, to the most valuable, or strongest, these are the standard Poker hands.

*High Card:* A Q 10 6 2
The lowest-ranking, most common hand in Poker, appearing at least fifty percent of the time. It has no combinations whatsoever. The highest unmatching card determines the rank between two or more high card hands at the showdown. Cards are ranked Aces highest, then Kings, and so on down to deuces. If hands contain the same highest card, then the next highest is used for comparison.

*Two-pair:* A A 8 8 2
Two pairs of cards and an unmatched fifth card. The highest pair determines the rank of the hand if two players both have two-pair hands. If the high pairs are identical, the hands are compared on the basis of their second pairs. Chances for this hand are one in twenty-one.

*One-Pair:* Q Q 3 6 A
Contains just one matching pair of cards. In case of competition between two one-pair hands, the higher pair (or, if both are the same, the highest unmatched card) decides the winner. Every one in two and a half deals produces one of these hands.

*Three Of A Kind:* 6 6 6 K Q
Three matching cards plus two unmatched. The rank of the triplet decides the rank of the hand when two three-of-a-kind hands come face to face in the showdown. Chances for a triplet are one in forty-seven.

**Straight:** Ace of diamonds, King of clubs, Queen of diamonds, Jack of Spades, 10 of hearts. All five cards in sequence, but in mixed suits. The straight shown is the highest of its class; the straight 5 4 3 2 A is the lowest. There is one chance in 255 of being dealt a straight.

**Four Of a Kind:** 5 5 5 5 9
Four matching cards, plus an unmatched fifth. If two players hold four-of-a-kind hands at the showdown, the higher-ranking foursome wins. It isn't often that two hands of this type come into competition, however. The chances of the hand being dealt are one in 4,165.

**Flush:** A 9 6 7 4 of diamonds
All five cards of one suit, but not in sequence. In case of a showdown between two flushes, the hand with the highest-ranking card wins. If the highest cards match, then the hand is decided on the rank of the next lowest, and so on. In the extreme case of the hand above being compared to the almost identical flush in spades, A 9 7 6 3, the hand shown would win on the basis of its 4. One deal in 509 results in a flush.

**Straight Flush:** J 10 9 8 7 of hearts
All five cards both in sequence and of the same suit. Aces may be used as the high rank (A K Q J 10) or as the low rank (5 4 3 2 A). Of two straight flushes, the one containing the higher cards wins. A Jack-high straight, for instance, is stronger than a 10-high straight. The highest possible Poker hand is the royal flush, Ace through King to 10. Chances of being dealt a straight flush are the smallest of all, only one in 64,974.

**Full House:** K K K 2 2
A triplet and a pair. In case of a conflict between two full houses, the hand with the highest triplet wins, no matter how the pairs compare. Chances for a full house are one in 694.

# FIVE CARD STUD POKER

*Two to ten players*

*Standard deck of 52 cards*
*Chips for betting*

*OBJECT: To win chips by holding the best hand, or by making other players think you do*

Whereas Draw Poker can be a heady, unpredictable game in which a worthless hand can take the pot in a bluff, Stud Poker is somewhat subdued, although the competition is no less acute. Several features make Stud Poker an excellent game for a large group. Because there is no draw, the game moves quickly; and up to ten people can play, since there is no fear that the deck will be used up. There are more rounds of betting to increase the action. And four cards of each player's hand are revealed, so opponents can better figure their odds.

There is rarely an ante in Stud Poker. The dealer starts the game by giving each player two cards, one placed face down, the "hole card," the other face up, the "up-card." The player with the highest up-card has the option to open the pot, after which play proceeds to his left. To fold, a player turns his up-card face down. The procedure for calling and raising bets is otherwise the same as in Draw Poker (p. 162).

When the first round of betting is over, the dealer deals each player another up-card. Another round of betting begins, started by the player whose up-cards show the strongest hand, and proceeding to his left. The second round is followed by another deal, a third round of betting, another deal, which brings the total number of cards in each player's hand to five, and finally a fourth betting round. After this last round, the players who remain in the game turn over their hole cards, and the highest hand takes the pot. The deal passes to the left, and another hand begins.

A hand of Stud Poker is detailed below. This particular sample hand is Stud Poker at its best. Unfortunately, the moment a high pair is revealed in any player's hand, the other players tend to fold. Even a single card as high as an Ace may make players nervous enough early in a game to fold their cards. With such nervous folding, players seldom stay long enough to complete straights and flushes, and the course of the game becomes overly predictable. The Seven Card variation of Stud that follows this sample game on p. 175 increases the zest of the play.

*Uncle Henry*

*Susie*

*Aunt Betsy*

*Charlie*

*John*

## Sample Game

ROUND 1:

Uncle Henry:

Uncle Henry:

Susie:

Aunt Betsy:

Charlie:

John:

Aunt Betsy opens the pot, since she has the highest up-card. Charlie, to her left, reckoning that his Queen in the hole is as strong as any card showing, calls her bet. John folds, turning his up-card face down. Uncle Henry stays in, since both his cards are relatively high. Susie raises him on the strength of her hole card, a 5 which makes a pair with her up-card. The remaining players match her raise.

ROUND 2:

Uncle Henry:

Susie:

Aunt Betsy:

Charlie:

Susie's up-cards are highest, so she opens the betting this time. Aunt Betsy matches the bet, figuring that her Queen and Ace are strong enough to carry her through. Charlie, in the hope that he may pick up a Queen to pair with his hole card, stays in as well. Uncle Henry, the last to bet, has snagged himself a pair of Jacks, the best hand on the table so far. Recalling that Susie raised on the first round, Henry correctly assumes that Susie has a pair of 5's, and judges from both Charlie's and Aunt Betsy's cautious betting that they are staying in the hopes of picking up a high pair. Not wishing to scare off the others, he simply calls the bet.

ROUND 3:

Uncle Henry:

Susie:

172

Aunt Betsy:

Charlie:

Aunt Betsy, with her revealed pair of 6's, bets first. Charlie folds: The two other visible Queens diminish his chances of getting another Queen to pair with his hole card, and his up-cards are of no help. Uncle Henry calls Aunt Betsy's bet. Susie is in a quandary: She faces on the one hand Uncle Henry, who could have a pair of Jacks or 7's, either of which could be higher than her pair of 5's; and on the other hand Aunt Betsy, who already has her beaten "on sight" with a pair of 6's. Rather than folding, however, she brazens it out in the hope that the two other players will think her hole card forms a pair with either her King or Queen. She raises the bet, and the other players call her raise.

ROUND 4:

Uncle Henry:

Susie:

Aunt Betsy:

Aunt Betsy has the option of opening the betting again, but she prefers to pass and see what the other players will do. Uncle Henry, who has not been taken in by Susie's bluff, opens the betting. Still bluffing, Susie raises the bet. Aunt Betsy is fooled, and folds. Now it is Uncle Henry's pair of Jacks against Susie's pair of 5's. He calls her bluff, and takes the pot.

# DEALER'S CHOICE AND WILD CARDS

Unlike games such as bridge—in which the slightest deviation from established procedures brings horrified gasps, strong protests, and a quick rush for the rule book—Draw and Stud Pokers are rarely played in informal groups without one or more rule changes to liven up the game, or to suit the idiosyncrasies of the company. Some changes, especially the use of "wild" cards, are used so frequently that some consider them the established norm. Others are so outlandish that it's unlikely two people in any given company have heard of them. They're all unique in their ways and it is a pleasant pastime just to try one after another. Experiment with the Poker variations explained on the following pages, try different combinations, or invent your own game. Just be sure you make all your "house rules" clear before the game begins to avoid fights between players, each of whom is doing it "their way."

Dealer's Choice, in which each player gets a turn to name his own rules at his deal, is a popular way to use the variations. In this game each new dealer specifies the rules for the upcoming hand. The first dealer, for example, could choose Draw Poker With Deuces Wild;

*Some of the classic wild cards, from left to right: the Joker, deuces, suicide King, mustached Kings, and one-eyed Jacks.*

the second dealer, a bit more adventurous, could announce that the next hand is to be High-Low Spit In The Ocean With Aces and Mustached Kings Wild; while the third, his taste whetted, might elect Shotgun or Pass the Garbage. No matter how absurd the rules, whatever the dealer dreams up is the next game played.

To liven up any Poker variation (or the standard games) certain cards can be declared "wild." A wild card is one which can assume any value or suit desired by the player who holds it, allowing him to complete whatever combinations he wishes. With a wild Joker added to the pack, for example, the hand Q 8 4 3 of hearts plus the Joker can be declared a hearts flush.

Although not acceptable among adult players, children may add other strange attributes to wild cards. For instance, wild cards may leave "holes" in the deck which can be skipped over in straights. With 4's wild, for example, the hand 7 6 5 3 2 constitutes a straight. Wild cards also make possible—to those who like their games strange—a new type of hand, the five of a kind. The hand 8 8 8 8 2, with deuces wild, ranks above a royal straight flush; the deuce is considered a fifth 8 of unnamed suit.

Wild cards often open up the possibility of a hand that assumes more than one value. In deuces wild, a player might declare the hand Ace, 4 and 8 of hearts, plus two deuces to be three Aces, but he would do better to call his hand an Ace-high hearts flush. The rule is that the hand is whatever it is first declared to be at the showdown. No changes of mind are allowed.

The choice of wild cards is completely arbitrary. Most commonly one or two Jokers will be added to the deck, or the deuces will be declared wild. Almost as frequently one-eyed Jacks (there are two of them) are wild along with the deuces. For variety, there is no reason you can't make the mustached Kings (three of them), or the "suicide" King (the King of hearts sticks his sword into his head), or red Queens wild as well. Another alternative is "low card wild," in which the lowest card in a player's hand, and other cards of the same denomination, are wild for that player.

*Seven Card Stud:* On the first round, each player is dealt two face-down hole cards and one up-card. This is followed by three more rounds of one more up-card each, and a final, fifth round in which a seventh card is dealt face down, giving each player a total of three hole cards and four up-cards. Each is followed by a round of betting, as in Five Card Stud.

At the showdown, each player selects five of his seven cards to constitute his hand. A hand of more than five cards, such as three pairs, has no standing; it ranks only as a two-pair hand with an odd card.

In contrast to Five Card Stud, the chances of filling a flush or straight are greatly improved. If your first three cards are of the same suit, or if they form a sequence, it is definitely worthwhile to stay in. If your fourth card furthers a straight or flush, you still have three more chances of completing a hand that's an almost sure winner. If your fourth card doesn't fit, however, better to fold than to take a long shot, unless that fourth card has given you a high pair and no one else's hand shows anything better.

Seven Card Stud offers several unique advantages over both Five Card and Draw Poker. Since most of your opponents' cards are exposed, you don't waste time vainly going after a card that has already been dealt. For example, if you are after a third Jack to augment a pair, you might as well forget it if you see a Jack in an opponent's hand. Conversely, there's all the more chance of picking up a particular card if it isn't already showing on the table.

Seven Card also has the bluffing potential that Five Card lacks, and may offer opportunities which even avid Draw Poker players envy. If, for example, your four up-cards are showing two pairs, a confident high bet may scare even a three of a kind holder into the mistaken belief that you hold a full house. Similarly, a visible four straight or four flush can take the pot if you bet with authority—even if you have nothing in the hole to back it up.

# POKER VARIATIONS

*High-Low:* Any Poker game can be played "High-Low." In High-Low, the highest and the lowest hands at the showdown split the pot. Though this cuts possible winnings in half, it gives each player twice the chance of winning and encourages players to stay in the game in the hope of winning with a low hand. At the showdown, players announce whether they are going for low or for high before they reveal their hands. This leads to interesting results, as often a player may win for high with only a pair if all his opponents were going for low.

High-Low Seven Card Stud offers the option of going for both high and low simultaneously. At the showdown, a player with the hand 9 8 7 6 5 3 2, for example, could declare that he was going for both the high and low categories, claiming the straight 9 8 7 6 5 for high, and the hand 7 6 5 3 2 for low. If this player wins in both categories, he collects the whole pot; otherwise the pot is split with the player who defeats him in one or the other category.

## UNORTHODOX POKER HANDS

*If Poker buffs around the world have managed to come up with a menagerie of Poker variations, haven't they come up with new hands as well? The answer is, they have, and the inclusion of one or more of the hands below is great fun, making more opportunities for surprise winners.*

*The Blaze is a hand consisting entirely of face cards.*

*There are four Blazes: Blaze Four: four of a kind, plus another face card, as in K K K K J.*

*Blaze Full: A face card full house, as Q Q Q J J.*

*Blaze Three: Three of a kind plus two other face cards, as K K K J Q.*

*Simple Blaze: Two pair plus another face card, as Q Q J J K.*

*Blaze Four ranks as the highest four of a kind, outranking four Aces. Because of their rarity, the other three Blazes also rank very*

The "swinging Ace" is often used in High-Low Poker. With this arrangement, the Ace can be either the highest or the lowest card, depending on how it is declared at the showdown.

*Lowball:* Lowball is simply a logical extension of High-Low. After all, if the low works all right in High-Low, why not all by itself? In Lowball, the lowest hand wins the game. Straights and flushes have no rank in the game at all, and the Ace is the lowest card in the deck. The strongest (and lowest) hand in the game is 5 4 3 2 A, often called the "wheel." In Lowball with wild cards, the wild cards are often given the value of zero, that is, one point below the Ace. With Jokers wild, the hand 5 4 3 2 Joker has the value of 5 4 3 2 zero, beating the unbeatable 5 4 3 2 A.

Lowball can be used as a variation of Draw, and both Five and Seven Card Stud.

*Spit In The Ocean:* This is a variation of Draw Poker in which each player receives four cards, and a common card is dealt face up in the middle of the table. Each player can consider this "mutual" card as a fifth and wild card in his own hand. Furthermore, all cards of the same denomination as the mutual card become automatically wild. Drawing and betting are the same as in Draw Poker, but at the showdown each player reveals his hand and declares its rank, using the mutual card in any way he wishes. Stud With A Spit is similar: A single mutual card is dealt after each player has four cards in hand.

*Around the World:* This game is a further development of Spit In The Ocean, hybridized with some aspects of Stud Poker. Each player is dealt four cards. A mutual card is dealt face up in the middle of the table; it is not wild but each player may mentally regard it as part of his hand. A round of betting follows, then a second mutual card is dealt face up, followed by a second round of betting. This continues until four face-up mutual cards have been dealt and bet upon. At the showdown, each player reveals his hand and declares which of the mutual cards he is using to complete his hand of five. He may use as few as one, or up to all four of the mutual cards to constitute his hand.

*Cincinnati:* Without a doubt, Cincinnati is the wildest of the mutual card variations. Cincinnati is also fondly known as Lamebrains. You'll see why.

Each player is dealt five face-down cards, and a mutual card is dealt face up in the middle of the table. The first round of betting follows, with each player betting on his hand plus the mutual card. Before each new round of betting, another face-up mutual card is placed on the table, until there are five mutual cards revealed. From his hand and the mutual cards, each player selects the five cards he will bet on or declare at the showdown.

The zaniness of Cincinnati comes in determination of wild cards. The lowest of the five mutual cards dealt becomes wild, and all cards of the same denomination are wild too. The problem is not knowing whether the lowest mutual card will remain low by the last deal. An example of the predicament a player can be in by the showdown:

| Charlie: | Jack and 8 of diamonds, 10 and 2 of hearts, 2 of clubs |
|---|---|
| Mutual Cards: | Jack of hearts, 5 and 2 of diamonds, Queen of clubs, 6 of spades |
| John: | Queen and 6 of diamonds, 5 and 4 of spades, 7 of hearts |

Until the fifth and last round of the game, John was doing well. As long as the mutual 5 was the lowest card on the table, it and all other 5's were wild. That gave John a possible four Queens (the Queen in his hand, the mutual Queen, the mutual wild 5, and the wild 5 in his hand). On the last round, unfortunately, the low-ranked deuce dealt as the mutual card changed the picture completely. Charlie, who had previously stood for no more than a full house (the pair of 2's in his hand and three Jacks formed from the one in his hand, the mutual Jack, and the mutual wild 5) is suddenly holding five Jacks (his own, his two wild deuces, the mutual Jack and the mutual wild deuce). He wins the game.

Note, however, that Charlie might also have chosen to declare a royal straight flush in hearts using a mixture of the cards in his hand and the mutual cards (his two wild deuces standing in for Ace and King of hearts, the mutual deuce for the Queen of hearts, the mutual Jack of hearts, and his own 10 of hearts). If Charlie had failed to see the possible five of a kind and claimed the royal flush instead, he could have been beaten by a low five of a kind. The declaration at the showdown may be crucial.

A variation of Cincinnati is designed to keep everyone in suspense by keeping the identity of the wild card a secret until the bitter end. Center cards are still dealt out one at a time, but the

*high, above the orthodox full house but below four of a kind.*

*The straight-like hands called Cats and Dogs are ranked in the following order, above a straight but below a flush:*

*Big Cat: King high, 8 low, with no pair, as K Q 10 9 8.*

*Little Cat: 8 high, 3 low, with no pair, as 8 7 5 4 3.*

*Big Dog: Ace high, 9 low with no pair, as A K J 10 9.*

*Little Dog: 7 high, 2 low with no pair as 7 5 4 3 2.*

*The "around-the-corner straight" is used commonly enough to be considered a quasi-standard hand. It allows the player to use an Ace to connect the high and low cards in a straight such as 3 2 A K Q, or 2 A K Q J. The around-the-corner straight is ranked as an ordinary straight. In the example given, the*

*three-high beats the two-high straight.*

*The following freak hands rank above three of a kind, and below a straight, in the order given.*

*Dutch or Skip-Straight: a straight formed of every other card, as Q 10 8 6 4.*

*Skeet: a 9, 5 and 2 plus other values in between so long as neither a pair nor a flush appears, as 9 7 5 4 2 in mixed suit.*

*Kilter: a 9-high hand that is neither a flush nor a four flush, and contains no pair, as 9 7 6 5 3. In a match between two Kilters, the hands are compared as in ordinary high-card hands.*

wild card is the last mutual card dealt rather than the lowest one. This is guaranteed to keep everyone on the edge of his seat until the climax.

*Shotgun:* Shotgun is designed to give Draw Poker the wallop of Stud by providing an extra round of betting. The alteration of the basic game comes during the deal. After three cards have been dealt to each player, the deal is interrupted by a round of betting. After the betting, the deal is completed and the game continues as in Draw.

*Double-Barreled Shotgun:* Double-Barreled is usually played High-Low, and begins the same as Shotgun, with the extra round of betting during an interrupted deal. After the draw, however, each player exposes one of his cards, and a round of betting follows. This is repeated, one card per round, until all cards are revealed. Players who have remained in the game compare hands in the showdown, and the highest and lowest hands split the pot.

*TNT:* TNT is to Shotgun as dynamite is to gunpowder. Each player receives three face-down cards, followed by a round of betting. Then four more face-down cards are dealt, one at a time, each followed by another betting round. Then each player discards two of the seven cards he holds, leaving each a standard five-card hand. Players then reveal their hands, one card at a time and in any order they choose, with a round of betting following each revelation. This prolonged showdown allows a player with a weak hand to conceal the worthlessness of his cards by exposing an incomplete straight or flush with a show of confidence, and enables a player with a strong hand to seem weak by revealing his poorest cards first.

*Pass The Garbage:* Each player is dealt a hand of face-down cards as in Draw Poker, but the hands are seven cards instead of five. After the first round of betting, each player selects from his hand the three most worthless cards, and passes them face down to the player on his left. From his new hand of seven cards, each player now discards any two he chooses, leaving him a standard five-card hand. Betting continues, and the showdown, usually played high-low, reveals who lucked out with his garbage.

*Take It Or Leave It:* As in Stud, each player is dealt a face-down hole card. But when the dealer deals the first face-up card to the player on his left, the player has the privilege of taking it or leaving it. A rejected card is passed clockwise from player to player, and if nobody (including the dealer) takes it, it is placed on the bottom of the deck. The dealer then deals the first player a face-up card which he must keep. The offering of a face-up card is then made to the next player, who again can take it or leave it. This continues until all players have one up-card, and the first round of betting follows. The Take It Or Leave It procedure is repeated for each succeeding up-card.

*Five and Dime:* Conservative players often object to the element of luck that drops wild deuces into the hands of less deserving opponents. To cure the malady in Seven Card Stud, someone came up with the bright idea of making players pay for their wild cards, or fold instead.

In this version, 5's and 10's are wild, but wild cards dealt as up-cards cost chips. A 5 up-card costs five chips, a 10 costs ten chips. This game used to be known as Woolworth, but inflation has robbed it of that name.

*Baseball:* This most ridiculous of variations is played like Seven Card Stud with 3's and 9's wild. It is based on the "logic" that since a baseball game has nine innings, a player can receive a wild 9 up-card without paying for it. However, three strikes are "out," and so is the player who gets dealt an up-card 3—unless he can pay for it by matching the entire pot on his bet; similarly, because four balls send a batter to base "free," an up-card 4 allows the player to ask for a free up-card to increase the cards in his hand.

*Diminutive Pokers:* To speed up games, and to accommodate large groups of people, the following variations have been devised:

FOUR-CARD: Played with only a four-card hand, which can either be dealt all at once with a draw to follow, or one at a time as in Stud. The ranking of hands from highest to lowest is: four of a kind, straight flush, flush, straight, three of a kind, two pair, pair, high card.

THREE-CARD: The same as Four-Card, but only three cards constitute a hand. The ranking is straight flush, three of a kind, flush, straight, pair, high card.

TWO-CARD: Styled Hurricane by its loyal public, this game is over before you know it. Each player is dealt two cards face down as in Draw, or one down, one up as in Stud. A pair takes the pot over a high card.

ONE-CARD: A good game for boring car rides, as there are few cards to handle. Each player is dealt only one card, on which he bets. The highest card wins, with Aces always high and deuces low. The game can also be played High-Low, the highest and lowest card splitting the pot.

*Striped Straights or Zebra: A hand without a pair or better which alternates red and black, as Jack of clubs, 9 of hearts, 6 of diamonds, 3 of spades.*

# SOLITAIRE BASICS

Solitaire or Patience games are probably the oldest type of card game, dating back to the time when cards were spread to divine the future. Winning a game of Solitaire is perhaps one of the most satisfying of all winning experiences; while losing—especially if you have almost made it—is one of the most frustrating.

Strangely, Solitaire games seldom remain solitary for long in a family. Everyone tries to join in, clustering around, poking, gesturing at cards, and giving helpful hints like, "Red Jack on the Black Queen!"; "No, don't move that card now!"; "The Ace, get the Ace!".

The best tactic, if you are one of those to whom Solitaire means solitary, is to sneak off with a deck of cards while no one is watching and play in a locked bathroom.

All Solitaire games have the same object: to create order out of disorder by putting all the cards into sequence by rank and in suit. Most games are won when all four suits are arranged from low to high in the order A 2 3 4 5 6 7 8 9 10 J Q K. In a few games the ranking of the cards is continuous, so that Ace can follow King, and so on.

Most Solitaire games (like the one called Klondike, illustrated here) have one or more of the following elements:

FOUNDATIONS: Four cards of the same rank, usually Aces, on which you "build" (stack or partially overlap) upward by adding cards of the next higher rank and in the same suit. Solitaire games that include foundations are won when all four suits have been built to completion in order by rank.

TABLEAU: A spread of cards in some distinctive pattern, laid out in front of the player. In most of the games, you can build onto the tableau cards by partially overlaying on top of each a card of the next lower rank, but usually in a suit of opposite color, so that the tableau pattern builds in columns of descending rank and alternating color.

STOCK: This is the special pile of cards in some games from which you can take cards for building onto either the foundations or the tableau.

HAND: In games where the tableau and/or stock don't use the entire deck, the remaining cards are the hand, and are turned up one at a time or in sets of three or more.

TALON: A trash pile made up of cards turned up from the hand which can't be played on the tableau or the foundation. Such cards are placed face up in the talon, and the top card is usually available for building onto the foundations or tableau.

*Foundations*

*Tableau*

*Hand*

*Talon*

*The Solitaire game illustrated here is Klondike, which does not have a stock.*

# KLONDIKE

*One player*

*Standard deck of 52 cards*

*OBJECT: To complete the foundations in suit and sequence*

This is the game used to illustrate the Solitaire Basics, opposite. Deal out a row of seven cards from left to right, the first face up, the rest face down. Then deal a card face up on top of the second pile, followed by single down-cards on each of the remaining piles to the right. Follow this with an up-card on the third pile, and down-cards on those to its right, and so on. When this is done, you will have a row of seven piles, each with one more card than the one before it. The top card of each pile is face up, while the ones below are all face down. This is the tableau. The remaining cards form the hand. Cards turned from the hand and not used form the talon pile.

As Aces become available during the game, by appearing as the hand is turned, or as top cards in either the talon or tableau piles, place them in a row above the tableau to begin the foundations. To win the game, you must build the four Ace foundations all the way up to King in suit and in sequence. The top cards of the tableau piles and the talon are always available to be built onto a foundation pile.

During the game, you can place a card from the talon pile or hand onto a tableau pile if the top card is of next-higher rank and opposite color. It is also possible to move a lone tableau card or an entire sequence of cards from one tableau pile to another, provided that all the face-up cards on the transferred tableau pile are moved as a unit; portions of sequences can't be moved. When building within the tableau or from tableau to foundation exposes a face-down tableau card, the card is turned over.

Any spaces formed in the tableau row can be filled by Kings. After all four Kings have been used to fill spaces, any card can be placed in an available gap.

To use cards in the hand, turn the cards over in packets of three at a time, and put them face up onto the talon pile. The top card from each packet of three is available for building on the tableau or foundations. If it is used, the next card in the packet becomes available. After running through the hand once in packets of three, the talon is turned over to become the hand again, and is turned face up in packets of three as before. The game is lost if you have run through the hand once or twice without being able to make any more plays.

In a somewhat more difficult version of Klondike, the hand is run through one card at a time, but it can be used only once. The game is lost if the hand is run through and there are no more available plays.

*A game of Canfield, complete with kibbitzers.*

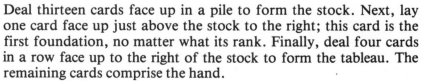

## CANFIELD

*One player*

*Standard deck of 52 cards*

*OBJECT: To complete the foundations in suit and in sequence*

Deal thirteen cards face up in a pile to form the stock. Next, lay one card face up just above the stock to the right; this card is the first foundation, no matter what its rank. Finally, deal four cards in a row face up to the right of the stock to form the tableau. The remaining cards comprise the hand.

As cards of the same rank become available, place them alongside the original foundation card. If the game progresses well, you will eventually have a total of four foundations above the tableau. The object of the game is to build up the foundations by

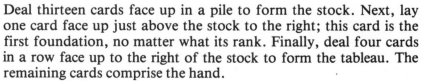

182

suit and sequence until all cards have been used. Ranking is continuous through King and Ace; if, for example, the first foundation card was a 6, the game would be won when all foundations were built up from 6 to King, followed by Ace to 5. The top cards of the tableau piles, the stock and the talon are always available for building on foundations.

The top card in the stock, as well as cards revealed as the hand is turned or the talon is used, can be built onto a tableau pile, provided that the card is of next-lower rank and opposite color. In addition, an entire tableau pile can be moved as a unit onto another pile, leaving an empty space. (Some play that it is also possible to move the top card of one tableau pile singly to another.)

While there are still cards in the stock, spaces formed in the tableau must be filled immediately with the stock's top card. When the stock of thirteen cards is exhausted, you have the option of filling spaces with cards from the hand or talon pile immediately, or leaving the spaces free until you need them.

Cards from the hand are turned over three at a time and placed face up in the talon. The top card of the talon is available for play on the foundations or tableau; when a card is used, the one beneath it becomes available. After running through the hand once in packets of three, turn the talon over to become the hand again, and turn cards three at a time as before. Continue this until you've won the game . . . or lost it.


# FOUR SEASONS

*One player*

*Standard deck of 52 cards*

*OBJECT: To complete the foundations in suit and sequence*

Deal five cards face up in the form of a cross. This is the tableau. Deal a sixth card face up in the upper left-hand corner of the cross. This card, whatever its rank, is the first foundation. The remaining cards constitute the hand.

As cards of the same rank as the first foundation become available, place them in the remaining corners of the cross until eventually the foundations and the tableau together form a 3 by 3 square. The foundations are built up, in suit and sequence, until all fifty-two cards have been used. The ranking of the cards is continuous, so that Ace follows King. The top cards of the tableau piles and the talon are always available to add to the foundations.

You can play a card from the talon onto a top tableau card of next-higher rank. Some play that red must alternate with black, but other players lay cards on the tableau in descending sequence, regardless of color. Unlike Klondike or Canfield, in which cards are overlapped in the tableau to form columns, the tableau piles in Four Seasons are kept squared up so that only the top card is visible. Only top cards can be transferred from tableau pile to tableau pile. The card beneath becomes the new top card and is then available for play. Any spaces appearing in the tableau can be filled with top cards from the tableau, the hand, or the talon.

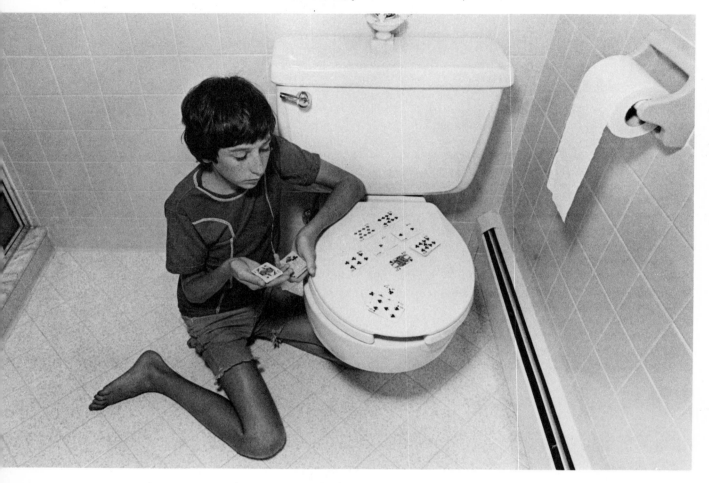

*Four Seasons takes less space than other Solitaires, and miniature cards shrink it even further.*

Run through the hand by turning the cards over one at a time. If you can't use a card, place it face up in the talon. Cards can be played from the top of the talon; whenever the top card is used, the one beneath it becomes available. You get only one chance to run through the hand. If you reach a standstill after the hand is exhausted, you've lost.

# IDIOT'S DELIGHT

*One player*

*Standard deck of 52 cards*

*OBJECT: To complete the foundations in suit and sequence*

Deal nine cards face up in a row. Follow this with an overlapping row of eight cards face up, beginning at the first pile and continuing to the right. Then deal out overlapping face-up rows of seven cards, six, five and so on down to a final row of one card, always starting at the first pile. This is the tableau. There will be only seven cards remaining in the deck. Spread the remaining seven cards face up below the tableau so that all are visible; these comprise the hand.

As Aces become available during the game, place them in a row between the hand and the tableau. The foundations are built up in rank and suit from Ace to King. All seven cards in the hand are available at all times for building onto the tableau or the foundations. The tableau piles can be built upon by overlapping top cards with cards of next lower rank and of opposite color. You are allowed to move cards between tableau piles, but only top cards can be moved. Sequences can't be moved as a unit. The top cards in the tableau are available for building onto the foundations. Spaces appearing in the tableau can be filled with any card from the hand, or the top card of another tableau pile.

The game is won when all fifty-two cards have been placed on the foundations, and lost when there are no more moves to make.


## SCORPION

*One player*

*Standard deck of 52 cards*

*OBJECT: To complete the foundations in suit and sequence*

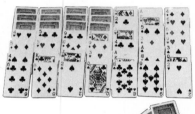

Deal out three rows of seven cards each: first four face down and then three face up. The rows should overlap toward you so that the top edges of all the cards are visible. Follow this with four additional overlapping rows of seven cards each, all face up. The seven rows are the tableau, and the three cards remaining in the deck are leftovers, called the "widow." Scorpion, unlike most other Solitaires, isn't played with foundations, hands or a talon pile. All building is done directly on the tableau.

The entire game is played by moving cards of next-lower rank in the same suit onto the face-up top cards of the tableau piles.

---

# CHEATING AT SOLITAIRE

You've been at that game of Klondike for over half an hour now; all the Aces are out, and all you need is the 6 of spades to totally clean off the board. But where is that lousy card? You run through the hand once; you try the hand twice. You scan the board desperately for any move you can make that might free a face-down card. You look for any move whatsoever. Nothing.

Let's be realistic. Who, after coming within a hair's breadth of winning, is going to gather up the cards serenely, smile calmly, and begin shuffling once again?

Most players, reaching an impasse after an especially hopeful game, react in one of two ways: They gnash their teeth, beat the table, tear their hair or otherwise express their disappointment . . . or they make a play that isn't exactly in the rulebook. After all, what harm will one sly move do? The cards don't object, and—if you have worked things out right—no one is watching.

Effective methods of cheating vary from game to game. In games like Klondike and Canfield, where play hinges on turning up cards from the hand, it's very simple to "accidentally" change the order of the cards in the hand a bit, by moving a card from the top to the bottom, or by giving the hand a quick cut. In games that are held up because of a missing card buried somewhere face down, a quick search for the offending card and a subtle rearrangement of the tableau is often efficacious. In Scorpion, Idiot's Delight and No Name, where two or more cards often get "crossed" in such a way that you need one in order to release the other, all problems can be solved by the nonchalant transfer of a card to a more desirable location. Vary your minor infringements on the rules as the situation seems to demand—always soothing your conscience with the least flagrant adjustment.

Cards can be played onto a pile regardless of how deeply they are buried, but when a card in the middle of a tableau pile is moved, all cards lying on top of it have to be moved along with it as a unit. When pile-moving exposes a face-down card, turn it up and continue. Spaces in the tableau can be filled only by Kings. When the game has come to a standstill, deal the three cards from the widow out onto the first three tableau piles, and continue the game, if possible.

Scorpion is won when the entire tableau has been organized by suit into four piles, from King down to Ace.

# NO NAME

*One player*

*Standard deck of 52 cards*

*OBJECT: To complete the foundations in suit and sequence*

Martin Gardner, a math whiz and games lover, was taught this Solitaire by a friend who learned it from his father—who in turn was taught it by a mysterious Englishman during the twenties. It is among the best Solitaires, but according to Gardner's book appears to have no name.

Deal the entire deck face up into overlapping rows of eight cards each. You will run out of cards as you deal the last row so that the first four of the resulting columns will end up with seven cards each, while the rest will have only six. This is the tableau; there is no hand.

As Aces become available, place them in a row above the tableau. The foundations are built up in the usual way—ascending rank and matching suit. Cards available for building onto the foundations are top cards from the tableau piles and all cards from the "temporary" spaces described below. The game is won when all cards have been built onto the foundations.

A card of next-lower rank in the same suit can be played on the top card of any tableau pile. But only one card can be moved at a time, and that card must be the top card of a tableau pile. To help you out, you are given four temporary spaces below the tableau. Throughout the game, you are allowed to transfer one available card from the tableau to each temporary space, freeing the card that was below. If you wish, for example, to reach a 7 of diamonds below a Queen of Spades in one of the tableau piles, you can put the Queen in one of your temporary spaces in order to make the 7 available for use in building onto a tableau or foundation pile. You run the risk, however, of using up your four temporary spaces with cards you can't play, forcing an early end to the game. Therefore, this game requires more foresight than any other Solitaire.

Spaces appearing in the tableau can be filled by any available card, from either a temporary space, or the top of a tableau pile.

## BEAUTIFUL CARDS

*You can choose a deck of cards for either the beautiful outsides or the beautiful insides. The cards shown here all have rather plain backs, but the faces of the cards are lovely. In most "special" decks only the face cards have been redesigned—as characters from Shakespeare, perhaps, or from Alice in Wonderland. But Japanese cards may reproduce paintings or other landscapes on numeral as well as face cards. They may come in a sandalwood box or a beribboned case, to boot. Few people realize that once you have removed the "Major Arcana" (see page 30) from a deck of Tarot cards, the remaining cards can be used as a standard deck if the knights (a fourth face card) are also removed. When numeral cards are unorthodox, they may take some getting used to before you can play with them easily.*

# & Counter Games

# Chapter 6
# Board & Counter Games

The games in this section all use small pieces of one sort or another, from dice to chips and counters. Although not all include a board, each can be accommodated within a small playing space on floor or table. Games which are similar but require a larger space, more players or greater activity (Roulette for example, or Nok Hockey) can be found in Game Room Games.

Board and Counter games differ more from one another than those in any other group. So do the idiosyncrasies of their devotees. The brilliant Chess player is a unique individual who would not be caught dead in a Bingo parlor. Yet the Bingo fan is every bit as devoted to his passion, and so is the marathon MONOPOLY player, the Craps better, the SCRABBLE fiend, and the Backgammon ace. You are less likely to find people who love board games in general than you are to find people who love one, and one only.

To suit as many idiosyncrasies as possible, we have tried to include a huge variety of games here—if not in complete form with rules and strategy, at least in review form to give some idea of structure and equipment. There is no way, however, to keep up with the field. Each season produces scores of new games, a few of which may rise to insane popularity within months. Luckily, most new games are descendants of old standbys so there is a way to make order of this chaos of progeny. Read the games here, and play a few until you know the kind of game you like. Then, when you crave novelty, ask at the store for a game that is something like it. They are sure to have a brand-new offspring with still another intriguing twist.

The passion that flares during many of these games can lead to trouble among friends and family. Why feelings should run higher with Checkers than with Gin Rummy is a mystery, but there it is: mates won't speak to one another, children weep, faces redden, doors slam, and the game board is thrown across the room. A clue to the eruptions may be that board games often simulate real life. There are more battle games than any other kind, from ones that provide armies and bombs as playing pieces to those fought with "men" on a checkered board. Even in the simplest children's games the goal is often "home," and the journey to safety fraught with scary hazards. Real life feelings may sneak into such enactments.

Where it seems possible to convert a sharp-edged game into a more leisurely pastime, we have suggested ways of doing so. But if temper seems chronic with a particular individual no matter what you try, you have little choice but to endure it or refuse to play.

# JACKSTRAWS (PICK UP STICKS)

*Any number of players*

*A set of jackstraws*

**OBJECT: To score the most points by removing sticks from a pile one at a time without moving those around them**

Each jackstraw is a colored stick about 6 inches long, tapering at both ends something like a knitting needle. The colors of the sticks indicate their scoring values. Usually the green sticks count for three points, red for five, blue for ten, and the one black stick counts for twenty points. The full set is about fifty sticks. Hard wood jackstraws are less capricious in their movements than plastic. There are also sets made to look like tools—rakes, shovels, hoes, ladders. These are attractive, and also fun to play with.

Select the first player. He holds the jackstraws in a bundle a few inches over the table or floor, and lets them drop. Starting with the first player, each person in turn tries to pull one jackstraw at a time out of the pile without jiggling any of the other sticks. When a player accidentally jiggles a stick, he must put back the stick he was trying to take out and let the next player try. This goes on until all the sticks have been taken.

You are allowed to get the sticks out in any way you can by using your hands. You can twist a stick to free it, or you can raise it slightly by pushing down its end, then grab it with your other hand. If you draw the black stick, you are allowed to use it as well

as your hands in order to get at the other sticks, delicately lifting or deftly flicking a stick from the pile with it.

The player with the highest score by the end of the game based on the values of the sticks he has picked up is the winner.

# LABYRINTH

*One, two or more players*

*A Labyrinth game*

*OBJECT: To guide a marble through the maze, past the pitfalls, and into home.*

The Labyrinth is a wooden or plastic box, the top of which is a maze design dotted with numbered holes. The top is mounted so that it tips backward, forward and sideways when two knobs on adjacent sides of the box are rotated. By skillful use of the knobs, you can tip the maze this way and that, guiding a steel marble through the maze, and past the holes, to the end of the course. The game is amazingly difficult at first, lasting only a second, and ending with a plunge down the first hole. With practice, coordination and a very light way with the knobs develop, and it is indeed possible to complete the course.

Labyrinth can be played solitaire, or as a contest of skill among several people. The idea is to get your marble as far as you can through the Labyrinth before the nearly inevitable mistake plunges it down a hole. Since the holes are numbered in the sequence in which you must pass them as you maneuver the course, it's easy to keep track of how far you've gone. The player to get the farthest within, say, a day or a week of attempts, wins the match. Or, if you prefer shorter contests of skill, give each player three tries. The one to get farthest in those three tries is the winner.

Be sure all contests are witnessed, to prevent exaggeration.

# CHINESE CHECKERS:

*Two to six players, playing individually or as partners*

*Chinese Checkers set*

*OBJECT: To be the first to move all your pieces from one point in the star across the board and into the opposite point of the star*

The Chinese Checker playing area is a six-pointed star. The star is dotted with holes or depressions in which marbles can rest. The holes are interconnected by thin lines in a hexagonal grid pattern. Along with the board come six groups of fifteen marbles each in contrasting colors. Some sets, though of the same basic design, substitute groups of colored pegs for marbles. At the beginning of the game, each player takes one point of the star, and sets his marbles within it. If only two are playing, they take opposite points and use fifteen marbles each. With more players, each sits anywhere he likes and uses only ten marbles.

## MISSING MARBLES

*Except for the brand-new Chinese Checkers set fresh from its box, we have yet to see a set that had all its marbles. Nor have we found a place that sells replacements. Ordinary marbles will do. Among several bags of mixed streaked marbles, you should be able to find enough reds, yellows, blues and greens to replace those that rolled down the heating ducts, or wherever it is marbles go.*

*Counters for board games can be replaced with items like thimbles, or small plastic figures of animals. When counters must match in color, as in Parcheesi, groups of matching buttons or bottle caps work well. Missing checkers are a greater problem, but you can always rob a Backgammon set—the pieces are the same. Chess pieces are the hardest of all to replace. Perhaps the average age of Chess players is some guarantee against carelessness.*

## CHINESE CHECKERS FOR SMALL CHILDREN

*You can't let children who may swallow marbles play with a Chinese Checkers set, but for those small children who know better, the gay board and bright marbles will prove so attractive that you will hardly be able to prevent them from playing. How do you play with, say, a two-year-old? Without rules, is the answer. You take your marbles and let him take his. That will help him learn the basic colors. Then you make a pattern with yours, and he makes a pattern with his. That will help him learn words like line, straight, and zigzag. If you like, you can show him how to step his marble one space, or jump it, or take turns or fill up a whole point of the star. Or he can just make designs of his own with one or more colors. All these apparently idle activities are actually necessary learning before a child is ready for even the simplest board game.*

Choose one player to go first. One at a time, going clockwise around the points of the star, players take turns moving one marble toward the point of the star that lies opposite their starting point. The first player to get all his marbles entirely into the opposite point of the star is the winner.

Marbles may be moved in two ways: by steps, and by jumps. When you step a piece, you move it one hole forward, backward, or sideways along a grid line and into a vacant adjacent hole. That is the end of that move; a step may not be followed by a jump in the same turn. When you jump your piece, you jump it from its hole over another marble (your own or another player's) to the empty hole beyond. Again, the jump must follow a grid line forward, backward or sideways. A jump may land your piece where it can jump again, and you are allowed to continue jumping as many times as you can, changing directions at will. Pieces that have been jumped over aren't captured, as in ordinary checkers, nor is there any compulsion to jump when you can. But jump moves and step moves cannot be combined.

Because a long series of jumps can get a marble farther forward in one turn than many stepping turns, it's a good idea to devote most of your your time to building straight or zigzag "ladders" of marbles which you can then use for jumping across the board. While you are doing this, your opponent will be sending out marbles and building his own ladders. Try to take advantage of his pieces to penetrate deep into his side of the board, and block his prospective long jumps by moving into vacant holes he would require for those jumps.

The end of the game, when players may all have their marbles close to or partially within the point that is their goal, may be critical. If you neglect to leave a jump into the very tip of the point, you will waste many turns stepping marbles individually into place. Practice various patterns within the point that will allow you to move all your marbles in with the least number of moves.

# DRAW DOMINOES

*Two to four players, but the game is best with two*

*Domino set*

*OBJECT: To be first to get rid of your entire hand of dominoes*

Dominoes are rectangular tiles of wood or plastic. Each piece is divided into two halves by a center line, and each half has one or more spots on it, or is blank. The most common Domino set is the "double-six" set of twenty-eight pieces, where the highest number of spots on any domino half is six. The pieces range from the lowest, with two blank halves (0-0), to the highest, with six spots on each half (6-6). Between these two pieces are all possible combinations of spots from none to six, such as 5-3, 0-2, 4-4. Pieces with a greater total number of spots are said to be "heavier" than those with fewer spots. For longer Domino games, or to accommodate many players, there are the larger "double-nine" sets of fifty-five pieces, and "double-twelve" sets of ninety-one pieces.

All Domino games share a common pattern. Players take turns building a pattern of dominoes laid end to end, each adding one domino to the pattern in his turn. This pattern, which is laid face up on a flat surface, is called the "layout." Two dominoes can follow one another if the number of spots on their touching ends matches. In most games "doublet" dominoes (ones with the same num-

ber of spots on each half) are placed crosswise against the matching end of the layout. The next domino is simply laid on the further side of the doublet, giving the layout something of the look of a totem pole. To keep the layout within the playing space you can form corners.

Players sit opposite one another, or in a circle. Turn all the dominoes face down and mix them up. Choose the first player, by having each draw from the face down dominoes. The one who gets the highest (or heaviest) domino goes first. Put the dominoes back in the pile and mix them in. Each player then draws his hand. With two players in the game, each takes seven dominoes; three or more players take five each. The dominoes can be held in a player's hand, or lined up on edge in front of him, so he can see them but his opponents can't. The dominoes left over after each player draws his hand are called "the boneyard." Keep the boneyard over to one side. It is used to draw from during the rest of the game.

The first player puts down any domino he chooses. His opponent can then place one of his dominoes against either end of the first domino, provided the numbers of spots on the touching ends match. This begins the layout, to either end of which the players alternately add matching dominoes. Doublets are placed crosswise rather than end to end. When a player doesn't have a domino that matches either end of the layout, he must draw dominoes from the boneyard until he has found one he can use.

The first player to use all the dominoes from his hand yells, "Domino!" and wins the game. If the boneyard is used up before any player has won, the player with the lowest number of spots in his hand wins. Very often Dominoes is played for points, the winner scoring a number of points equal to the total spots left in his opponents' hands. The first player to score fifty or one hundred points after several games of Dominoes is the winner of the bout.

**Block Dominoes:** Block Dominoes is played like Draw, but there is no boneyard to draw from. This variation is much better for three, four or five players, than for two.

Hands are of seven dominoes each with two or three players in the game, and of five dominoes each for four or five players. When a player can't play a domino in turn, he passes and hopes for better luck next time around. The first player to get rid of his pieces wins, or, if the players are all unable to move before anyone has gone out, the player with the least number of spots is the winner.

**All Fives (Muggins):** In this game, one of the most popular of Domino variations, players compete for points won during the game as well as points gained for going "Domino" first. When a player is able to add a domino to the layout so that the total of the spots at the layout's free ends is equal to a multiple of five, he scores that total. Preparation for All Fives is the same as in standard Draw. In a two-handed game each player gets seven dominoes; five dominoes go to each player in a three- or four-handed game.

The game is played as in standard Draw, but the first doublet,

*This game of Dominoes, started by older children, was taken over by younger brothers. This explains the fact that many of the outside pieces are incorrectly placed, and that the pattern is illegal. They seem to be enjoying themselves anyway.*

# THE DOMINO TOPPLE

An odd thing about dominoes is that in most families they are used less often for games than for other sorts of play. This is especially true of old sets, from which pieces have been lost, and of collections of dominoes in which portions of two or more sets have gotten mixed together. Dominoes make marvelous miniature building-blocks, are handy in all sorts of sliding collision games across smooth table tops, and are indispensable for that classic physics demonstration, the Domino Topple.

A Topple is easy to set up, and fascinating to watch. On a level surface, carefully stand the dominoes up on their narrow ends, spacing them about an inch apart. Arrange them in a straight line, or in fanciful curves; any pattern will do so long as when one domino falls forward, it will hit the one just in front of it. When your line is in perfect readiness, give the first domino a little tap, and the entire line of dominoes should fall over in an even wave of destruction.

After you have mastered the basic Topple, you may wish to try variations on the elementary theme. You can try curving the line of dominoes into the initials of your name, or forking the chain into two or more branches and then bringing the branches back together. With a large set of dominoes, it is possible to construct staircases for the toppling tiles to climb up and then climb down, or to arrange your line of dominoes to climb up a precipice, where the last falling tile will go over, and trigger another chain beneath. With ingenuity, bridges and overpasses can be arranged, to make your Topple spectacular indeed. An accidental brush of your hand as you construct, however, can cause your entire extravaganza to topple prematurely.

One word of advice, learned from experience: If your chain is very, very long, and the thought of rebuilding it after an accidental topple is excrutiatingly painful, leave periodic gaps. When the pattern is otherwise complete, gently fill them in.

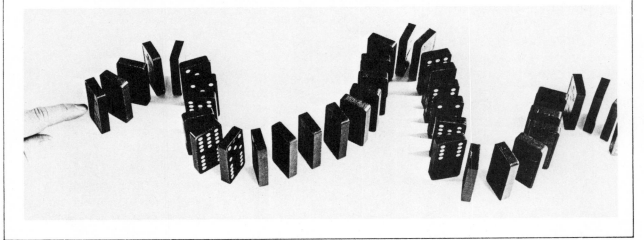

called the "sniff," can be laid either in the standard crosswise manner, or lengthwise like other dominoes. The sniff opens up three new branches for dominoes to be laid against, each on one of the sniff's free sides. When the sniff has been used to its fullest, there are a total of four pathways leading from it, and all can be built upon. All doublets after the sniff are laid crosswise as usual and don't open up any additional branches.

Depending on how many sides of the sniff have been used, the layout can have two, three or four free ends. A side of the sniff that has not yet been used, even though it is available, is not considered a free end for scoring purposes. A player scores the total of the spots on the free ends of the layout when his play makes them total a multiple of five. When the doublet is laid at one of the layout's free ends, the spots on the entire tile must be figured into the total to make a multiple of five. If the sniff is placed lengthwise, only the spots at one end are counted; but if it is placed crosswise, all its spots count toward the free-end total, as with any other doublet. When a player is unable to play so that the sum of the free ends are a multiple of five, he may still place a domino as in Draw, but he does not score.

A player may choose to dig into the boneyard even when it isn't necessary for his play, if he feels that he'll find a domino that he can use to score.

The game ends when one player has used up all his pieces, and cries "Domino!" or when the boneyard is used up and no player can take his turn. The player with the lowest number of spots in his hand wins the difference between his hand and his opponents', and adds those points to the total he won during the game. The player with the highest number of points is the winner.

The beginning of a game of All Fives might go like this:

Sally begins the game with a 4-1, so she scores five points immediately. Jim plays a double-4 at the four-spot end of the first domino, scoring five points as well; since his first doublet is the sniff, Jim isn't required to lay it crosswise or count all of its eight dots.

Emma, having no better domino to play, puts a 1-3 against Sally's 4-1. The total is seven, giving Emma no points.

Sally, taking advantage of the open 3 on Emma's domino, places a 4-2 on one of the sniff's sides, scoring five points.

Jim, not to be outdone, adds a 5-4 to another side of the sniff to score ten points.

This gives Emma a chance to play her double-5, a valuable piece. She lays it crosswise against Jim's piece, scoring a grand total of fifteen points (remember, all the spots on crosswise doublets count).

However, Sally takes advantage of Emma's high score by adding a 4-0 to the sniff's fourth side. Blanks count as zero, so Sally also wins fifteen points.

There is an additional rule that can be used if it is agreed upon—and if it will not cause ill-feeling between the players. If a player completes a multiple of five and doesn't realize it, any other player noticing the total can call out "Fives" and collect the points himself.

*The "sniff"*

# TIC-TAC-TOE TO GO

Thought you'd had enough of Tic-Tac-Toe? Good things never die, as shown by the number of games available which are based on the Tic-Tac-Toe principle.

3-D TIC-TAC-TOE, made by several different manufacturers, adds a topographical twist to the basic game by putting it into three dimensions. A typical setup is played on three levels of clear plastic. Each level is divided into squares like a Tic-Tac-Toe board, with holes in each of the squares to allow colored glass marbles to mark positions (rather than

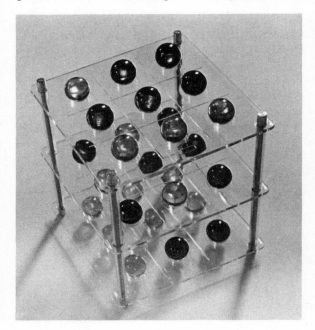

X's and O's). Wins are scored by getting three marbles in a row: along a straight line in a single level, up or down between levels, or diagonally in one, two or three dimensions.

CONNECT FOUR, made by Milton Bradley, is an upright frame that resembles an ant farm, except that its plastic walls are opaque. Both sides of the frame are pierced with holes, through which you can see the playing pieces as they are dropped into place through the open top. Two players take turns dropping checker-like discs (each player has his own color) through the top, each trying to get four discs in a horizontal or vertical row. As the frame begins to fill up with discs, there are fewer and fewer positions open, so that winning becomes a challenge.

SCORE FOUR, made by Lakeside, is like a three-dimensional version of CONNECT FOUR. The game is a block of wood with pins arranged in a 7 by 6 grid. Large wooden beads are used as counters, to go over the pins, and each pin is exactly four beads high. Like Tic-Tac-Toe, the idea is to get four beads of your color in a row: up a single pin, along a row or column of pins, or along any diagonal (even at a slant upward). Since each new bead has to be played either at the lowest level of a pin or on top of another bead, the game becomes very demanding, as each player tries to foil the other's plan by filling positions the other needs to occupy, or by filling levels the other wants.

## BINGO

*Any number of players*

*A Bingo set*

*OBJECT: To cover on your Bingo card any five squares in a straight line along a row, column or diagonal*

Bingo is traditionally a mild gambling game often played to raise money for church groups and volunteer fire departments. But many sets for home use have been designed. A typical home Bingo set consists of a set of cards, red chips to be placed on the cards, and a device for drawing numbers randomly (usually either a cage filled with numbered balls, or a bag with numbered chips). Each Bingo card is printed at the top with the letters B—I—N—G—O,

and underneath each letter is a column of five squares; the whole card looks something like a glorified Tic-Tac-Toe board. All but the center square are each printed with a number between 1 and 75. The center square is printed with the words "free play." No two Bingo cards are exactly alike.

The counters or balls for drawing are each printed with a letter and a number standing for a position on the Bingo card. The ball printed I-18, for example, stands for the number 18 in the "I" column of a card.

Select a player to be the "Drawer," and distribute a Bingo card and twenty-five red chips to each of the other players. Before the game begins, each player puts a chip on the center free play square of his card. The Drawer rotates the cage or shakes the bag before each draw, and takes out one ball or counter at a time. After drawing, he calls out the letter and numeral so everyone can hear, and puts the ball to one side, before drawing again.

As the Drawer calls out the letters and numbers, the other players listen attentively. When a chip or ball corresponds to the square on their card, they place a chip on that square. If a player has been able to place chips on five squares in a straight line (along a column, row or diagonal) he calls, "Bingo" and wins the game. His card is then checked against the balls or counters that were drawn, to make sure he hasn't made a mistake.

Along with this traditional Bingo, there are many variations of the game, such as Animal Bingo, and Word Bingo. All are excellent games for young children, and are useful for helping them learn whatever designations are used for the squares.

## SNAKES AND LADDERS

*Any number of players*

*Snakes and Ladders set*

*OBJECT: To be the first to reach the hundredth square*

Snakes and Ladders, also made by Milton Bradley Co. under the name CHUTES AND LADDERS, is an exciting race-type children's game in which the winning depends solely on the roll of the dice.

The board is divided into 100 squares (ten on each side). The squares are numbered in order from 1 to 100, and snakes (or slide-like chutes) and ladders are scattered over the board. Different boards have different arrangements, but in all setups, the ladders always lead upward to higher numbers, while the snakes (or chutes) lead downward to lower numbers. Along with the board come a die, and colored plastic counters for each player to move along the board.

Set up the order of turns. Choose counters, and place them in the square marked 1. Each player in turn rolls the die, and moves his piece the number of spaces shown, following the sequence of numbered squares. Then he gives the die to the next player, who takes his turn.

Whenever a counter lands on the foot of a ladder, it can be moved up the ladder to its top, skipping all the squares in between.

But when a counter lands on the head of a snake (or the top of a chute) it gets "swallowed," and must slip down to the square at the snake's tail (or at the bottom of the chute).

You are only allowed to reach the 100th square on an exact throw of the die. If you are near the 100th square and your throw is higher than what you need to reach it, first move your counter forward the number of spaces necessary to reach the last square, and then move it backward the number of spaces left in your throw. For example, if you are at square #98, you need to throw a 2 to win the game. If you throw a 6 instead, you first move your counter forward the two squares to #100, but then you must move it four squares backward, ending up at #96. Now hope for a 4.

The first player to reach the 100th square is the winner.

# PARCHEESI

*Two to four players*

*Parcheesi set*

*OBJECT: To move your pieces around the board and into the center before your opponents*

Parcheesi originated ages ago in India, where it is still the national game. Many domestic games manufacturers have taken the game and updated it, and in so doing have introduced minor variations in the basic rules. The rules described here are typical, although the game you purchase may be somewhat different.

The Parcheesi board is a path of squares arranged in the form of a cross. Each player has a home circle in which he places his four pieces before play begins. Next to each circle is a colored square, through which his pieces enter the cross to begin their trip around the board. The players also each have a center circle, which is the final goal for their pieces after they have completed their journey. Four sets of counters in contrasting colors are provided with the set, along with a pair of dice.

After taking his position on the board, selecting his set of four counters, and placing them in his home circle, each player throws a die to see who will go first. Ties are thrown again, and the player who throws the highest number goes first. The rest follow in order, going around the board to the left.

On his turn, each player throws both dice once, moves his counters or pieces (if he can) according to the throw, and passes the dice on to the next player. At first, each player is concerned only with getting his pieces onto the board. To put a piece into your colored starting square, you must throw a five with one or another of your dice. For each five you throw you can take one piece from your home circle and put it on the colored starting square.

Once one or more pieces are on the board you may start moving them around it clockwise. The dice count individually. If you roll a 6-3, for example, you may move one piece six squares forward and another piece three, or choose to move the same piece nine squares forward. (So that other players clearly see what you are doing, move the value of one die, then pause before moving the value of the other die.) If you roll a 5-4, and you already have pieces on the board, you might choose to enter one piece onto the board from your home circle and move another piece four squares; or you might both enter and move the same piece; or you might decide to forego entering any pieces at all and just move the piece already on the board. If you roll doubles, you get to roll again after moving. Some versions allow you to take the sum of the tops and bottoms of the dice when you roll doubles.

Two pieces of the same color on any square form a "block," which prevents any other piece (even of that color) from landing on or passing the blocked square. If, for example, two pieces occupy a square that is three steps ahead of one of your pieces, you won't be able to move your piece forward at all if the numbers you roll are three's or over.

If one of your pieces is alone, and an opposing piece lands on its square, your piece is "captured," and sent back to the home circle. You have to wait for a five again to re-enter it. Fortunately, there are "safety" squares, marked in blue or with a star, scattered over the board. If your piece rests on one of these, it can't be sent back home when another piece lands there. Sending back an opponent's piece is an excellent way to gain a lead; and some games award you a twenty-square bonus for a capture.

When a piece has gone all the way around the board and is nearing its starting square, rather than beginning the route over again, it enters an alternate, colored avenue which leads into the center. Once on this avenue, your pieces are safe from capture. Pieces are moved up the center avenue in exactly the same manner as they are moved elsewhere on the board, with the exception that to move a piece into the center circle you must roll the exact number of squares required. If, for example, you have a piece which is four squares from the center and you roll a 3-6, you can't use the six to move your piece forward into the center. You may, however, use the 3 to move it within one space of the promised land, but you will still need to roll a 1 to terminate that counter's journey.

The first player to get all four of his pieces into the center is the winner.

## CHOOSING LOTS

*If "Me first" causes many arguments in your family, the decision on who gets the first turn can be made by choosing lots. In fact, the entire order of play can be decided by this neat method. Break toothpicks or matches (one for each player) to varying lengths, so that no two are alike. Have someone arrange them between his thumb and fingers as shown, so no one can see how long they are. The person who chooses the longest gets the first turn, the shortest the last turn, and the other players take turns according to the lengths they chose in between. The chorus of "Me first" may arise as to who chooses a lot first. There is no solution.*

# FIRST BOARD GAMES

For a child under the age of six or seven, the rules of many board games are too complicated to follow, and the object of the game doesn't make much sense. Yet what child wants to be left out when the older members of the family are enjoying themselves in a hearty game of Parcheesi, or are wrapped up in a Checkers match?

Fortunately, various games have been designed for young children which present simple, unfrustrating rules, and have definite, self-evident goals.

CANDY LAND, manufactured by the Milton Bradley Company, is the prototype of first board games. The players start by putting their gingerbread-man pieces on the first square of a long, winding track. Then they take turns picking colored or picture cards and moving to a matching square on the board. The first to reach "Home Sweet Home"—an iced gingerbread house—is the winner.

WINNIE THE POOH, made by Parker Brothers, is also an excellent game for children who can't yet read, and it also helps them learn their colors. Players reach into a bag of colored chips, choose one, and advance their piece on to the next square of that color. The board has hazards, but the goal—a jar of honey—is rewarding.

Some of the more grown-up games, especially Parcheesi, Bingo and Snakes and Ladders have the advantage of combining simple rules with interesting results even though they were not especially designed for young children. These form a shared playing ground where the older and younger members of the family can play in equality with one another without the younger becoming frustrated or the older becoming bored. Try them after children have learned the basics of rules, turns and goals from the simpler games.

*There are many commercial Lotto games available, and all are excellent games for young children. A Lotto game consists of picture cards, and boards showing six to nine pictures that match the pictures on the cards. No two boards are alike, but there is a card to match each picture on the boards. Each player gets his own board. The cards are turned over one at a time, and the object each card depicts is called out. The player who has that picture on his board gets the card, and places it over his matching picture. The player whose board is covered first is the winner. Subjects range from animals to alphabets, clothes, furniture and so on. You can make your own Lotto sets from magazine pictures and either shirt cardboards or heavy paper.*

*You will need two copies of each magazine you use. Cut out one picture to paste on a card, and an identical one from the second copy of the magazine to paste on a board. You can make a Lotto set consisting of two nine-square boards and a set of matching cards from only eighteen pictures and their duplicates. Sharp scissors are the only tool you will need, and white glue or rubber cement to paste the pictures down.*

# WARI

*Two players*

*48 pebbles, shells, beans, buttons or other counters*
*Sand or dirt to scoop the playing board from, or 12 cups or bowls*

*OBJECT: To capture more counters than your opponent*

Wari is a widespread, popular game in Africa and the Middle East. Its great advantage is that it is a challenging game to play, yet the Wari "board" can be scooped from sand or dirt, or set up with ordinary cups or saucers.

The Wari board is simply twelve depressions arranged in two rows of six depressions each. If you wish, each player can also keep a "reservoir" beside him for the pieces he has captured. Depressions can be scooped out of dirt or sand for outdoor play, or you can use a set of cups or saucers. The forty-eight counters needed for the game can be pebbles, nuts, ball bearings, dried beans or any similar objects. The counters needn't be uniform in either size or color.

At the beginning of the game, the two opponents each take one of the two rows and sit facing one another at opposite sides of the board. Four counters are placed in each of the twelve depressions. Choose which player will go first. Players take alternate turns until the end of the game.

In his turn, each player removes all the counters from one of the six compartments on his side of the board. He "seeds" these counterclockwise around the board, by putting one counter into each of the next successive compartments. For example, if the player has five counters in the compartment he has chosen, he takes all the counters out and puts one of those five counters into each of the next five compartments, going counterclockwise to his right. If a player chooses a compartment with only one counter in it, he takes the counter out and puts it into the next compartment over.

Depending on the location of the chosen compartment, this seeding process may or may not continue onto your opponent's side of the board. If there are eleven or more counters in a compartment, the seeding will go all the way around the board and come back to the starting point or beyond, so that it is possible to seed a compartment twice during the same move. The compartment you emptied, however, cannot be seeded in the same turn in which you emptied it. If your seeding comes all the way back to the emptied compartment, you must skip over it and continue to seed beyond it.

When the last counter you sow on your turn falls into a compartment on your opponent's side where there are already one or

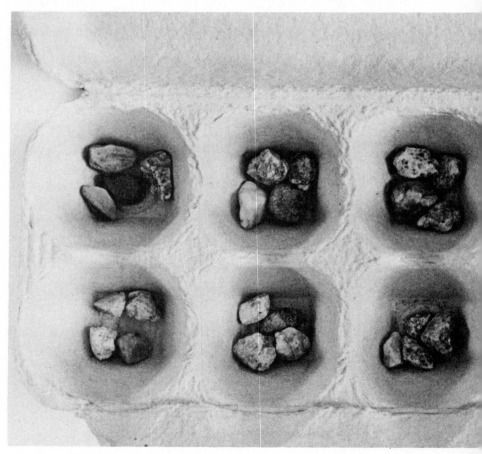

*This Wari board is just an egg carton. It doubles as a container for the pebbles used as counters.*

two counters (making a total count of two or three), you "capture" all the counters in that compartment. Remove them from the cup and put them beside you, or in your reservoir. This leaves empty the compartment from which you made your capture. If, after you have made a capture, there are either two or three counters in the compartment immediately preceding it on your opponent's side of the board, you are allowed to capture that compartment as well. If you can make that capture, the same rule applies to the compartment preceding that one, so long as it is on your opponent's side of the board and contains either two or three counters. If you are lucky, and sow three or four adjacent cups in your opponent's territory in such a way that there are two or three counters in each cup including the last one you sowed, you may capture several compartments in a single turn.

The game ends when all the cups on one side of the board are empty, so that one player has no move to make. However, you are not allowed to deliberately set this situation up by capturing all your opponent's pieces from all his compartments in one turn, or by making a small move between compartments on your own side when you could have sown one or more counters onto your opponent's side. In other words, he must be allowed the privilege of putting himself out of the game by seeding his last available counters onto your side of the board.

When one side of the board is empty, the player who still has counters on his side takes them all off and drops them in his reservoir. Then the counters in each reservoir are tallied, and the player with the most counters is the winner.

# CRAPS

*Any number of players*

*Pair of dice*
*Dice cup (optional)*
*Chips or money (optional)*

**OBJECT: To win bets by throwing certain combinations on dice**

Each cubical die is numbered from 1 to 6 in such a way that the opposite sides of the cube always add up to 7. In addition to the dice, you will need an open area, such as a wide table, or a section of floor or ground to play on. Most players insist that there be a wall or other backstop to throw the dice against.

Craps has become one of the biggest casino gambling games played in the United States, but it started out as a private, informal game. It can be played for real money, chips or tokens, or just for fun. Craps is suited for any number of people in any situation where there is room to throw the dice: the back of a station wagon, the interior of a tent, a cozy living room, or a baking sidewalk.

Form a ring around the playing area, and choose one player to throw the dice first. The privilege of throwing the dice generally passes from player to player to the left around the ring, but the turns aren't rigidly fixed—new players can come in at any time, and old players can choose to skip their turn.

Each player throws the dice as many times as he wants to, until he decides to stop, or he is forced to stop by a losing throw of the dice. The dice then pass to the next player in turn, who can decide to shoot, or to skip his turn. Dice may be thrown from a dice cup, or simply from a cupped hand. In many circles, one or both of the dice have to hit the backboard in order for a throw to be legal; this prevents crooked throws. But the requirement isn't necessary in a friendly gathering.

Each player's first throw on his turn is called the "come-out." There are three possibilities for dice combinations on the come-out:

A NATURAL: You throw a "natural," a 7 or an 11. You win the roll automatically, collect your bet (if any), and start a new come-out roll if you wish.

CRAPS: You roll "craps," a 2, 3 or 12. In this case you've lost the roll (along with any bet you've made), and pass the dice on to the next player.

POINT: You roll a "point," a 4, 5, 6, 8, 9 or 10. When this happens, you must try to "make" your point by continuing to roll the dice until you've thrown the same number over again. If you are successful in throwing your point over again, you've won both the roll and bets; and you may keep the dice, lay a new wager, and roll a new come-out. If, however, you roll a 7 before you have made your point, you lose the throw, and the dice pass to the next player.

Players continue throwing the dice in turn, until the game breaks up by general agreement. If the game has been played for money or chips, those who have come out ahead can all consider themselves winners.

## Betting

In private Craps games, players bet with one another, and several wagers can be laid between different players on the same throw of the dice.

***The Center Bet:*** Each time he gets ready for a new come-out, the shooter places his bet of money or chips in the center of the playing area as a wager that he'll win the throw. One or more players then match all or part of the wager with their own money. If the shooter's wager is not completely matched by the total put in by other players, the shooter can call off the bet entirely, or remove the unmatched portion of his bet. If the shooter wins his throw, either by rolling a natural on the come-out or by making his point, he rakes in all the money or chips in the center bet. If he loses, then the individual players who matched his bet take in the amounts they bet, and share out equally among themselves the shooter's stake.

In addition to the center bet, "side bets" can be made between two or more players for any odds agreed upon. These players may or may not also have money or chips staked in the center bet. Side bets are generally laid along an edge of the playing space.

***Flat Bet:*** This is the basic bet made before any throws on whether or not the shooter will win his throw. The "right better" (who may be the shooter himself) bets on the success of the throw, while the "wrong better" (who may also be the shooter) bets that the throw will fail.

***Point Bet:*** After the shooter throws a point, other players may bet on whether or not he will make his point.

***Off-Number Bet:*** This is a bet, made before any throw, that the shooter will throw some specified number before throwing a 7.

***Come Bet:*** Two players may agree to this bet at any time during a player's turn. This bet treats the shooter's next throw as a come-out throw, even if it is not, and wagers on whether or not the shooter will win that throw. Say, for example, the shooter is in the process of trying to match a 5 point. Two players might make a "come bet," treating his next throw as if it were his first. The shooter then throws a 7 and loses his center bet, but the player who made the come bet wins, since a 7 on the come-out is a natural. If the shooter had thrown some point other than the 7, the wagerers of the come bet would wait with bated breath for the shooter's next few throws, to see if he made that point or rolled a 7 first.

***Hard Way Bet:*** This is a wager, usually at high odds, that the shooter will throw an even number with double dice (such as an 8 with 4-4) during his turn. If the shooter fails to throw the double number, or throws the specified number with mixed dice, or throws a 7, the one who laid the wager loses.

***Proposition Bet:*** This is an arbitrary bet that another player will agree to. Examples are:

## YAHTZEE

*YAHTZEE, by Milton Bradley, is a game in which you roll five dice to score for certain combinations akin to poker hands, such as straights, and two's and three's of a kind. Each combination carries a different point value that you apply toward a final score.*

*Each roll you make may offer you a choice of two or three combinations to claim. Since you are only allowed to claim a certain type of combination once during a game, you must choose wisely in order to get the highest possible score.*

A bet that a certain number will appear within a specified number of rolls.

A bet that a particular combination of the dice will appear, such as a 4-2.

A bet that any of a group of numbers will appear within a certain number of rolls—such as all odd numbers, all numbers between 7 and 3, and so on.

A proposition is only limited by the players' imaginations, and usually is so arranged that the one who proposes it has significant odds in his favor over the one gullible enough to accept the deal.

# THE ODDS

In order to bet with a reasonable chance of winning in Craps, it's best to have a good grasp of the odds. The chances of winning the center bet when you are the shooter are about 251 to 244 against, or a 1.4 percent disadvantage. Another way of saying this is that if you were to play 495 times, you would be likely to lose 251 times and win 244 times. When you bet against the shooter's success, however, the odds are correspondingly in your favor. Of course odds are only likelihoods, not guarantees. The whole fun of betting by odds is that fortune only follows the odds in the long run, not necessarily during the short one.

The odds against rolling any given number are based on the number of different combinations that can add up to a point. A 4, for example, can only be made by a double-2 or a 3-1, whereas a 9 can be made by four different combinations: 6-3, 5-4, 7-2, and 8-1. For each number the odds are:

| Number | Odds Against |
|---|---|
| 2 | 35 to 1 |
| 3 | 17 to 1 |
| 4 | 11 to 1 |
| 5 | 8 to 1 |
| 6 | 31 to 5 |
| 7 | 5 to 1 |
| 8 | 31 to 5 |
| 9 | 8 to 1 |
| 10 | 11 to 1 |
| 11 | 17 to 1 |
| 12 | 35 to 1 |

When the shooter has rolled a point, the chances of making that point before rolling a 7 are as follows:

| Point | Odds Against |
|---|---|
| 4 | 2 to 1 |
| 5 | 3 to 1 |
| 6 | 6 to 5 |
| 8 | 6 to 5 |
| 9 | 3 to 2 |
| 10 | 2 to 1 |

The odds against winning a Hard Way bet are:

| Bet | Odds Against |
|---|---|
| 4 (2-2) | 8 to 1 |
| 6 (3-3) | 10 to 1 |
| 8 (4-4) | 10 to 1 |
| 10 (5-5) | 8 to 1 |

When you accept a bet, make sure that the odds are balanced by the amounts you stand to win or lose. If, for example, you are offered a wager on whether the shooter will get a 5 on his next throw, the wager should be eight for one (eight chips if he gets a 5, one if he doesn't). If the wager is that the shooter will throw a 5 within his next two turns, the odds against are halved to 4 to 1, and the betting stakes should be adjusted accordingly.

# BASEBALL

*Any number of players, but the game is best with two*

*One die*
*Pencil and paper*

**OBJECT: To score the most points by throwing certain numbers on a die to simulate a baseball game**

Baseball is played with a single die. It is usually played between two people, but can be played with three or more. Draw a baseball diamond on a piece of paper, putting in all three bases and home plate. Then tear out three bits of paper to stand for men. Throw the die to determine whether you or your opponent will be up at "bat" first. The player who throws the highest number is batter.

Baseball tries to simulate the ball game. While you are at bat, a throw of 1, 2 or 3 stands for a single, double, or triple, respectively. When you make hits, advance your paper men around the paper diamond to correspond to a real baseball game. Every time a man reaches home base, you score a run. For example, say you throw a 2, and you already have one man on second and another on third. Move your two runners to home plate, and move your "hitter" around the diamond to second base. A roll of 4 is a home run, and all the men already on the diamond score as well as the hitter. If you roll a 6, your batter has struck out. If you roll a 5, it's as if your batter hit the ball, and it was successfully fielded and thrown, giving the other team a possible double play. Not only is the man at bat out, but men on base may also be out, as follows:

> If only one man is on base, he is out.
>
> If you have men on first and second bases, the man on second is out.
>
> If you have men on second and third bases, they are both safe.
>
> If you have men on all bases, only the man on first is out.

When a man is out, remove him from the diamond. After three outs, your inning ends and you pass the die to your opponent. After you have each played nine innings (or some other number), the one who scored the most runs is the winner.

## DROP DEAD

*This game is played with five dice and any number of people. Each player in turn rolls the dice until he "drops dead" as described below. Then he notes his score on a piece of paper, and passes the dice on to the next player.*

*For every throw of the dice, you score the total of the spots showing. (For example, you score fifteen if you roll 3-6-1-4-1.) However, if you make a roll in which a 5 or a 2 appears, your score for the throw is zero. Furthermore, you must remove any dice which showed a 5 or a 2, and play from then on with fewer dice. So, if you roll 4-3-5-1-2, you score zero for that turn, and your next roll will be with only three dice. Eventually, you will be reduced to one die. When the last die comes up a 5 or 2, you "drop dead," and pass the dice on to the next player.*

*After everyone has dropped dead, the player who scored the most points is the winner.*

*The game can be made more suspenseful by giving each player only one throw of the dice at a time. After a throw, mark down the score and how many dice that player has left, then pass the dice on to the next player. The dice continue to go around the circle until everyone has dropped dead.*

# MASTERMIND

*Two players*

*MASTERMIND Set*

*OBJECT: To guess the peg pattern set up by your opponent*

MASTERMIND, a popular game of logic produced by Invicta Plastics, is something like Twenty Questions played on a board. One player sets up a hidden sequence of four colored pegs, and his opponent tries to figure out that sequence in the fewest turns.

The game board has eleven rows of four large peg holes into which fit pegs of dark blue, light blue, green, orange, red and yellow. The eleventh row is covered with a shield so that only one player can see the sequence of pegs in it. Each of the other ten rows represents one move, or turn. To one side of each row of large peg-holes is a group of four smaller holes. These are for the narrow black and white "logic" pegs, which give the player the information he needs to figure out his opponent's secret.

Select one player to be the first Mastermind. While the Mastermind looks the other way, his opponent chooses colored pegs and sets up a sequence of four pegs on the eleventh row. He then hides the pattern behind the plastic shield so the other player can't see it.

The Mastermind now tries to guess his opponent's hidden arrangement of the pegs in as few moves as possible. On each try the Mastermind makes, he sets up a trial series of pegs in one of the ten visible rows, starting with the row nearest him and moving one more row toward his opponent in each turn. After each trial his opponent responds by sticking logic pegs into the four small holes alongside that trial row: one white peg for each of the Mastermind's pegs that is the right color but in the wrong position, and one black peg for each that is correct in both color and position. Therefore, when the Mastermind has solved the mystery, his correct trial row gets four black pegs. However, the positions of the logic pegs do not in any way correspond to the positions of the colored pegs, so the Mastermind cannot tell which of his colored pegs are right or wrong. After the Mastermind has solved the sequence, or has been stumped by finishing the last row incorrectly, the players switch places and the new Mastermind gives it a try. The player to guess the sequence in the least number of trials wins the match.

The first row the Mastermind guesses is completely random, but after that he uses logic to help him on his next trial. For example, say on your first row you place a red, dark blue, orange and green peg in that order. In response your opponent sticks in two white pegs and no black ones. Since there are only six possible colors, and two of the four you guessed were incorrect, you realize that the two colors you left out of your first trial, light blue and yellow, must belong to the sequence. So on your next trial you use these two colors in the place of any two other colors. (Remember, you don't know which two of the four were correct.) Also, you change the positions of the two colors you are reusing, because even if by chance they were the correct ones, they were not in the right positions. When your opponent responds to your next row, you are sure now to have at least two colors correct (the two you substituted), and possibly three, or even all four. Even if two colors are still wrong, you are sure to get them all correct in row three. If the logic pegs were to tell you that all four colors were correct, but none were in the right positions, your future turns would be only a question of trying different positions, and watching in each move for black pegs to tell you that the position of one of the colors is correct. By constantly shifting the positions of the pieces, and by experimentally substituting one color for another to see what happens, it is possible (though not easy) to deduce the correct peg pattern before your tenth move.

The game can be made more difficult or less. MASTER-MIND can be made simple enough for younger children by removing two colors from the set, leaving four. The game is then played with black logic pegs only, standing for colored pegs which are in the right positions. For top flight Masterminds, you can allow colors to be duplicated in the hidden sequence, or allow less than four pegs. Therefore, a sequence might be two red pegs and a green, four orange pegs, or no pegs at all! Remember that the logic pegs are always put in to correspond to one peg of the correct color or both color and position in the Mastermind's trial, so that if two red pegs are in the solution and the Mastermind puts down one red peg, he receives only one white logic peg for his guess, not two.

*BATTLESHIP*

*BATTLESHIP, manufactured by Milton Bradley and based on a traditional pencil and paper game, is a mock battle at sea between two opponents. At the beginning of the game, each player positions a number of plastic battleships, destroyers and cruisers in the peg-holes of a 10 by 10 grid on his side of the board. Each player's fleet arrangement is hidden from the other's view by a screen across the board. Taking turns, the two players name positions on the board where they suspect the other's ships are located. Every time a player names a correct position, he "destroys" an enemy ship. The player who destroys his opponent's entire fleet is the winner.*

## SCRABBLE

*Two to four players*

*SCRABBLE set*
*Pencil and paper*

***OBJECT: To score more points than your opponents by forming high-scoring words***

SCRABBLE is a proprietary game manufactured by Selchow and Righter Games. Players vie with one another to form words on the board that interlock like a crossword puzzle. The more letters a player uses to form a word, the rarer the letters he uses, and the better the word's position on the board, the more points that player scores. At the end of the game, the player who has scored the greatest number of points is the winner. The basic set includes the board, 100 letter tiles, and four racks to hold players' tiles.

The board is divided into 225 squares (15 by 15), on which letter tiles are placed. Most of these squares are grey non-premium squares, but sixty-one of the squares scattered in a pattern over the board are premium squares, which change the scores of single letters or of whole words placed on top of them.

There are twenty-four double-letter-score squares (light blue) and twelve triple-letter-score squares (dark blue). Both of these change the value only of the letter placed upon them. There are also seventeen double-word-score squares (pink), and eight triple-word-score squares (red). The pink center square, marked with a star, is also a double-word score square. Multiple-word squares change the total value of the whole word, no matter which letter of the word is placed on them.

The 100 tiles are each imprinted with a letter and a point value that roughly corresponds to the rarity of the letter, both in the English language, and among the set of tiles. The rarer letters have the higher point values. The blanks, which have no point value at all, can be used as any letter needed to complete a word, but once used, they remain fixed as that assumed letter during the rest of the game.

Players sit around the board in such a way that each will be unable to see the others' tiles. Each places a rack in front of him to hold his tiles. Turn all the letter tiles face down and mix them up well. For convenience, they can be kept inside the box top. Each player draws a tile from this "stock" of tiles, and the one who draws the letter nearest to the beginning of the alphabet goes first. The tiles are returned to the stock, and it is again mixed up. Each player now draws seven tiles from the stock and places them on his rack, keeping them hidden from his opponents. The first player begins the game using letters from his rack to form a word running along a horizontal or vertical line of the board and covering the starred center square. Diagonal words are never allowed. Any English word found in a previously agreed upon dictionary is legal, so long as it is not abbreviated or hyphenated, and does not have a capital initial letter. The first player announces his score and draws enough tiles from the stock to replenish his group of seven tiles. Scores for each player are kept on a piece of paper.

Going around to the left, the second and subsequent players take turns using their letters to form new words on the SCRABBLE board. After taking their turns, players replenish their groups from the stock. New words must always run vertically or horizontally, and interlock with a word already on the board.

A new word can interlock with an old one at right angles, for example:

```
      P
      E
RENOWN
      T
```

The player scores for his own word only.

A new word can be formed by adding one or more letters to a word already on the board—for example, adding G to RILL to form GRILL. The player who adds the G scores for the whole new word GRILL.

A player can form his own word parallel to one which has already been formed, so long as all adjacent letters form complete interlocking words:

```
S H I N
  T O R T
```

The player who puts down TORT scores for IT and NO as well.

Blanks are wild tiles, and can stand for any letter a player chooses; but once fixed, the letter assigned to a blank remains the same throughout the game.

A player can, if he wants, exchange one, some, or all of his tiles for new ones during his turn, rather than forming a new word.

He does this by dropping his unwanted letters into the stock, shifting the tiles around, and drawing as many new tiles as he needs to bring the tiles in his group up to seven. The play then passes on to the next player.

Words are scored by adding up the point values of their letters, multiplied by any premium squares which were covered. If a letter lands on a double- or triple-letter square, the value of that letter is doubled or tripled before being added into the word's total score. For example, if you form the word FLACK, and the K falls on a double-letter-score square, the total score will be $4 + 1 + 1 + 3 + (2 \times 5) = 19$ points. If part of a word falls on a double-word or triple-word premium square, the score for that entire word is multiplied by two or three, even if the letter on the premium square is a blank.

Premium squares are cumulative. If a word covers both a triple-letter and a double-letter word square, the letter on top of the triple-letter square is tripled before the double-word premium is figured. Premium squares can only be used by the player who originally covers them; you get no extra points for modifying a word which already covers a premium. In the example of adding G to RILL given above, the player could only score the total of the letter points even if RILL was originally placed on a double-word square.

If you form two or more words at the same time, you are scored for all of them, counting any premium squares you've covered. If you use all 7 letters on a single turn, you are awarded a bonus of fifty points.

When the stock is exhausted, the game continues until one player has used up all his letters, or until no one can form further words. Players then subtract the total points of the letters they have from their total scores during the game. If the game ends when one player "goes out" by using all his letters, he adds to his score the total point values of the letters left in his opponents' hands.

The player with the highest score is the winner.

## Strategy

SCRABBLE is a cheerful game to play noncompetitively, just taking turns making words and trying to get high scores, without keeping track of who is winning. Unfortunately, there tends to be at least one member in every SCRABBLE-playing family who has earned the right to be called a SCRABBLE "fiend," and who has a way of turning friendly games into nerve-wracking battles.

The innocent, inexperienced player who first matches wits with a seasoned fiend has a surprise coming to him. While our player struggles to form a word—any word—using the letters in his group, and finally places the word LINE on the board (for all of four points), his opponent is building a five-, six-, seven- or eight-letter word designed to land a high-scoring letter on a triple-letter square or to cover a double-word premium. Somehow, incredibly, the fiend clears his hand—collecting the fifty-point bonus—not once but twice during the game. Whenever our new player has, after great concentration, come up with a five- or six-letter word, his opponent saps his triumph by capping the word with a suffix or adding a prefix. And wouldn't you know it, the

| Letter | Quantity | Point Value |
|--------|----------|-------------|
| A | 9 | 1 |
| B | 2 | 3 |
| C | 2 | 3 |
| D | 4 | 2 |
| E | 12 | 1 |
| F | 2 | 4 |
| G | 3 | 2 |
| H | 2 | 4 |
| I | 9 | 1 |
| J | 1 | 8 |
| K | 1 | 5 |
| L | 4 | 1 |
| M | 2 | 3 |
| N | 6 | 1 |
| O | 8 | 1 |
| P | 2 | 3 |
| Q | 1 | 10 |
| R | 6 | 1 |
| S | 4 | 1 |
| T | 6 | 1 |
| U | 4 | 1 |
| V | 2 | 4 |
| W | 2 | 4 |
| X | 1 | 8 |
| Y | 2 | 4 |
| Z | 1 | 10 |
| blank | 2 | 0 |

fiend manages to land that suffix on a double-word square, giving the fiend twice our player's score just by adding one or two additional letters.

The end result of the game: Inexperienced, 130; Fiend, 421.

There are really only two ways to deal with such an expert: decline to play with him, or learn to fight fire with fire. If you choose the second course, here are a few hints to help you hold your own:

There are ten letters which carry values of more than four points: F, H, J, K, Q, V, W, X, Y and Z. When you draw one of these high-scorers, take full advantage of it by using it in conjunction with a premium square; either put it on top of a double- or triple-letter square, or use it in a word which covers a multiple-word-score square. If no premium square is immediately available, hang on to your high-scorer until one is, unless the prospect of reaching a premium soon seems unlikely. Hang on to a U, in case you draw a letter Q later. Blank tiles, though they don't carry any points themselves, are extremely valuable, letting you use your high-scorers in otherwise impossible words. Some good shorties to remember are : QUIZ, QUIP, QUERY, XENON, AX, AXE, OX, COX, VEX, ZOO, ZED, ZEAL, ZIG, ZEST, FEZ, JOY, JET, JELL, JAR, RAJ, SKY, SKI, JAY, ORYX (all there in black and white in Webster's Collegiate Dictionary).

A leisurely way to pick up a few points is to add a suffix or prefix to an opponent's word. Therefore, it is often handy to keep a common group or two in your hand, if possible, such as -ED, -EST, -ING, -ENT and RE- (or -ER). There is often a chance to make a noun plural with an S, but since there are only four S's in the game, it is usually better to save an S for a particularly high-

# HOW TO GET OUT OF PLAYING A GAME

It's a great misfortune that the people of the world are divided into the two broad categories of Those Who Play Games Every So Often, and Those Who Play Incessantly. Because of the natures of the two groups, differences often arise between them.

"Hey, Fred, want a little game of backgammon?"

"No, sorry, I'm eating."

"I've got the board right here; you can eat and play at the same time."

"I really don't want to, I'm sorry."

"I know you don't mean that. I'll just set the board up here by your plate. You're red. Ready?"

Somehow, people from the Incessant category don't seem to listen, and the milder Every-So-Oftens shy away from putting their message in firmer terms for fear of hurt feelings. Often, you can be railroaded into playing a game when you didn't want to in the first place. If you win, there's no help for you, because once the games addict has lost, he'll insist on playing again . . . and again.

There are few proven methods for refusing a game. If you refuse mildly, you will be heckled with, "Are you sure?" for hours to come. If you lie, saying, "Gee, I don't know how to play that game," instruction is sure to be offered. If you say you hate the game, that is an insult to all its devotees.

There is only one effective course to take when turning down an invitation to play. If a firm "No," (twice repeated) doesn't have any effect, close your eyes and hold your breath to tell him you are serious. It works every time.

scoring opportunity. Always keep your eyes wide open for a suffix or prefix that will land the whole new word on a premium square.

Another way to come up with high scores is to form more than one word at once. For example, if one of the words on the board were MAD, you could add HEWN at right angles to the word, forming:

```
      H
M A D E
      W
      N
```

You would then score for both words, MADE and HEWN (a total of seventeen). Also keep in mind that if you form two words by covering a single premium square, that square applies for both words. To use the example shown above, if the square underneath the E were a double-word premium, the scores of both MADE and HEWN would be doubled.

More than two words can be formed at once by laying a new word parallel to an old one. If the word NOT were on the board, you could add OLIO to it, forming:

```
O L I O
N O T
```

You'd then score for OLIO, ON, LO and IT (a total of 10), even though you only used a total of four points from your hand.

You might also try for the fifty-point bonus you collect when you use all seven letters in your hand. Though the opportunity somewhat depends on luck, you can give fortune a helping hand by keeping a balanced distribution of letters on your rack. If you have double letters in your hand (such as two D's), try to use one of them as soon as possible. The most common letters are the ones to keep in readiness; two or three vowels, and the consonants L, N, R, S, T, D or G. Letter frequencies are listed on one side of the board itself for ready reference.

# MONOPOLY

*Two to eight players*

*MONOPOLY set*

*OBJECT: To remain financially solvent and to drive your opponents into bankruptcy by buying and developing real estate*

MONOPOLY, owned and manufactured by Parker Brothers, was the first of the "real life" board games, in which players face some of the same problems and compete for some of the same goals that they encounter in day-to-day living.

In many ways, MONOPOLY is the embodiment of the American ideal. Each player starts out the game with the same amount of money in his pocket and with exactly the same prospects stretching in front of him as the others. It is up to him, through the exercise of his business cunning, to pull himself up by the bootstraps, and to drive his opponents into bankruptcy; luck is all but canceled out in the eventual outcome of the game. Perhaps this accounts for the game's enduring popularity, unequalled by any other proprietary board game.

The MONOPOLY board is designed as a loop divided into squares representing real estate properties, railroads, utilities, a jail, random "Chance" squares and other aspects of the vicissitudes of life. Along with the board come a pair of dice, title deeds to the properties, thirty-two houses and twelve hotels for developing real estate, play money, tokens to move around the board, and "Chance" and "Community Chest" cards.

Before beginning the game, shuffle the Chance and Community Chest cards and place them face down in their marked spots on the board. Spread out all the title deed cards so that they are easily visible to each player. Then give each player $1500 in

play money in the following manner: Two $400's, two $100's, two $50's, six $20's, five $10's, five $5's, and five $1's.

Select a banker. His job will include the meting out of salaries, the collection of fines and taxes, the dispensation of bonuses, the sale of property and houses, and the supervision of real estate auctions. The Banker should be quick with arithmetic, organized, and possess a well-developed sense of humor. The Banker takes charge of all the spare play money, plus the unsold houses, hotels, and title deed cards. If the Banker also plays in the game (and he usually does), he should be careful to keep his personal finances separate from the bank's money. If the bank runs out of money during a long game, the Banker has the authority to issue more money by writing the denominations on any spare pieces of paper.

Each player selects a token to represent himself in his travels around the board, and places it on the corner square of the board marked GO. Each player throws a die, and the one to throw the highest number takes the first turn. The remaining players take their turns going around to the left.

The play itself is simple. On his turn, each player throws the pair of dice and moves his token that number of spaces clockwise around the board. Depending on the space he lands on, the player can then take any of the actions described below (buying, building, or selling) before giving the dice to the next player. Between all turns, any player can also buy, build or sell as freely as during his own turn. Any number of tokens can occupy the same square without affecting one another. Players' tokens go around and around the board until the game ends with all but one player bankrupt.

If a player rolls doubles, he takes his turn as usual, and then rolls the dice again and takes another turn.

The different types of squares on the board are as follows:

GO: Each time you go around the board, you collect $200 in salary. This is paid to you by the Banker every time you land on or pass the GO square, whether you reach it by throwing the dice or by drawing a Chance or Community Chest card which sends you there.

JAIL: You are sent to Jail when any of the following occurs:

  You throw doubles three times in a row.

  You land on the corner square marked "Go to Jail."

  You draw a card marked "Go to Jail."

When any of these three circumstances occurs, move your token directly across the board to the Jail portion of the Jail square without collecting your $200 salary; your turn ends immediately. (Since one of these eventualities is bound to happen sooner or later, chances are you'll spend some time behind bars.) Although you are now in Jail, you still retain your rights, and are allowed to buy or sell property, collect rents, and erect houses and hotels. If you land on the Jail square in the ordinary course of moving around the board, you keep your token on the "Just Visiting" portion of the square, and move forward on your next move as usual.

Understandably, it is a bit more difficult to get out of Jail than to get in. Just as there are three ways to be arrested, there are

three means of escape:

Pay a $50 fine to the bank on one of your next three turns. When you have paid the fine, roll the dice and move the specified number of spaces forward.

Use a "Get Out of Jail Free" card if you have already drawn one from Chance or Community Chest. Show the card to your opponents, place it back under the pile from which you drew it, and throw the dice. You might also buy this card from an opponent willing to sell it to you.

Throw doubles on one of your next three turns. If you are successful, move your token the specified number of spaces out of Jail; but even though you've thrown doubles, do not take an additional turn. If you can't get a Get Out of Jail Free card, and if you have not escaped jail by throwing doubles after your third try at it, you must pay the $50 fine, throw the dice, and move out.

**CHANCE AND COMMUNITY CHEST:** When you land on either of these spaces, draw the top card from the face-down stack specified, and follow the directions on the card. Some of these cards reward you ("Bank pays you a dividend of $50"), some change your position ("Advance token to Illinois Avenue"), while some penalize you ("You are assessed for Street Repairs, $40 per house, $115 per hotel"). Upon drawing a card from the Chance or Community Chest pile, show the card to your opponents, act on it, and then return it face down to the bottom of its pile.

If you draw a Get Out of Jail Free card, you may keep it until you use it to get out of Jail; then return it to its pile. You might also try to sell this card to one of your opponents for somewhat less than the $50 fine for getting out of jail.

**INCOME TAX AND LUXURY TAX:** If you land on Luxury Tax, you are required to pay the bank $75.

You have two alternatives, however, if you land on "Income Tax." You may pay a flat fee of $200 to the bank, or you can pay ten percent of your total assets. Assets include all spare cash, the printed values of all your houses and hotels, the mortgage values of mortgaged properties, and the board prices of any unmortgaged properties you might own. Unfortunately, the official rules state that you must decide whether to pay the flat fee or ten percent before adding up your total worth, so it is a good idea to keep a rough running total in your head of how much your assets come to. Or, if your group approves, you can opt to drop this rule in light of its inconvenience, and decide whether to pay ten percent or $200 after calculating your worth.

**FREE PARKING:** The Free Parking space calls for no action at all. If you land on it, you get no money or other reward; in Parker Brothers' words, it is just a free resting place.

The rest of the squares on the board are properties that can be purchased. There are twenty-two real estate squares, arranged by three's and two's in neighborhoods of common colors—"color groups." Then there are four railroads and two utilities (Water and Electric). Whenever your token lands on an unowned property, whether by a throw of the dice or by being directed there by a Chance card, you have the option of buying it from the bank for the price listed on the square. To buy the property, give the Banker

**TITLE DEED**
**TENNESSEE AVE.**

RENT $14.
| | |
|---|---|
| With 1 House | $ 70. |
| With 2 Houses | 200. |
| With 3 Houses | 550. |
| With 4 Houses | 750. |

With HOTEL $950.

Mortgage Value $90.
Houses cost $100. each
Hotels, $100. plus 4 houses

If a player owns All the lots of any Color Group the rent is Doubled on Unimproved lots in that group

the necessary money, receive the title deed for the property, and place the deed face up beside you so that your opponents can all see your holdings.

If you decide not to buy the property for its printed value, the Banker immediately puts the property up for auction. Any player, including you (who initially turned the property down), can then bid on the property, starting at any price. The highest bidder takes the land.

When you land on a property that is already owned by another player, you are required to pay him rent for the privilege of using his square for one turn. If it is mortgaged, you pay no rent at all. The basic rent for undeveloped land, which is listed on each title deed card, doubles in value for undeveloped lots when a player owns all the properties in a color group, even if some of those properties are mortgaged. This makes it an advantage to have a monopoly on all the land in a color group. Rent increases dramatically with each house placed on the property (see Building Houses), and some properties bring in more rent than others.

## SONS OF . . .

The first game board designed as a closed loop rather than as a trail with a "start" and "finish" was a genuine invention. So was the idea of introducing play which reflected some aspect of everyday life. Since the first such board game, many others have been modeled on similar principles; players travel around and around the board instead of to a definite goal, as they attempt to accumulate money, love, possessions or power. One of these is THE GAME OF LIFE, made by Milton Bradley, in which players must make such crucial decisions as whether or not to go through college, enter business or a profession, or marry. At the end of the game, the player who has picked up the highest number of "success" points wins the game.

In ANTI-, created by Anspach, Inc., each player represents a "trustbuster" who, with the aid of law suits and antitrust legislation, seeks to wipe out three large monopolies controlling the board at the outset. The winner of the game is the one who has accumulated the highest amount of budget money and "social credits" at the end of the game.

The homemade game shown here is based on gangland life, complete with hit men and organized murder. It is pleasingly gruesome, and satisfyingly long.

*Over the years, many rules have sprung up; so much so that many people have never played strictly by regulation. (One player is known who swears that if you roll double-ones, you get one of each type of bill.)*

*A few of these home-grown varieties are:*

*Free Parking Jackpot: In the standard game, the Free Parking square is simply a resting place. In this game, it represents a jackpot for the one lucky enough to land on it. At the beginning of the game, a $500 bill is placed in the center of the board. From then on, all the money players pay for fines, taxes, and building and street repairs goes into the center. The player to land on Free Parking gets the jackpot.*

*The $500 bill isn't replaced after the first jackpot is won, but fines and taxes continue to accumulate for successive jackpots.*

*GO Jackpot: Ordinarily, players landing directly on GO collect $200 as usual. In this variation, those who land on the square itself collect $400, while those passing it collect only the normal $200.*

*Prisoner's Rights: In this variation, the player in Jail loses all his rights to buy and sell properties, collect rent, mortgage holdings and erect housing. This makes the Jail cell a much more undesirable spot to be stuck in. (In ordinary play, it is sometimes useful to rest in Jail for several turns as your opponents wipe one another out.)*

*After leaving Jail, all your rights are restored.*

If you land on an unmortgaged railroad owned by another player, you pay him a fare based on the total number of railroads he owns. The fare for a ride is $25 if he owns only that one railroad, $50 if he owns two, $100 for three, and $200 for four.

Similarly, if you land on an unmortgaged utility owned by an opponent, the service charge is higher if he owns both of them. When you land on an owned utility, don't touch the dice. Leave them where they are lying, and pay the owner five times the amount shown on the dice if he owns one utility, and ten times the amount if he owns both.

As you see, you will be paying a lot of money in rents and fees during the game, but hopefully everything that you pay out will be more than made up for by rents you receive on your own properties. Be alert to other players landing on your unmortgaged property, because another player is only obligated to pay your rent during his turn. If you fail to demand your rent before the following player throws the dice, you lose all claim to it.

BUILDING HOUSES: When you own all the real estate in a color group and none of the lots are mortgaged, you may begin building houses on your lots. This is highly desirable, because as you develop your properties their rental prices jump, especially after the third house. During your move, and also between the moves of the other players, you can, if your finances allow, purchase one or more houses from the bank for the price shown at the bottom of your title deed, and place the plastic house or houses on the colored bar of the property square or squares.

However, MONOPOLY sports a zoning regulation that requires that you build up each color group evenly, so that there is never a difference of more than one house between lots in the same color group. For example, if you place a house on one of the lots of a completely undeveloped color group, the next house you build in that color group must go on one of the other undeveloped properties. Before you can put two houses on a lot, all the other properties in that group must have at least one house on them already. Houses can never be moved from one lot to another, or sold by anyone but the bank.

When selling houses back to the bank to raise cash, they must be sold evenly, so that no two lots in the same group differ by more than one house.

Even after you have a house on one or more properties in a color group, you still collect the same double base rent on any undeveloped lots in that group, just as you did when you first completed the group.

After you have four houses on each property of a complete color group, you can begin erecting hotels on that group's lots. A hotel is equal to five houses, so in order to buy a hotel from the bank you must pay the price of a fifth house and return to the bank all four houses already on the lot; for this you receive one large red hotel to place on your property. Hotels follow the "build evenly" regulation too; if you have a hotel on one lot, you must have either four houses or a hotel on each lot in the same group. Only one hotel per property is permitted.

The MONOPOLY set comes with only thirty-two houses and twelve hotels, and in many games this leads to a "building shortage" toward the end of the game. If two or more players want to buy more houses than the bank has on hand, the Banker runs an auction, houses going to the highest bidder. When all the bank's houses are exhausted, no more buildings can be erected until a player sells some of his houses back to the bank, or converts four of his houses into a hotel. The canny player will take advantage of the building shortage by refraining from converting groups of four houses into hotels, in order to prevent an opponent from developing potentially lucrative properties.

PRIVATE TRADING AND SELLING: In games with larger numbers of players, it becomes difficult for any player to gain possession of a complete color group simply by being lucky enough to land on all the properties before they are snatched up by the other players. Trading, and buying and selling between players becomes vital at this point. Only unimproved lots (those without houses), railroads and utilities can be transferred between players; all houses or hotels on the lots in question and adjoining lots on the same color groups must be sold back to the bank at half their original purchase price before private sale of the land. You might agree, for example, to sell Marvin Gardens and a railroad to another player in return for States Avenue and $500 in cash, giving each of you a complete color group, and you some extra cash as well.

RAISING MONEY: Suppose you have just landed on New York Avenue and buying it will give you a complete color group; you've just landed on another player's property and owe him rent; or you've been assessed for building repairs (Chance card) and you need $150 quick . . . but you don't have the money. There are several ways of raising quick cash:

        Sell property or your Get Out of Jail Free card to another player for whatever amounts you can get for them.

        Sell houses and hotels back to the bank for half their original purchase price.

        Mortgage undeveloped properties with the bank.

If you are unable to raise the requisite money through private transactions, your first action should be to mortgage with the bank single undeveloped real estate lots, an odd railroad, or an unmatched utility. Turn your title deed upside down, so that the side marked "Mortgaged" shows, and collect from the bank the amount of money printed on the back of the card (which is always half the purchase price). You are still sole owner of the property, but you cannot collect rent on a property while it is mortgaged or build houses on any of the lots in its color group (although, if you hold the whole group, you still collect double rents on unmortgaged lots and collect the benefits for holding two or more railroads or utilities). If you are forced in the last extremity to mortgage a piece of land which is in a developed color group (one with buildings), you must sell all buildings in the entire color group back to the bank for half their purchase prices before mortgaging any property in the group. After mortgaging, you can later take the property out of hock as described below.

Houses and hotels may be sold only to the bank, and for half their original purchase price. When you are ready to build up again, you can repurchase your homes, but at their full list prices. Remember that houses and hotels must be sold evenly, according

# SIMULATION GAMES

In the general category of board games falls the large family of simulation games, which reproduce historical or fictional events. Each player takes the part of an army, a country, a faction or race, and tries to win in a simulated battle, diplomatic coup, or industrial takeover.

Generally, the rules of these games are extremely complex (rarely less than a book of forty pages), and the games themselves are protracted, sometimes stretching into weeks and months. Understandably, only certain types of people like these games, but those who do are usually wild about them. One person, receiving STAR FORCE, which simulates interstellar conflict between several space-traveling races, might be so appalled at the rule book (nearly 100 pages in length) that he puts the game away in a closet. But the next door neighbors' children, both under twelve, gleefully play a complex simulation of the invasion of the Roman Empire by Goths, Vandals, and other barbaric tribes. Those neighbors, cheerfully talking hoplite soldiers and rampaging war elephants for months, learn a great deal of history in the process. If there is a lesson to be learned here, it is perhaps that these games are best given to people who already love the subject matter a game represents—in all its complexity.

To give you some idea of the range and variety of the games, here is a random sampling of simulation games from various manufacturers:

OIL WAR: American Intervention in the Persian Gulf in 1979; Simulation Publications

DIPLOMACY: International Intrigue; Avalon Hill

WORLD WAR III: Nuclear Holocaust; Simulation Publications

RISE AND DECLINE OF THE THIRD REICH: WW II Strategy; Avalon Hill

TOBRUK: Tank Battles in North Africa in 1942; Avalon Hill

THE PLOT TO ASSASSINATE HITLER: 1940-45; Simulation Publications

PANZERGRUPPE GUDERIAN: The Battle of Smolensk, July, 1941; Simulation Publications

GOLAN: Syrian-Israeli Combat in 1973; Simulation Publications

THE BATTLE OF THE NATIONS: The Encirclement at Leipzig in the Napoleonic Wars, 1813; Simulation Publications

RAIL BARON: Railroad Expansion; Avalon Hill

WAR OF THE RINGS: Tolkien's Fantasy; Simulation Publications

STAR FORCE:  Interstellar Conflict; Simulation Publications

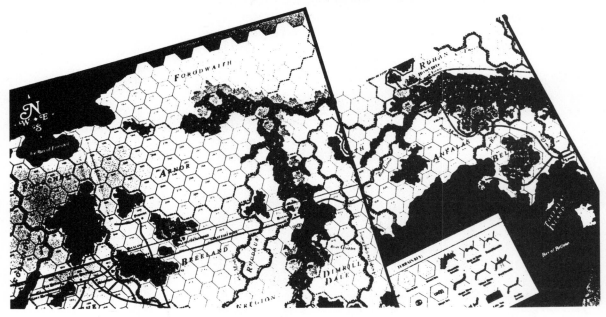

to MONOPOLY's urban development regulations, so that there is never a difference of more than one house between lots of a color group.

Hotels can be sold all at once. But because of the "build evenly" rule, if you decide to sell a hotel, you've got to sell houses or hotels on adjacent lots as well, so that you are left with no more than one house per lot in the color group of the newly vacant lot.

Alternately, hotels can be sold one house at a time by first exchanging the hotel for five houses, and then selling one or more of those houses, always keeping the "build evenly" rule in mind.

Because you sacrifice half of the price of your house in selling it back to the bank, try to use this as a last resort—only in order to avoid bankruptcy, or to pull off a highly lucrative purchase.

GETTING LAND OUT OF MORTGAGE: When you have increased your cash again, you can start paying off the mortgages on your properties. Do this by paying the bank the mortgage amount of your property (printed on the back) plus ten percent of the mortgage value as interest. For example, if you had mortgaged St. Charles Place for $70, you would pay the bank the principal of $70, but with $7 interest. When the mortgage has been paid off, turn the title deed right side up and begin collecting rent once again.

If you don't have the cash necessary to get the property out of hock (in fact you need still more money) you can try selling the mortgaged property to another player for whatever price you can get. If your opponent wants to make such a deal, he has two options:

He may decide to lift the mortgage on his new acquisition by paying the bank ten percent interest plus the mortgage principal.

He may pay the ten percent interest at the time of purchase, but elect to leave the property mortgaged. If he later decides to take the property out of hock, he must pay the principal plus an additional ten percent of the mortgage value.

GOING BANKRUPT: You have just landed on Pennsylvania Avenue, developed with four houses: you owe $1200 in rent, and your cash reserves amount to just under $300. Or, because of building repairs or taxes, you owe the bank more than you can pay.

You should first do your best to raise the necessary cash by selling houses back to the bank for half their purchase price. If you still don't have enough, your next step is to mortgage properties, or to offer your holdings for sale to another player. If your creditor is another player, perhaps he'll be willing to make a deal, accepting property instead of rent. If you are unable to raise the necessary cash to pay off your debts, you have no alternative but to declare bankruptcy. You declare bankruptcy by selling all your buildings back to the bank, and then turning over all your assets, including cash, title cards and mortgaged property, to your creditor. You then leave the game.

You are not allowed to deliberately cheat your creditor by selling your property to other players dirt cheap and then turning over the scraps; your creditor must receive either the full cash owed him, or all your transferable property.

When the creditor is the bank, property received from a bankruptcy is immediately auctioned off. Mortgaged properties are auctioned by the bank as unmortgaged.

The last player left financially solvent is the winner. Since games have been known to last many hours if not days, it is sometimes advisable to set a time limit at the beginning of the game. The wealthiest player at the end of the limit (or by suppertime) wins the game.

## OTHELLO (REVERSI)

*Two players*

*An OTHELLO set*

*OBJECT: To have the majority of the pieces in your own color at the end of the game*

The game of Reversi, popular in the last century, had almost sunk into oblivion when Gabriel, Inc. brought the game back under the trademark OTHELLO. It is now available at most toy and games stores. The board is divided into sixty-four squares like a checkerboard, but the squares are all of the same color. Sixty-four plastic playing chips are provided with the set. These chips are black on one side and white on the other.

After choosing one player to be Black and the other to be White, sit facing one another with the board between you. Each player gets thirty-two chips. Before starting the game, each player places two of his chips with his color face up in the four center squares of the board.

Starting with White, the two players alternately lay chips with their color face up on the board, positioning pieces so that they capture chips of the opposite color between chips of their own. When a chip is captured, it is not removed from the board, but is simply flipped over so that the color is now that of the player who made the capture, and indicates that he is the new owner of that square. This continues until the end of the game, when all the sixty-four squares are occupied.

You capture your opponent's pieces by trapping a piece in his color or a line of several of his pieces between two of yours. Your two pieces may capture his by standing at both ends of his line whether it runs diagonally or along a row or column. If the placement of a new chip in your color simultaneously traps more than one line of your opponent's pieces between two of yours, they are all flipped over to your color.

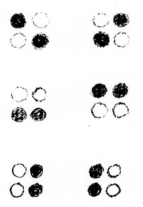

*These are all the possible starting set ups at the opening of a game of OTHELLO. Gabriel's rules allow only the diagonal patterns.*

In the illustration opposite, if White puts a chip on the square marked X, he captures two lines of black chips: one line of four chips running along a row, and another of only a single chip along a diagonal. These five chips are flipped over so that their white sides are face up, and belong to White until Black recaptures them. A chip may change hands many times in the course of a game. Note that the black chips marked by arrows are not captured as a

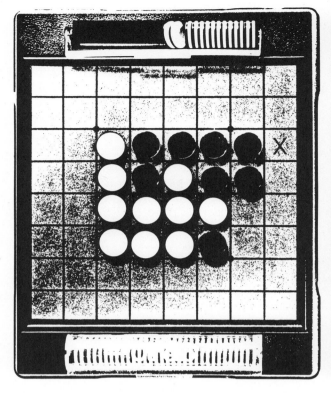
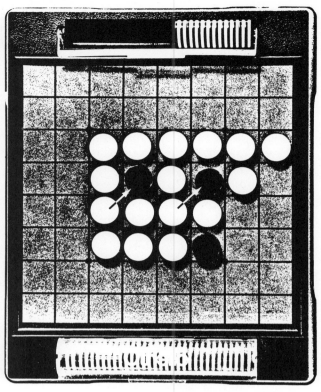

*White is going to place a chip on the square marked X.*                    *The result of White's move.*

result of White's action, although they are immediately hemmed in by whites as the captured pieces are flipped. Pieces can only be taken by the capture itself, not by its indirect results when captured pieces are flipped.

The only legal turns you can take are those in which you capture one or more of your opponent's pieces. Although this rarely occurs, if there is no square in which laying a chip will make a capture, you must forego your turn until it is again possible for you to capture.

At the end of the game, when all the squares have been occupied (or when the game reaches a point at which neither player has a valid play), both black and white chips are counted up. The player with the most chips in his color is the winner. In contests between equally matched adversaries, the game may end in a draw, with thirty-two white chips and thirty-two black.

## Strategy

The basic strategy of this game is not, as you might think, to take the maximum number of chips per move. This is because the balance of forces in the early part of the game changes so drastically from move to move that it is impossible to tell who is winning by just counting up the chips. If you capture a long row of your opponent's chips during one move, chances are sooner or later he'll recapture that same row, along with a few of your original chips as well.

The secret to winning the game is to occupy the corner squares, and the squares which run along the sides of the board.

# PLAY ON A MAP

Unlike games such as Chess and Backgammon, in which the design of the board is abstract, many popular games are played on boards designed as maps. The shape and structure of the map determines how the players interact, and the play itself is similar to enacting a drama.

The board for RISK, a game manufactured by Parker Brothers, is in the shape of a simplified world map, with countries shown in contrasting colors. Each player is given a group of countries to start off with, plus armies to defend his holdings while he attempts to expand his domain. Through dice-throw "skirmishes," players try to conquer adjacent countries without dangerously diminishing the strength of their forces. As a player conquers new countries, he is allowed to add to his armies as well. The winner of the game is the one who finally accumulates enough strength to take over the entire world.

STRATEGO, made by Milton Bradley, is another warfare game, but on the scale of a single battle rather than a world-wide campaign. The board is a battlefield map, divided into squares, with large ponds taking up much of the center. Each player is given a single army, including a marshall, generals, captains, lieutenants, bomb squads and a spy, as well as bombs and a flag. The object of the game is for one player to capture the other's flag, but to do that a player has to penetrate the other's forces. This is not easy, because the pieces are "ranked," so that men of one rank can only capture men of lower ranks. The bombs can be used to destroy anyone but members of the bomb squad, while a spy can capture only the marshall.

The board for CLUE, made by Parker Brothers, represents the map or floor plan of a mansion. The players are presented with one of a number of unsolved murders, which they must solve. They move from room to room, interrogating "witnesses" and hunting for clues. Finally, the player with the greatest ability for deductive reasoning wins by correctly stating the murder weapon, the site of the murder, and the murderer's identity.

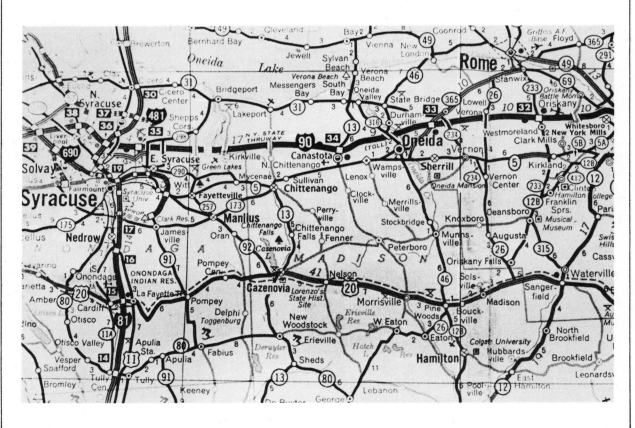

Once you have placed a chip of your color in a corner, it can never be captured, and stays where you put it for the rest of the game. Any rows of your color which include a corner are strengthened, sometimes to the point of invulnerability. If you manage to occupy two adjacent corners near the beginning of the game, you can seek to connect the two with a long line which, when completed, may easily wipe your opponent off the board. Possession of three corners almost assures a win; possession of four clinches the matter.

Setting up lines of your pieces along the side squares is almost as important as occupying the corners, because once you have "anchored" chips on side squares, your opponent will have difficulty capturing them without being captured in return. Furthermore, with a solid line of your color along the side, your opponent's colonies in the center are subject to systematic attack. No matter what goes on in the middle of the board, eventually the player who occupies the greatest number of side squares and corners will win the game.

# BACKGAMMON

*Two players*

*Backgammon set*

**OBJECT: To move your pieces around the board into your inner table, and then to bear off all your pieces before your opponent**

The Backgammon board is divided into two halves by a vertical "bar" down the center. One half of the board (traditionally the one nearest the light source) is the "inner table" and the other half is the "outer table." Along each side of the board are twelve thin, alternately colored triangles, or "points," which project toward the center of the board. For reference, the points are often numbered from 1 to 12 on both sides, starting at the far edge of the inner table. Each player has a colored set of fifteen checker-like pieces called "stones," and a pair of dice with a dice cup for rolling them.

Choose one player to be White and the other to be Black (some sets are red and black or red and white), and sit facing one another across the board. Set up the Backgammon board as shown on p. 234. Each player begins the game with two stones on his opponent's 1-point, five stones on his opponent's 12-point, three stones on his own 8-point; and five stones on his own 6-point.

The basic idea of Backgammon is for each player to race his opponent into his own inner table, but unlike most other board games, the movement in Backgammon is asymmetrical. Each player moves his pieces around the board away from his opponent's inner table, through his opponent's outer table into his own outer table, and from there into his own inner table. Some of the pieces, especially the two stones on the opponent's inner table, have a long way to go, while others have shorter trips, or even no trips at all. Because of the way the pieces are set up, White moves his pieces counterclockwise around the board and Black moves clockwise, so that the stones, traveling in opposite directions, interfere with one another and impede one another's progress. This is where strategy and competition come in, though excitement is made keener by the random element of luck.

To start the game, each player picks up one die and rolls it. If they roll doubles, they try again. The player whose die comes up the higher number goes first, but he uses the numbers on both of the dice to move his pieces on his first turn. From then on, players take alternate turns rolling both their dice and moving their stones accordingly.

When the dice are thrown, the numbers on the two dice, taken separately, show how many triangles one or more stones may travel. For example, if you roll 4-6, you can move one stone four points and another six to any available triangles. You can also, if you wish, move a single stone ten triangles forward by first moving it the number indicated by one die, pausing, and then moving it the number indicated by the other die; however, both the point at which you pause and the point at which you come to rest must be available triangles.

When you are lucky enough to roll doubles, you get to take the numbers of the roll twice. If you roll double-3's, for example, you have the choice of moving four stones three points each, of moving one stone a total of twelve points (three points at a time, with a pause at available triangles), or other combinations which use a three-step move four times.

Triangles that are available for landing on are those which: are not occupied by any stone; are occupied by one or more of your own stones (there is no limit to how many of your own stones you can accumulate on a point); or are occupied by only one of your opponent's stones. If a triangle is occupied by two or more of

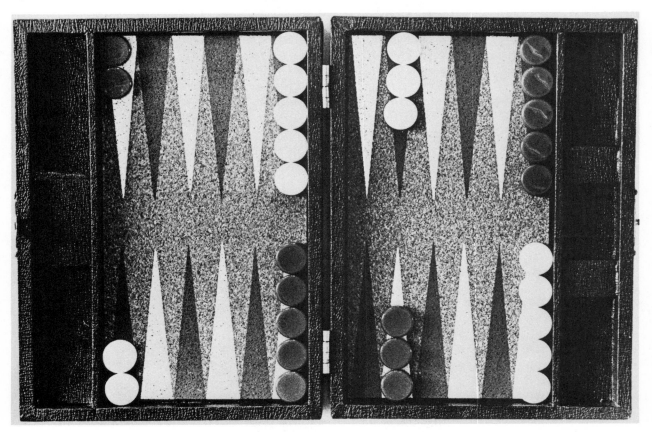

*In this photograph, the inner table is on your left. Number the points from that edge, starting with the 1-point. The 12-point is to your right, at the edge of the outer table. Black's side is at the bottom, White's side at the top.*

your opponent's stones, it is "blocked," and you cannot land on it. When so many triangles are blocked that you can't move the number of spaces specified by one die, move only the number of spaces specified by the other die. If you can't use the number on either die, play passes to your opponent.

HITTING: A solitary stone left on a point is called a "blot," and can be captured by an enemy piece. You "hit" a blot left by your opponent by landing on the point it occupies. The hit stone is then removed from the board and placed on the bar separating the two tables.

When one or more of your stones is on the bar, all movement of your other pieces is frozen, until you have re-entered your hit stone. To get a stone off the bar, you must throw the number of an unblocked triangle in your opponent's inner table, and place your re-entered stone on the triangle indicated. It can then begin its long journey to your inner table. It often happens near the end of the game that one of your stones is sent to the bar when all, or almost all, of the points on your opponent's inner table are blocked. When this happens, you may have to use up half a dozen turns throwing the dice before you can re-enter your stone. Occasionally, too, the hitting of an opponent's stone backfires. He may re-enter his stone on a point at which you have left a blot, thus hitting a piece you have finally managed to get to your inner table.

BEARING OFF: When all your pieces are on your inner table, you can begin bearing them off. This is done by rolling the dice and removing a stone from each of the points indicated, simply putting it aside near you. For example, if you roll a 2-4, you can remove one piece from point #2, and one from point #4, provided that you have stones on these points. Doubles count twice, as usual, so that a double-3 would allow you to bear off four stones from point #3. You may also use one or both of the numbers rolled to move your stones within your inner table to redistribute them rather than bearing them off.

When you roll a number that is higher than the highest point on which you have stones, you can bear them off from the highest point you occupy. If you roll a 4-5 but have stones only on the first three points, you can remove stones from point #3, or if that is unoccupied, from point #2. If one of your stones is hit after you begin bearing off (perhaps by an opponent's re-entering piece, or one that has lingered behind), you must re-enter your hit man on your opponent's inner table, and travel all the way around the board before you can resume bearing off. The first player to bear off all his stones is the winner.

## Strategy

*The Running Game:* This is the least devious and most common approach. Adopt it when you have thrown a few high rolls right at the game's outset. The strategy is to race ahead as fast as you can without going out of your way to hinder your opponent. Move out the two stones at the far end of your opponent's inner table as soon as possible; try to get them past the bar with all haste before your opponent has a chance to block their progress. Use doubles to their full advantage, moving two pieces at a time to avoid leaving blots. If the dice are favorable, you have a fair chance of getting through your opponent's outer table before he has a chance to organize his defenses.

*The Block Game:* To counter your opponent's dumb luck in gaining an early lead, you should adopt the defensive strategy of the block game. Your goal is to impede your opponent's forward progress by forming wide barriers of blocked points, hitting his blots frequently, and keeping his stones on the bar by blocking most of the triangles in your own inner table.

In the block game, your earliest action should be to break up the group of five stones initially on your opponent's 12-point, and to move them into your outer table. There you can use these stones, together with the stones on your own 8-point and 6-point, to form a blockade of points occupied by two or three stones. This blockade will interfere with your opponent's attempts to move his stones through your outer table.

Whenever possible, hit your opponent's single stones, being careful not to leave blots yourself.

While your opponent is struggling to break through your outer table blockade, cautiously move out the two pieces in your opponent's inner table, taking care not to leave either of them exposed to hits. Then, as they join up with your other pieces, begin moving your blockade en masse into your inner table. If you are then able to send an opponent's stone to the bar, he may find it impossible to re-enter until well after you've begun bearing off (which should be done carefully to avoid leaving blots which your opponent might hit on re-entering).

*The Back Game:* If your opponent has used the block game above to impede your progress, and there seems to be no chance of your ever catching up, try this: Instead of doing everything you can to get through your adversary's defenses, stay in his inner table. Form tempting blots for your opponent to take, and when you re-enter on his inner table, double up and let your pieces stay on the opposing side. Meanwhile, work on getting all your other pieces in groups of two on your inner table, to block it.

After your opponent has gotten all his pieces into his outer table, and is gleefully sending stone after stone into the inner table, he'll be forced, just by unfavorable rolls of the dice, to form blots from time to time. Whenever you can, hit his blots, and don't mind the fact that you may leave a blot in the process. If your blot is hit, you are set back a mere four or five points; but when you hit one of his blots, he's lost a minimum of twelve points—provided he's even able to re-enter on his first throw. Then, as your opponent is laboring to get his stones off the bar, get your stones around the board, and begin bearing off. This strategy is risky, and should only be attempted as a last resort; but when it succeeds, it succeeds in a pleasing manner.

## TRAVELING GAMES

Chess, Checkers and Backgammon are all available in traveling versions. In some the pieces are magnetic and the board is metal; in others the pieces are pegs that fit into either a wood or plastic playing board. The sets range in cost from the equivalent of a party favor (they make swell favors or stocking presents) to elegantly designed hardwood and leather-bound sets that are more in the price range of an "executive" gift. In the medium range of from eight to twelve dollars, you can get a very handsome set. All of them are ideal for VIP's who must sit through frequent airplane rides, for everyday commuters who like to play with a buddy on the train, or for kids who may be stuck in the back seat of a car during a tedious journey. Any of them would fit in glove compartment or briefcase, and many are small enough to earn the name of pocket game.

# CHECKERS

*Two players*

*Checkerboard and set of checkers*

***OBJECT: To capture all your opponent's pieces or to trap his pieces so that he has no move***

The checkerboard is divided into sixty-four squares (8 by 8) which are alternately dark and light. The checkers come in two contrastingly colored sets of twelve pieces each (usually black and red, but sometimes black and white).

Position the checkerboard between the two players in such a way that the dark corners of the board fall to the left of each player. Choose which player gets the black pieces. Black always goes first. Each player sets up his side of the board by placing his pieces on the dark squares of his first three rows. After the player with the black pieces takes the first move, the two players take their turns alternately until one wins the game.

Checker pieces are always confined to the dark squares, so their moves are all diagonal. The simple, uncrowned checkers with which the game begins have two possible moves:

Noncapturing move: Pieces move diagonally one square forward toward the opponent's side of the board into an unoccupied square.

Capturing move: the piece jumps diagonally over an enemy piece, and the enemy checker is removed from the board. If a piece can make another capturing jump after completing a previous one, it must do so, making as many capturing jumps as it can all in one turn. In making such multiple jumps, a checkers piece can zigzag to right or left as many times as is necessary, so long as each jump it makes is in the forward direction.

When there is a choice between making a capturing move and making a noncapturing move, you must capture. This cardinal rule of Checkers states that, "If you can jump, you must," even if in jumping you expose your piece to capture by your opponent. However, if you have a choice between two or more jumping

*This is the situation as Black begins his two-for-one tactic.*

*Black puts his piece into a position that forces White to jump him.*

*White jumps, but on the next turn Black will be able to take both of his pieces.*

moves, you are under no obligation to choose the one which takes the most pieces.

When you move a piece to the row farthest away from you (and nearest your opponent), your piece is "crowned," by topping it with another checker of the same color. (If none are available, temporarily place a checker of another color underneath the crowned piece.) When pieces are crowned, they become "kings," and have the privilege of moving backward toward their own side as well as forward. In making multiple jumps, kings can change directions, not only zigzagging diagonally, but backward and forward as well toward their own or their enemy's territory. If an uncrowned piece lands on the last row during a jump, it can't in the same turn resume its jumping as a king; a piece's move ends the instant it is crowned.

When you have captured all your opponent's pieces, or trapped his pieces so that they can't move, you win the game. If both forces become so reduced that neither player can capture the other's pieces, the game is a draw, and neither player is the winner.

### Strategy

Here are a few of the simplest Checkers principles—just enough to give you a feel for some of the game's excitement. Much more appears in the many books that have been written on the game.

The most basic of all Checkers tactics is the two for one capture. This relies on the rule that jump moves are mandatory even when they're undesirable. In the situation pictured here, Black moves a piece into jeopardy, knowing that when White is forced to jump, the move will open up a double jump for Black. This gives Black a net gain of one piece, although he had to sacrifice one of his pieces to get it.

Another basic position is the "cross," shown in one of its ramifications here:

When the Black king moves between the two White kings, one or the other of them is bound to be captured. Each White king is blocking the other's capture of the Black king, yet they cannot both move out of jeopardy at the same time.

*To accomplish a cross, Black must be in a position to get his king between two of White's pieces.*

*From that position, no matter where White moves one king, Black will be able to capture the other.*

*Black is pinned. Whichever way he moves, White will capture him.*

Near the end of the game, an important way of holding your opponent's kings at bay is by "pinning" them to a side—positioning a piece so that the opposing king will be captured whenever it moves. A typical pin: White king has the Black king trapped. Black has only two squares open to him, both of which expose him to instant capture.

In addition to these tactical maneuvers, here are a few strategic goals you might want to keep in mind:

Try to gain, hold and control the center of the board, backing up your pieces so that they are protected from capture. This tends to block your opponent's advances, and force him to make moves which will weaken him.

Keep two or three pieces on your first row, in order to prevent your opponent from easily getting his pieces crowned.

If you are at a disadvantage near the end of the game and are being chased by several of your opponent's kings, try to stay in the center of the board, and avoid being trapped along the sides or in the corners.

### CHESS BY MAIL

*If you practice at chess notation (page 245) enough to triumph over your initial confusion, you can use it to play Chess by mail with friends or family. Each of the players keeps a Chess board set up to show the game in progress. You make a move, and note it in your letter; your friend makes the appropriate move on his own board, then takes his turn and writes his move to you. This is one way to assure a steady flow of letters from children at camp or girlfriends on vacation— assuming they are avid chess players.*

# CHESS

*Two players*

*Chessboard and set of chessmen*

**OBJECT: To penetrate your opponent's defenses, and capture his king**

The game of Chess, the origins of which are ancient and somewhat mysterious, is very much like a simulated battle between two armies. The pieces have different ranks and abilities, advance into each other's camps, and attempt to capture one another. The Chess board is identical to a Checkers board—a large square divided into sixty-four smaller squares in an 8 by 8 pattern. Each player has a set of sixteen pieces under his command: eight pawns, two rooks, two bishops, two knights, a queen and a king. The opposing armies are of contrasting colors, usually white and black.

The chessboard is positioned between the two players so that the black corners are to the left of each player. Players choose which color they will use. White always has the first move.

Position the Chess pieces as shown on p. 243. The taller pieces—rooks, knights, bishops and the king and queen—are lined up along the row of squares nearest you. The pawns form a protective barrier in the row beyond. The pieces are arranged so that each piece of one color is directly across from its matching piece on the opposite side—queen faces oppositely colored queen, king faces king. The White queen is always on a white square, and the Black queen is always on a black square.

Starting with White, players take their turns alternately, changing the position of one piece per turn until the game's end. The game may end when one player wins by capturing his opponent's king, or with a draw when neither player has enough power to overcome the other. The game may also end with a "stalemate," when a player cannot make any legal move during his turn—either because his only moves would open his king to

immediate capture (it is illegal to endanger your own king), or because his pieces are so blocked that there is no vacant square to move to. There is no winner when a game ends in a draw or a stalemate.

When a player is threatening his opponent's king with capture, he calls out, "check," in the way of a warning, and his opponent is obliged to get out of check, either by moving his king away from danger, by blocking the attack with a piece interposed between the king and the threatening man, or by capturing the attacking piece. When a player has so maneuvered that his opponent's king will be taken no matter what, he calls, "Checkmate," and wins the game. It is not necessary to go through the formality of actually capturing the king and removing the piece from the board, so long as the players can clearly see that is the only eventuality.

## The Moves

Each chess piece has its way of traveling from one square to another. Pieces capture opposing men by moving to the square oc-

*Queen*

*King*

*Rook*

*Bishop*

*Knight*

cupied by that enemy piece, removing the enemy piece from the board, and taking its place.

QUEEN: The powerful queen can move in any direction, backward, forward, sideways, and along the diagonals. There is no limit on the number of squares a queen can move. So long as her way is not blocked by a piece of her own color, the queen can move as far as desired along a row, column or diagonal, though she cannot change direction during the same move. If an opposing piece lies along the queen's path, she captures it, taking its position and ending that move.

KING: The king can move one square in any direction into an unoccupied square. He may move backward and forward along a column, sideways along a row, or one square on any of the diagonals. If an enemy piece is within its one-square range, the king makes a capture. However, the king is not allowed at any time to move to a square where it could be immediately captured by an enemy piece.

ROOK: Another powerful piece, the rook (castle) can move any unobstructed distance forward, backward and sideways along the rows and columns. It is not allowed to move diagonally. It captures in the same manner in which it moves, taking any enemy in any direction along a row or column. The king and rooks are involved in the complex "castling" move, which each player can utilize once during the game. In castling, the king moves two squares toward either of the rooks on his row, and the rook leaps lightly over the king to occupy the square the king passed over. This is the only Chess move that involves two of a player's pieces. Castling is permitted only if: neither the king nor the rook involved have been moved from their original positions at any time during that game; all the squares between king and rook are vacant; the king is not in check, and neither the square the king must pass over nor the one on which he lands are under attack.

Castling is useful in order to bring the two rooks together for an attack on the enemy, and to move the king to a more protected spot.

BISHOP: The bishop moves forward and backward along the diagonals for any distance that is unobstructed by another piece. He captures in the same way he moves. Because of the way the pieces are set up at the beginning of the game, one of each player's bishops moves only on white diagonals, while the other moves only along black. Because half the squares on the board are inaccessible to each bishop, the loss of either of them weakens the abilities of its partner.

KNIGHT: The knight makes an odd, limited move resembling an "L," and is thus the only piece that changes direction within a turn. He first moves two squares along a column or row and then moves one square at right angles to the first direction, landing on a square of opposite color from the one at which he began. Knights have the unique privilege of being able to ignore pieces that lie along their route, as if the way were clear—just so long as the square they eventually land in is vacant, or contains an enemy piece to be captured. Knights are useful for penetrating crowded areas of the board where most other pieces would be blocked.

PAWNS: The pawns, the least powerful and most numerous Chess pieces, have the option of moving either one or two squares straight forward toward the enemy camp on their first moves. On all subsequent moves, however, a pawn may move only one square forward. Unlike any of the other pieces, pawns do not capture in the same way in which they ordinarily move. Instead, a pawn captures an enemy piece by moving diagonally forward one square; this is the only time that pawns can move in any direction other than straight forward. Although pawns don't threaten anything directly in front of them, they are useful to block opposing pawns. Keeping one pawn diagonally behind another is a protection too; if the forward one is captured, the rear pawn may capture the enemy piece in return.

If a pawn manages to reach the last row at the farthest end of the board, it is "promoted," by being exchanged for any other piece desired, usually a queen. Before the beginning of your next turn, substitute the piece you wish for the promoted pawn. Occasionally pawn promotion may give you multiple pieces, such as two or three queens. Since there are no extra queens in a chess set, the extra queen can be indicated with an upside-down rook, a checker, or a queen from another Chess set.

*Pawn*

### THE EN PASSANT CAPTURE

*Pawns have an anomalous capture given to them as a result of their option to make their first move two squares. When an opposing pawn moves two squares on its first move in a situation where it could have been taken by one of your pawns if it had moved only one, you may act as if the opposing pawn had moved only one square, by moving your pawn diagonally to the square the enemy pawn passed over, and removing the enemy piece from the board. This, the "en passant" capture, can only be done immediately after the opponent has moved his pawn the two squares. In most family games, situations where the "en passant" capture can be used come up only rarely, and most people playing Chess informally prefer to ignore this rule as an unnecessarily confusing one.*

### Strategy

Chess is easy enough to learn in the course of half an hour, but the definitive strategy for the game has never been discovered—despite the fact that hundreds of lengthy dissertations have been printed. The best way to become a competent player is to wage many games against players of different levels and approaches. Eventually, you will get a feel for the structures of attack and defense, and the interrelationships of the pieces. The following are a few of the basic concepts.

DEVELOPMENT OF FORCES: A piece is "developed" when it is moved out of its original position into an area where it has room to maneuver, threaten, and retreat. The early portions of many games are mainly a rush to develop pieces before an opponent gains the advantage, which usually goes to the first player to get a greater number of pieces out into the open.

There are two basic traps in Chess in which you can injure your opponent's forces without running much risk yourself. These are:

**The Fork:** *A fork occurs when one of your pieces threatens two or more of your opponent's pieces at the same time. This is especially deadly when one of the pieces threatened is a king. One way or another, your opponent will be forced to lose a piece.*

*A classic fork is this one, where the White knight threatens the Black rook and the Black king at the same time. Black has only one choice, to move his king out of jeopardy. White takes the rook, and is out of danger before Black can threaten in return.*

**The Pin:** *A pin occurs when one of your long-range pieces threatens an opponent's piece in such a way that he cannot move out of the way without exposing his king to check, or allowing a valuable piece to be taken.*

*The White Bishop is pinned to its square. If it tries to change positions, the White King is placed in check by the Black Queen.*

Try to develop your pieces so that the development of one doesn't interfere with another's, so that pieces protect one another, and so that each piece has the greatest potential for threatening the opponent's side of the board.

CONTROL OF THE BOARD: As in Checkers, control of the four center squares of the board is a strong advantage. Long-range pieces like rooks, bishops and queens have the greatest command of the board in the center, while a knight posted in a center square has the effect of interfering with most of your opponent's plans for developing his pieces toward an attack. Possession or control of the center squares effectively cuts your opponent's army into two, and hinders his moving of pieces from one side of the board in order to protect the other.

Your pieces need not be physically occupying one of the center squares in order to have control. Often it serves well just to guard the center squares with pawns or other pieces in order to keep the center out of your opponent's hands.

THE PAWN LINE: The pawns serve both as your shields from enemy attacks and as expendable men to harass and threaten opposing pieces that are getting too near for comfort. Unfortunately, by getting in the way, pawns also hinder attempts to develop the stronger pieces. It is necessary to move the line of pawns forward without leaving holes and gaps which enemy pieces might penetrate. Advance your pawns in such a way that each pawn protects its neighbors; when you move a powerful piece beyond the line, try to use the pawns to their best advantage by setting them up to guard the more valuable piece. "Doubled" pawns, two of the same color in the same column, weaken the structure of your defensive line.

Although pawns are often sacrificed in order to develop a particular strategy, remember not to underestimate the value of a pawn. In a tight game, a pawn or two can easily make all the difference, especially as they near the point at which they can be exchanged for queens.

# CHESS BY MAIL

A special notation is used to record Chess games, and to pose Chess problems in newspapers and magazines. Each piece is represented by a letter as follows:

Q—queen    B—bishop
K—king     N—knight
R—rook     P—pawn

Since there are two bishops, knights and rooks, these two pieces are further identified with an initial K or Q, depending on whether the piece is nearer the king or queen in their original positions at the start of the game. For instance, the rook at the far left corner is White's queen's rook, or QR for short.

Each square on the board is identified by row (rank), and by column (file).

The files are distinguished by the pieces which are set up along them at the beginning of the game. For White, the column at the far left of his board (far right for Black) is where his queen's rook is set up, so the file is called the "queen's rook file." Similarly, the files where the queen, king, bishops and knights are initially set up take their names from those pieces.

The ranks (rows) are numbered from 1 to 8, starting at the first rank on the viewer's side. If you are looking at the board from White's point of view, and want to speak about the square in the upper left hand corner of the board, you need only say QR8 (queen's rook 8). This same square from Black's point of view is QR1 (queen's rook 1), since he is numbering from the opposite direction.

Chess records indicate a move with the hyphen. "White P-KR4" means that White is moving a pawn to king's rook 4 (moving the pawn on his far right two squares forward, or "up").

When Chess games are recorded, the board is looked at from the point of view of the player who is making the move.

Other Chess notations are:

x—means "takes," as in BxP, bishop takes pawn

0-0—castles with the king's rook

0-0-0—castles with the queen's rook

?—bad move

!—good move

ch—check

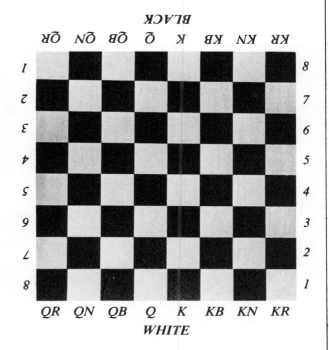

Look at this upright to see White's notation. Turn the page upside down for Black's point of view.

# Game Room Games

# Chapter 7
# Game Room Games

Supplying a game room requires a substantial investment. There is no single piece of equipment that you could call inexpensive. For this reason, consider the needs and habits of your own family carefully before rushing out to buy a permanent and costly piece of game room equipment. If you have a quiet family that socializes little, Roulette is not the best choice. With only a couple of people playing, there will be few wins, and not much excitement. But video games for one or two players might suit you fine, as might Darts, or Ping-Pong. On the other hand, households that bustle with their own and the neighbors' children would find it worthwhile to buy Bumper Pool, Air Hockey, or Pachinko; these games move quickly, so more players can get turns.

It is a good idea to measure your available space carefully. A Ping-Pong or Pool table might fit into your area, but remember that you need several yards of space at each end of a Ping-Pong table, and at least 6 feet of space all the way around a regulation Pool table. The layout of your room has to be considered too. Darts may fit in a small space, but playing the game anywhere near a door or passage, where people may wander into the path of a dart, is dangerous. Electric games such as Pinball, Pachinko and Air Hockey should be plugged in close to the machine, so there is no danger from wires that can be tripped over, or from the fire hazards of extension cords. Only a very large basement will accommodate both Ping-Pong and Pinball, whereas Bumper Pool and Pachinko might fit. Video games take up very little space, and so do the dozens of games that can be stored inside a home computer. Games like Roulette and Nok Hockey can be stored out of the way when not in use, but a Pool table is there to stay.

We have covered a large variety of game room games in this section. A few can be played by quite young children, and we have suggested other ways for preschoolers to use similar equipment. For the most part, the equipment in this section is best for children over eight years old and for adults. Included are active, fast-moving games excellent for those who are physically restless, games that require quick coordination of hand and eye, and games that exercise only the restless intellect. A combination of all three kinds is ideal to keep a family interested in a game room over a long period of time: one game to blow off steam, one for the thrill of dexterity, one for intense mental effort (and maybe Roulette for a bit of relaxed gambling) would be a good selection.

# SLOT CAR RACING

*Two players*

*Slot car set and two cars*

*OBJECT: To be the first to complete the race course with your car*

Slot car race track games are made by several manufacturers. They consist of snap-together plastic tracks which you can assemble in any of a variety of patterns, depending on the individual set. The simplest track is the basic oval loop, but more challenging courses may include several bridges, many curves, and one or more intersections. Each track has two "slots" running along its length to guide two model cars around the course. Each car is about the length of a thumb. The tracks are electrified (at a harmless level) to provide the cars with power. Current controls (one for each of the two cars) allow each player to change the amount of electricity his car receives, affecting its speed.

At the beginning of the race, each player picks a track lane, puts his car in that lane at the starting line, and takes the current control for that lane in hand. One or both players chant, "Ready, set, go!" and start their cars racing down the track. Players have to change the speed of their cars continually in order to win the race. If you let your car go too fast, it will wipe out on a curve. If you play it cautiously, and make your car go too slowly, you will lose the race.

The first car to go around the track an agreed-upon number of laps and reach the finish line wins the game. If one car crashes, the survivor wins the race.

The appeal of this game is not only in the excitement of the race itself, but the frequently beautiful model cars that are available for it. The least expensive models are correspondingly plain, but more expensive ones may be replicas of famous racers or classic antiques, or intriguing space-age fantasies.

# NOK HOCKEY

*Two players*

*Nok Hockey set*

**OBJECT: To score the most points by knocking the puck through your opponent's goal hole**

The Nok Hockey playing area is a rectangular board with raised sides, about 4 feet long and 2½ feet wide. The goals are slit-shaped holes, one at each end of the board, protected by diamond-shaped blocks of wood positioned several inches in front of them. A round wooden puck and two miniature hockey sticks for hitting it, comes with the set. However, many Nok Hockey players prefer to use their thumbs in a twisting motion to propel the puck down the field with high velocity. To play thumbs only, your knuckles touch the board, your thumb sticks out straight like a hockey stick, and the motion is achieved by a quick twist of the wrist.

Each player takes his position at an end of the board. He will shoot for the goal at the opposite end. Put the puck in the center of the field, in the "face-off" circle. Select one player to go first. The first player shoots the puck from the face-off circle. From then on, players take turns attempting to propel the puck through the opposite goals. Unless a goal is made, each player shoots the puck in his turn from wherever it has come to rest on the board.

Players are not allowed to block shots, but since the diamond-shaped blocks of wood prevent any frontal attack on the goals, the only way you can make a goal is by ricocheting the puck off the sides of the board and through your opponent's goal at an angle.

You score a point when you shoot the puck through the opposing goal. After a goal, put the puck in the face-off circle. The player who did not score the last goal takes a shot, and the game proceeds as before.

Penalty shots are awarded when a player shoots the puck over the side of the board, blocks a shot, or jiggles the board. His opponent picks up the puck, puts it on top of the block of wood in front of the penalized player's goal, and from that vantage point shoots directly at the goal. The play resumes from the center if a goal was scored, or from the point where the puck stopped if no goal was made.

The first player to reach a predetermined number of points (usually eleven) wins the game.

## AIR HOCKEY

*Two players*

*Air Hockey set*

**OBJECT: To score the most points by knocking the puck into your opponent's goal**

The surface of an Air Hockey table (which is a bit smaller than a Pool table) is punctured with many tiny holes. An electric blower in the base of the table is turned on, and jets of air shooting out of the holes support the puck on a thin cushion of air, making its motion almost frictionless. At either end of the table are goal slits similar to those in Nok Hockey. A round plastic puck comes with each Air Hockey set, along with two plastic bumpers for hitting it.

The play in Air Hockey is breathtakingly fast. Select one player to start the action. He places the puck in front of his own goal, and, using his bumper, knocks the puck toward his opponent. Playing simultaneously, each player attempts to knock the puck into his opponent's goal while defending his own goal. The puck has almost no friction to slow it down, and it bounces off the sides of the table readily. This means that it can carom half a dozen times off the sides at high speeds and slip through your goal before you even realize it's headed your way. Therefore, many players adopt the strategy of letting an opponent hang himself—they play defensively close to their goal while waiting for one of their opponent's reckless shots to ricochet backwards into his own goal. This happens rather frequently in the game, and is an easy way to pick up points; when the puck flies into a player's goal his opponent scores the point, regardless of whose shot it was. The player who has just been scored against takes the puck out of his goal, puts it down in front of him, and hits it away. The game then continues as before.

If one player knocks the puck off the table, the other player picks it up, places it in front of his goal, and hits it into play.

The first player to reach a predetermined score (such as twenty-one) is the winner.

# DARTS

*Two or more players, twelve years or older*

*Dart board and darts*
*Pencil and paper*

**OBJECT: To get the most points by throwing the darts into high-scoring areas of the dart board**

The standard dart board is divided into six rings. The center ring is called the "inner bull's-eye," and the one just outside it is called the "outer bull's-eye." The third ring out, a wide one, is a "single-scoring ring," followed by a thin "triple-scoring ring." This is followed by another wide single-scoring ring, and finally the thin outermost "double-scoring ring." All the rings but the two bull's-eyes are subdivided into twenty wedge-shaped "sectors," each carrying a different point value. These values are printed along the rim of the board. Sometimes the reverse side of the dart board is a simple bull's-eye, and this pattern is better for beginners, or for relaxed play. The darts are heavy, and extremely sharp. They are dangerous, and should definitely never be played with by young children. Keep them out of reach when not in use. Play Darts only with responsible people, and in calm surroundings.

Hang the dart board on the wall, with the sector marked "20" on top. (To prevent holes in the wall, it might be good to mount the dart board first on a piece of plywood or pressboard.) Be sure the board is well away from doors, windows and hallways, in an end of the room through which people will not be passing.

With chalk, or another marker, mark a throwing line about 8 feet from the board.

To choose a throwing order for the contestants, each player throws a dart at the board. The one whose dart sticks into the board nearest the center goes first. Players take turns, each throwing three darts at the board in his turn. After each turn, calculate the score, record it, and give the darts to the next player in turn.

Only darts that stick in the board can score. Darts in the inner bull's-eye count fifty points, and in the outer bull's-eye, twenty-

*The front of a standard dart board.*

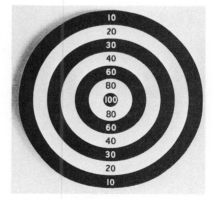

*The back of this one is a simple bull's-eye.*

# HOMEMADE DART BOARDS

Like many people, you may find the standard dart board requires more dart-throwing skill than you had bargained for. Unfortunately, simpler dart boards, such as the bull's-eye type, are not easily found.

To remedy this problem, it's easy to rig up a board to your personal specifications. Get a square of thick composition board, available at lumber yards. A cork-veneered bulletin board would also do. Get a large piece—at least two feet on a side—since darts have a tendency to miss smaller targets.

Nail the square up on a wall in the same way suggested for a standard dart board.

Then, using marking pens, draw your preferred target on a large piece of construction paper and tack it up on the board, or pen it on directly. You can draw a baseball diamond and try to run the bases, or draw a picture of a bull's head instead of a bull's-eye. The do-it-yourself design shown here looks suspiciously like those children's baby sister. The paper bull's-eyes sold in sports shops for B-B guns and archery make excellent targets too, and novel targets can be made from newspaper and magazine illustrations. When the target has been filled with holes, just replace it.

five. Darts in the different point rings score according to the sector they fall within. Points are doubled or tripled if the dart lands in one of the special thin rings. For example, if a dart lands in one of the wide, single-scoring rings and is within the sector marked "12," it scores just twelve points. But if the same dart had landed in the outer double-scoring ring, it would count for twenty-four points, and thirty-six points if it had landed in the triple-scoring ring.

Many Darts players use the rule that scoring can't begin until you have gotten a dart into the double-scoring ring. That throw and all subsequent throws are then scored.

Dart scores are traditionally deducted from a previously chosen number (usually 301 or 501), so that the first player to reach zero wins the game. Along with this custom comes the rule that you must reach zero exactly on your winning throw; if you make a throw which carries you below zero, the throw doesn't count and you lose your turn. Since this scoring method is an unnecessary complication, most people play darts informally in a straightforward manner: the scores you throw are totalled up from the start, and the player who reaches a selected number first is the winner.

*Around the Clock:* Here is another Darts game using the standard board. This one eliminates the necessity of keeping any score at all. Throwing three darts in a turn, each player tries to hit the numbered sectors in order from 1 to 20. The first player to hit them all in order and reach the 20 wins the game. An optional rule, which adds even more interest to the game, says that if a player hits the sector he was trying for with his last dart, he gets to go again.

# PING-PONG

*Two players, or four playing as partners*

*Ping-Pong table, balls and paddles*

**OBJECT: To score the most points by hitting the Ping-Pong ball onto the opponent's side of the table in such a way that he fails to hit it back correctly**

Ping-Pong tables are 9 feet long and 5 feet wide. A low net is stretched across the table, halfway down, and a white line divides the table in two lengthwise. Ping-Pong paddles are short-handled, made of lightweight wood. There should be one for each player. Ping-Pong balls have a way of getting lost or cracked rather easily, so it's a good idea to keep a stock of a dozen or so.

After choosing sides of the table, flip a coin to decide who will serve first. The game begins as the first server takes the Ping-Pong ball and hits it with his paddle so that it hits his side of the table, bounces over the net, and bounces on the other side of the table. His opponent, after waiting for the ball to bounce once, hits the ball back over the net. This continues, with the ball volleying back and forth over the net, until one player misses the ball, or hits it illegally. Then the ball is served again and the game resumes.

To return the ball legally, you must let it bounce once on your side of the table; then hit it with your paddle so that it flies over the net without hitting your side of the table, but does bounce on your opponent's side. If the ball brushes the net in going over, it is still legal; but if the ball hits your hand or a piece of your clothing, doesn't make it over the net, bounces on your own side after you have hit it, or overshoots the table so it fails to bounce on your opponent's side, your return was no good.

Every time your opponent fails to return the ball, or makes an error in service or volley, you score one point. The first player to score twenty-one points (or some other predetermined number) is the winner. However, if both you and your opponent reach twenty, you have to continue playing until one or the other wins by two points.

In the regulation game, the service switches sides every time five points have been scored. One way to keep track of this is to add the scores together after any point is made. When the total of the scores is a multiple of five, you know that it is time to trade service. For example: you are serving; you score a point, making the score thirteen to twelve. You add the scores together, getting twenty-five points, a multiple of 5. In informal games, it is easier just to let the player who is nearest the Ping-Pong ball after it has been missed serve the ball next.

The regulation doubles game, in which there are two players on each side of the table, is more complicated than the singles game. The rules governing to whom the ball goes and when, and who has the serve, are very confusing, and not especially vital to family play. You can do very well just playing the game like the singles version, letting partners alternate in their services.

### PUFF THE PING-PONG BALL

*Ping-Pong balls hold an endless fascination for kittens and young children. If your cat drives you to distraction batting the ball about, you can easily keep it in a box away from him. But children open boxes easily, even if the boxes are high up on shelves. One way around the irritating clickety-clack of a Ping-Pong ball ricocheting from walls and floor is to introduce your child to a silent game called Puff the Ping-Pong Ball. Place the ball on the floor, preferably on carpeting, Your child gets down on all fours and puffs at the ball to make it move. This will be enough for a while, but when the game gets stale, add obstacles like sneakers and books (perhaps they are already there) for him to blow the ball around or use as targets. Two children playing together can race their balls to a goal, with or without intervening obstacles.*

## WASTEBASKET TOSS

*Young children who love to throw, but are still a hazard to family and furniture when they do so, might settle for Wastebasket Toss. Place a wastebasket, carton or other large container in the middle of the room. Give the child crumpled paper balls, a sponge ball, or a beanbag. He can toss his missile from a certain distance to try to get it into the wastebasket; but more likely he will maneuver closer and closer to the target, like the boy in this photograph. He started at a distance all right, as the first picture was snapped. But by the last shot he had crept up on his target until he stood directly over it, and simply dropped his beanbag in. No matter. Children will make such games harder for themselves as their skills improve.*

# BUMPER POOL

*Two players*

*Bumper Pool table, balls and cues*

*OBJECT: To shoot all your balls into your opponent's pocket*

A Bumper Pool table measures about 3 to 4 feet on each side, and is felt-covered. At the center of each of two opposite ends is a pocket for the balls to bounce into. Unlike ordinary Pool, the Bumper Pool table sports eight or more rubber-covered knobs projecting from the board. Each pocket is flanked by a knob on each side, and the remaining ones are arranged in a pattern in the center of the table. These "bumpers" interfere with the motion of the balls, and make the game more unpredictable. Each player gets a cue stick and a set of five Bumper Pool balls. One of the two sets is white, the other red. Each set has four solid-color balls and a fifth which is marked with a single spot.

After selecting the ends of the table they'll be playing from, each player arranges his five balls from left to right along his end. (There are little marks on the table on which to position the balls.) The single spotted ball goes in the center of the line, just in front of the player's pocket.

Simultaneously, opponents take their sticks and, at a signal, hit the center spotted balls so that they carom off opposite sides and head toward the opposing pockets. The one whose ball comes closest to the opposing pocket, or goes in, gets the first shot. If the spotted balls both go into the pockets, or end up at exactly the same distance away, this procedure is repeated with one of the solid-colored balls.

After this first simultaneous shot, opponents take turns trying to shoot their balls into the opposing pocket. There is no cue ball in this game. You shoot your balls directly with the cue. However, you can't shoot any of your solid balls before you pocket your spotted one. After that, you may shoot your balls as you choose. You may shoot a ball in an attempt to get it into your opponent's pocket, to knock an opposing ball into an inconvenient corner, or to block your own pocket against your opponent. If you successfully pocket a ball, you get an extra turn. If your ball accidentally knocks your opponent's ball into either of the pockets, his ball stays there to his credit. If your ball flies off the table, or you accidentally knock your ball into your own pocket, you are penalized by having that ball placed in the center of the table within the pattern of bumpers. Getting it out can be difficult.

The first player to pocket all his balls is the winner.

## EIGHT-BALL POOL

*Two players*

*Pool table, balls and cues*

*OBJECT: To knock your balls into the pockets before your opponent, and then to pocket the 8-ball*

A Pool table is a very large felt-covered table with a raised rim. It is about twice as long as it is wide. In the four corners, and on the two long sides, are holes through which the balls drop; these are called the "pockets." One quarter of the table, called the "head string" area, is marked off with a line across it, while at the other end of the table is a dot called the "footspot."

Complete Pool equipment includes long sticks called "cues," often bought separately so their lengths correspond with the reach of each player, a large, white "cue ball" used for hitting the other balls into the pockets, and fifteen smaller balls numbered from 1 to 15. Balls #1 to #7 are in solid colors, balls #9 to #15 are striped, and the 8-ball is solid black. A triangular form is used to group the balls together at the start of the game.

Eight-ball, though it is not the standard form of Pool, is the one favored by most families. The rules are simple, there's no need to keep score, and there's just enough luck involved that even a poor player who has been losing all through the game can win at the very end.

Place the triangle onto the table and drop all the smaller balls into it. Position the 8-ball in the center. Swirl the triangle around a bit on the table to even up the balls, then position it so that the apex of the triangle sits on the footspot, pointing down the table toward the headstring line. Decide who will go first, and lift the triangle gently from the balls.

The first player puts the cue ball anywhere behind the headstring line. Using his cue stick, he jabs the cue ball in its center, propelling it into the triangle of numbered balls. This "breaks" the formation, and drives the balls in different directions. If, on his first turn, the player "pockets" one of the solid or striped balls by knocking it into one of the Pool table pockets, all the balls of

that type (solid or striped) become his group, and he shoots again. If he pockets two balls, one of each kind, he gets to choose which type he'll be shooting for, and then he goes again. If the first player fails to pocket any balls at all, he and his opponent take turns shooting until one or the other of them succeeds in pocketing a ball, thereby determining who gets which group.

After the break, the players take turns shooting the cue ball at balls in their own group, trying to knock them into the pockets. More than one ball can be knocked into the pocket in one shot, and you can use any combination of collisions between balls, or between balls and the table rim, that seem likely to help pocket a ball. If you successfully knock a ball into a pocket on one shot, you get to shoot again until you miss.

If you accidentally knock an opponent's ball into the pocket, it stays there and your turn ends. If you knock one of your own balls into a pocket at the same time, your opponent's ball stays there, but you are allowed to continue your turn. If you knock the 8-ball into a pocket at any time before you have pocketed all the balls of your group, you immediately lose the game. If you "scratch" the cue ball, by knocking it into one of the pockets, your turn ends; any balls you may have pocketed on that shot are taken out and placed on the footspot. If a ball flies off the table, it is put back on the footspot.

Ordinarily, after your opponent misses by failing to pocket one of his balls, you must shoot the cue ball from wherever it stopped at the end of his turn. However, if he scratches, or misses so badly that he fails to hit one of his own balls at all, or hits so weakly that neither his own ball nor the cue ball are propelled into the rim of the table, you are allowed to pick up the cue ball and put it anywhere you like on the headstring line.

### Endgame

When you have knocked all the balls of your group into the pockets, you must try to pocket the 8-ball. Before taking a shot at it, you must also announce which pocket you are aiming for. This is generally the most risky part of the game. You immediately win if you pocket the 8-ball, but you lose instantly if any of the following occurs:

You miss the 8-ball completely, or hit it without enough force to knock it or the cue ball into the rim.

You knock the 8-ball into a pocket other than the one you announced in advance.

You scratch the cue ball by knocking it into a pocket.

You hit one of your opponent's balls before you strike the 8-ball.

This really only leaves you two alternatives for your shots at the 8-ball: Either you must put the 8-ball into the pocket you have specified, or you must hit the 8-ball with enough force to push it or the cue ball into the rim without pocketing it. The player who first succeeds in pocketing the 8-ball is the winner, or a player automatically wins because the other has lost for any of the reasons listed above.

## ROULETTE

*Any number of players*

*Roulette wheel and betting cloth*
*Chips*

*OBJECT: To accumulate chips by successfully betting on which number a ball will settle on after a spin of the Roulette wheel*

Roulette wheels, available at many games departments, are mounted on ball bearings within round bowls, so that they spin freely. The perimeter of the wheel is divided into thirty-eight colored sec-

tions, each section corresponding with a little pocket in the wheel. The sections are numbered from 1 to 36 in no particular order, plus the two numerals 0 and 00. Except for zero, and double zero, which are green, the sections are alternately black and red. When the wheel is spinning, a little marble or ball bearing jumps randomly from pocket to pocket, finally settling in one pocket or another as the wheel slows down.

The betting cloth (or layout) has squares corresponding to all thirty-eight compartments of the Roulette wheel, plus extra boxes standing for number characteristics (odds, evens, blacks, reds, highs and lows) and other designations explained later. Chips of various denominations are used for placing bets on the betting cloth.

Roulette is a game the entire family can play at once, with only the "House" having a special advantage. Tremendous sums can be won or lost, hopes soar and then are dashed to the ground, the betting becomes fast and furious, tempers run short—then the chips are packed up, the set put away, and everyone cheerfully retires for supper.

Select one player to represent the "House." He has the duty of spinning the wheel, calling out the results, paying off, and raking in the bets. Since the House has an advantage of a little more than five percent on every bet on the table (and over seven percent on the five-number bet described later), it is only fair to let someone else win for a time after one player has been the House for a while. Let the player who has lost the most chips take the House's place. It's a good idea for the House to carry a pocket calculator to figure the payoffs.

To work the Roulette wheel, grasp the center knob and spin it rapidly counterclockwise. When the wheel is moving quickly, toss the marble into the works so that it travels around clockwise. As the clockwise moving marble and the counterclockwise moving wheel collide, the marble is tossed around wildly until it finally settles down in one of the numbered pockets.

You can make bets at any time before and during the time the wheel is spinning, but not after the marble has begun to settle down. Bets are made by putting one or more chips down on any of the squares on the betting cloth. The squares you pick carry different payoff odds. For example, if you put two chips in the layout square marked 20, which carries payoff odds of 1 to 35, you stand to win thirty-five times your bet—70 chips—if the little marble stops in compartment 20. If the wheel were to stop anywhere else, you would lose your two chips. You can have bets in any number of squares at the same time, or make no bets at all for a particular spin.

There are various kinds of bets you can make, various ways to place them, and various payoffs.

*Single-Number Bet:* Put a chip or chips in the center of one of the numbered squares of the layout including the 0 and 00 squares. In the photo, the chip on 3 is a single-number bet. If your number comes up, you win thirty-five times what you bet. Otherwise, you lose your wager.

*Two-Number Bet:* To bet that either of two adjacent numbers will come up, place your chip(s) on the vertical or horizontal line

separating them. This is the type of bet that the chip placed on the line between 8 and 11 is making. If either number comes up, you are paid seventeen times your wager.

*Three-Number Bet:* Place your chip(s) on the vertical line on the outside of a row of three, to bet that any of the numbers in the row will be the winner. This is the kind of bet the chip placed on the line on the outside of the row of 16, 17 and 18 is making. If any one of these three numbers wins, the payoff is eleven times the wager.

*Four-Number Bet:* Lay your wager on the intersection of the lines touching any four numbers. The chip placed at the intersection of the lines bordering 25, 26, 28 and 29 is making a four-number bet. When any one of these numbers wins, you are paid off at eight times your bet.

*Five-Number Bet:* Lay your chip(s) on the outside line of the row 1, 2, 3 where it is intersected by the line separating 0 and 00 from that row, as shown. This placement means you are betting that any one of the numbers in either the 0, 00 or the 1, 2, 3 row will win. This bet pays off at six times the wager. There is no other five-number bet possible.

*Six-Number Bet:* To bet that any of the numbers in two adjacent rows will win, put your chip(s) to the outside of the layout on the intersection between the outside line and the line that separates the two rows. In the illustration, the chip at the upper right on the cloth will win if any of the numbers in the rows 31, 32, 33 or 34, 35 or 36 is spun. The payoff is five times the bet.

*Column Bet:* Put your chip(s) on one of the blank spaces below a column to bet that any of the twelve numbers in that column will pay off. If one of the numbers comes up, you win double the amount you bet.

*Dozen Bet:* Heavier lines divide the numbered layout into three blocks of twelve squares each. Put a chip in one of the spaces marked 1st 12, 2nd 12 or 3rd 12 to bet that a number in the adjacent block of 12 numbers will win. The payoff is 2 to 1, the same as a column bet.

*Characteristic Bets:* The remaining spaces of the betting cloth all pay off 1 to 1, so that if you bet one chip, you stand to win only one additional chip. These squares are the "characteristic" squares marked 1-18 (Low), 19-36 (High), Even, Odd, Red, and Black. If you bet on one of these squares and the spin satisfies the specified characteristic, you win. Neither 0 nor 00 satisfies any of the characteristics, so the house always wins characteristic wagers when one or the other of the zeroes is spun.

After a spin, the House should first collect all the incorrect single-number bets, then the wrong characteristic bets and combination bets. After the board is cleared of "chaff," the House pays off the winning wagers.

## PACHINKO

*Any number of players*

*Pachinko machine*

*OBJECT: To keep your turn going for as long as possible by winning bonus balls*

Pachinko is an electric game that works something like a Pinball machine, but it hangs on the wall rather than resting on the floor. For this reason, Pachinko will fit into a small game room where there is no space for Pinball.

The face of the Pachinko machine is round, and filled with tiny brass pins, spinners, levers, and holes that reveal the game's interior, plus little plastic hoppers that open and close like the petals of a flower. Below the face is a long ramp, which emerges from the machine and then disappears back into the interior next to a shiny lever.

At the beginning of the game, you drop many dozens of small steel balls onto the ramp beneath the face. You flip the lever, which sends a ball flying up into the face. The ball then plummets downward, ricocheting off pins, hitting spinners and levers, which set bells ringing and lights flashing. If you are lucky, the ball will hit one of the bonus spinners, or fall into a hopper. In either case the machine will award you bonus balls, which roll out of the machine's interior onto the ramp. A bonus may be a modest number of balls, or a jackpot. If your ball does not hit a bonus spinner or a hopper, it simply vanishes into the machine's interior. Keep hitting the lever to send up balls one at a time, and hope you win a large jackpot. When you use up all your balls, reset the machine, retrieve the balls from the reservoir inside, and place them on the ramp. If other people are playing, it is the next player's turn. If you are playing alone, begin again.

# PINBALL

*One or more players*

*Pinball machine*

**OBJECT: To score the highest number of points**

The details of each Pinball game differ, but basically the design is a slightly tilted boxlike table surmounted by a scoring board. Bumpers, depressions, and sometimes thin wire triggers spread over the surface of the table respond to the touch of a steel ball as it rolls against or over them. The bumpers, depressions and triggers not only deflect the ball in its course down the table, but also relay an electric signal to the scoring board to give the player points, or extra balls. Buttons on the sides of the table control one or more pairs of flippers located toward the bottom of the slope. Left- and right-hand flippers are activated independently to flip the ball back uphill, prolonging its travels and increasing the number of points a player can score on each ball. Depending on the machine, players are supplied with from three to five balls for each turn.

To begin the game, turn the on-off switch to the On position. Pull the plunger on the right side of the Pinball machine to release one ball at a time. The ball shoots at high speed to the upper end of the table, to begin its travels down the slope and eventually out of sight through an opening into the interior of the table. As the ball rebounds off bumpers, settles momentarily into a depression, or touches a trigger, bells ring, lights flash, and a score is recorded on the scoreboard. As the ball nears the flippers at the bottom of the table, try to hit it with them to propel it uphill again. Once a ball slips past your flippers, it won't score any more, and drops out of play. Pull the plunger again to release another ball.

The electrical devices that lie in the path the ball is most likely to take score the lowest number of points. Devices toward the sides of the machine, where the ball is least likely to hit, score the highest number of points. Among these, a few may award you extra balls. And if your score goes over a certain limit, you are given a free game, with whatever number of balls your machine is equipped to deliver.

When a player has used his last ball, his game is over and his final score is displayed. On fancier machines, a player's game may be stopped prematurely by the only illegal move in Pinball: tilting the machine by jiggling it to influence the course of the ball. The scoreboard flashes "Tilt," and no more balls are delivered until the machine is started up again for the next game.

Players adept at using the flippers can prolong the game dramatically by keeping a single ball in play longer for high scoring, by getting extra balls to play, and, if the score is high

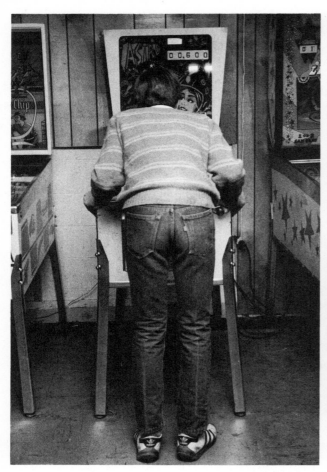

enough, by getting extra games. If more than one player is competing, take turns at the Pinball and keep track of your scores. The player with the highest score for a single game after a predetermined number of games is the winner. Or, you could keep score cumulatively, so that a player who wins an extra game has a special advantage. In this case, compare scores after a certain number of turns, rather than games, to take account of the fact that a player might win extra games in his turn.

*HOME PINBALLS*

*Pinball games, once found only in candy stores and amusement centers, are now available for the home. Since they are complicated electrical devices, they are expensive. Prices start at several hundred dollars, at stores that specialize in game room equipment.*

## VIDEO COMPUTER GAMES

*One, two or more players, depending on the game*

*Video game device*
*TV set*

*OBJECT: Each of the many games available has a different object*

Since the introduction of Odyssey by Magnavox in 1972, video games have proliferated, until now the number of different games you can play on your home TV set is enormous. Video game devices are self-contained in small boxes. To use them, follow the directions that come with the devices for attaching the game to

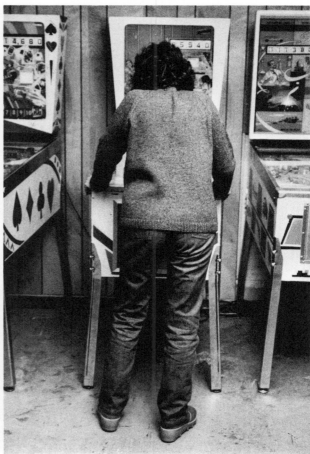

your television set's antenna leads. After this simple operation has been performed (a screwdriver is usually the only tool required) you need only switch your TV to a vacant channel, turn the game power switch to "on," and compete with the machine or another player in any one of many athletic events—without leaving the comfort of your armchair.

Video devices differ from one another in cost, in versatility, and in the selection of games and options they offer. Moreover, every year newer and often better games appear on the market. Some produce games in full color when hooked into color television sets, while others produce only black and white images. Look into all the possible video games in your price range before deciding which device suits you best.

A typical example of the basic, least expensive type of video game is the Apollo 2001 made by Enterprex. A similar game, TV Scoreboard, is sold by Radio Shack. Both feature four standard video games: Tennis, Hockey, Squash and Practice. Turn on both your TV set and the game box, switch the selector dial to Tennis, and a black and white diagram of a tennis court will appear on your screen. Dotted horizontal lines at the top and bottom of the screen delineate the sideline boundaries of the court, and a solid vertical line down the center of the screen represents the tennis net. Two short lines in either half of the court are the tennis rackets. They can be moved up and down by moving levers on either side of the game box.

Push the button marked "serve," and a white dot will shoot out from one side of the court. By manipulating the levers, you and your opponent can move your rackets so that they intercept the ball and hit it, to volley it back and forth over the net. The game is set up so that the ball bounces off the rackets at unpredictable angles, and rebounds if it hits one of the sides of the court. Electronic bleeps that coincide with any hit or rebound give the game a sense of action. Whenever you or your opponent miss the ball, it quietly exits off the screen. The screen then displays the score in large numerals, and serves the ball again. The game ends when the first player reaches fifteen points. (The device continues to serve the ball, but it passes right through the rackets.) Press "reset" to start a new game.

Controls on the unit allow you to change the speed, the size of the rackets, to make the serve after a miss automatic or manual, and to change the number of rebound angles. All of these adjustments can make the game harder or easier to match your skill. When you become proficient at Tennis, you can move on to Hockey, in which you and your opponent each have two "sticks" (lines)—a goalie and a forward—both controlled by the single lever. In Hockey, you try to get the skidding puck through small goals—a more difficult game, excitingly fast and action-packed. Or you might try Squash, in which each player alternately intercepts the ball and bounces it back off a single wall at the end of the court.

To practice your speed and accuracy when nobody else is around, turn the set to "Practice." This gives you one racket and a single wall against which the ball rebounds at each hit. The practice is similar to practicing tennis against a backboard, but the controls allow you to adjust the difficulty to a relaxing or challenging level.

## THE COMPUTERIZED GAME

There was a time, not long ago, when you couldn't play Tennis in your living room. Or Hockey. Or Basketball.

Now you can, using some of the incredible electronic simulation games which have hit the market. Not only can you play Tennis, but you can race a hot rod, score a touchdown, guide your tank through a minefield, shoot down enemy fighter planes, and, if you can afford a home computer, you can land your space vehicle lightly on the moon, or chase Klingons across the galaxy.

All this has turned the old family game room into simultaneous court, arena, field and galaxy. These games and many more—the list is proliferating rapidly—are computerized. The circuitry for video games is connected into your TV set—since it is small, it is also relatively simple. Home computers offer more complex circuitry for extraordinarily flexible and interesting games. But whether the circuitry is contained within a small control box, is inside a colorful child's toy, or is in a refrigerator-sized machine many miles from your home terminal, such games are all computers.

## Video Action, Indy 500

This device, made by Research Labs, Inc. offers Tennis and Hockey games similar to the basic ones, but these are in full color. Furthermore, they can be played by two people, by four people playing doubles (using the four control knobs in each corner of the device), or by one player against a "robot" racket or stick controlled by the device itself. After four or five volleys, the ball speed automatically increases.

The device's big feature, as its name makes clear, is a racing game that can be played by one or two players. When you start the racing game, a continuous stream of simulated hot rods zooms downward from the top of the screen. You and your opponent are each provided with a single car at the bottom of the screen. Your two cars move from side to side rather than up and down. The object of the game is to dodge the other cars by moving yours to the right and left. Since the other cars gradually speed up, this becomes increasingly difficult. When the inevitable collision occurs, the screen flashes, there is an exploding noise, and a point is scored against you. The onslaught then resumes. The game ends when one player loses by suffering nine collisions.

## Face-Off

This device, made by Executive Games, Inc., offers a Hockey game in black and white that is exceptional in several ways. Instead of a one-directional lever to push, or a knob to twist, each player is given a swivel-stick to control his single hockey player. By swiveling your stick in the direction you choose, you can make your man go anywhere on the field you wish, in contrast to the fixed up-and-down or side-to-side motion in other games. Furthermore, when the hockey puck hits your man, it doesn't rebound as in ordinary video games. Instead, the puck "sticks" to your player as if he were actually pushing it with a hockey stick. When you have the puck, you can "skate" your player over toward your opponent's goal. If your opponent catches on in time, and intercepts your man with his, the puck comes loose and flies away, bouncing wildly off the walls. When you are ready to shoot at your opponent's goal, push the firing button, and the puck will shoot away in the direction you were traveling when you hit the button. The 8-point games are automatically scored by the device, and bleeps accompany the action.

Face-Off also includes a Soccer game, but the ball can only be kicked, not carried. The difficulty of both games can be adjusted by changing ball size, stick size and game speed.

## Fairchild Video Entertainment System

The most advanced video game currently on the market is the Fairchild Video Entertainment System, made by the Fairchild Camera and Instrument Corp. Though this small device looks like a portable tape recorder, it is actually a sophisticated microcomputer, which offers a theoretically unlimited variety of games. Sets of four games each are pre-programmed on electronic cartridges that plug into the game console. When you get tired of one set of

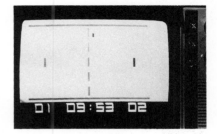

*Tennis*

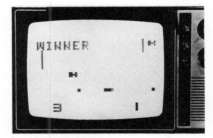

*Car Racing Game*

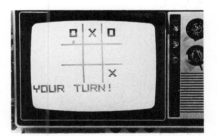

*Tic-Tac-Toe*

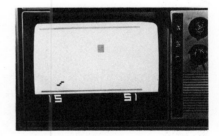

*Shooting Gallery*

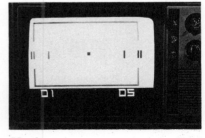

*Hockey*

271

games, pull out that cartridge and insert a different one. Fairchild already has several game cartridges on the market, and plans to continue producing new games regularly. This means that the system is not likely to grow stale.

The Fairchild offers the standard games of Hockey and Tennis in full color. However, these games are out of the ordinary in several respects. First, each player controls his men with a hand grip device attached to the game console by a long wire. The device, which looks something like a detonator, has a triangular knob at the top which can be moved backward, forward and from side to side, twisted, pushed in, and pulled out. Using these controls, you can move your men all over the field as well as control the rebound angle of the ball.

Furthermore, the games can be set up with a time limit of two, five or twenty minutes. At the end of the time limit, clocked digitally at the bottom of the screen, the player with the highest score wins. Special buttons allow you to freeze the action indefinitely while you take a break, and to adjust the difficulty of play.

Many other games are available on additional cartridges. One game, for example, allows you to play Tic-Tac-Toe against the machine. It takes the O's, you get the X's. After it makes a move it flashes YOUR TURN on the screen. When it wins (it usually does) it displays YOU LOSE TURKEY.

Other games, which are good for young children, are Doodle and Quadradoodle. These games allow you to make multi-colored doodles all over the screen of the set, still using the hand-held controls, but in different ways. And when you want to clear the screen and start another design, just push the plunger in.

*The Fairchild system hardware. Several cassettes are available, each programmed for a variety of games.*

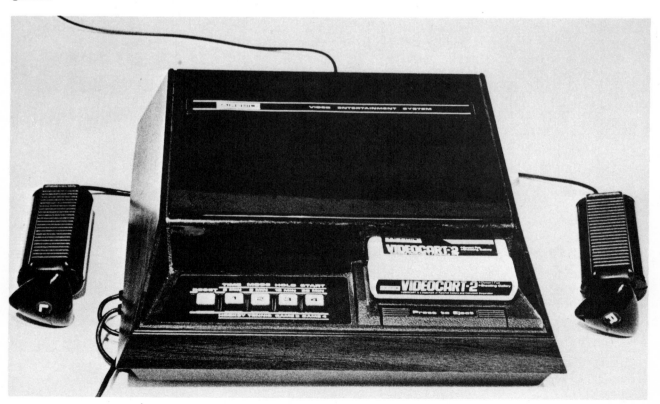

*A game of Desert Fox.*

A more advanced game (for adults) is Blackjack, which can be played against either the machine or another player. The machine gives you $500 to start, deals the cards, and asks for your bet (which you indicate by pressing buttons on the console). Cards are displayed on the screen, and the machine takes the role of the dealer, "hitting" you when you ask by giving you another card.

Shooting Gallery is a game in which "birds" fly diagonally across the screen. Your "rifle" is positioned in a corner. At the right moment, push down the plunger on your control to fire a shot. Every time you hit a bird, the machine racks up the score for you.

One of the most interesting games presently offered on a Fairchild cartridge is Desert Fox. In this game, the screen is set up to represent a battlefield spotted with land mines. You and your opponent control tanks that start out at opposite ends of the field. Your goal is to blow up your opponent's tank before he gets yours. Move your tank by pushing the knob on your control forward, backward, left or right, and rotate it by twisting the knob clockwise or counterclockwise. The tanks only fire shells in a fixed line, and the shells have only a limited range. Therefore, in order to blow up your opponent's tank, you must get within range of him, rotate so that your tank turret faces in his direction, and then push down the knob to lob a shell at him. Two safety zones in the corners can give your tank protection from enemy shells while you are firing.

Whenever a tank is blown up (whether it ran into a mine or got hit by a shell) it turns over on its side, the screen flashes, and the tank changes colors to simulate an explosion. Then, the tank recovers, and the game resumes. The game automatically scores the "destructions" of the two tanks.

## COMPUTER GAMES THAT TALK BACK

*One player*

*A responsive game playing computer*

*OBJECT: The object varies with the game*

Game equipment, whether a deck of cards or a football, is usually passive. The equipment itself doesn't compete against the players using it. When a game is played, it is either a match between breathing humans, or a match between a human and an agent of chance, as in Solitaire or Craps. With the exception of the Fairchild Video Entertainment System (which does actively compete at Tic-Tac-Toe and Blackjack), even the new computerized video games are passive. They may open up new ways to play, but the conflict is still between two human opponents, not between a human and a piece of hardware.

Lately, however, this picture has changed. Computer games are becoming increasingly active. Some are so animate that they've been given human names, and all respond, often quite conversationally, to the player. The introduction of the responsive games-playing computer has opened up a new and fascinating type of match: Man vs. Machine.

Most of the new computer games are only available to you if you have a home computer (page 277), or have access to a computer through a terminal at a local school or business. But a few small machines that will compete with you are now becoming available at toy and games departments, and more will follow.

### Simon

An example of this new class of computer games is made by Milton Bradley. SIMON is a musical memory game. The machine, which looks something like a flying saucer with four large colored panels on the top, gives you sequences of musical tones to memorize. One panel lights up with each note. After SIMON gives the sequence, you try to push the panels in the same sequence to reproduce the "tune." If you succeed, the machine moves on to a more difficult sequence; if you lose, it buzzes you. This can properly be classed as a game that sings.

### 2XL

A game which literally talks back is 2XL, manufactured by Mego. This game looks like a miniature robot and is equipped with several audio tapes. 2XL is designed as a children's quiz game: It makes jokes, giggles, and asks questions, which the child responds to by pushing one of four buttons in 2XL's chest. If the child answers correctly, 2XL commends him; if the answer is wrong, the child may get another try, or 2XL will explain the answer to him.

Other examples of computer games that compete with children are Auto Race, Football and Basketball, made by Mattel. These hand-held games look like pocket calculators, with small screens on which the action takes place. In Basketball, for example, move a little lever backward, forward and to the sides to move a small red dot (your man) under the basketball lines to make a shot. The computer defends the basket with its dots, and tries to interfere with your man's progress.

On a more sophisticated level—and therefore at considerably more expense—Chess- and Checkers-playing computer games are now available for the enthusiast who can seldom persuade another person to play with him for as long or as often as he wishes. These games, such as CHECKER CHALLENGER and CHESS CHALLENGER made by Fidelity Electronics, never get tired, never complain of being awakened at one o'clock in the morning for a match, and never get hung up on a move and keep you waiting. In short, they are the perfect opponents.

These devices feature a calculator-like keyboard, and a display screen built right into a regular Chess/Checker playing board. After moving your actual chessman or checker on the playing board, you tell the computer what your move was by pushing the keyboard buttons according to a simple numeric code

that corresponds to board positions. After thinking for a short time, the computer flashes its move on the screen (in numeric code), and you obligingly move his piece for him. These games recognize any incorrect or illegal moves you've made, and correct you. They can be set for beginner level, intermediate, or advanced. At the advanced level, they play a game that few people can easily beat. If you upset the Chess or Checkers pieces in any way, or you've taken a piece off the board and have forgotten where it belongs, you can request the computer to give you a run-down on the board.

## Boris

BORIS is a costly deluxe Chess-playing computer game manufactured by Applied Concepts, Inc. It comes in its own walnut case (which doubles as a box for the chess pieces and board), and it features a graphic display of the pieces on the screen, in addition to the standard numeric code. It keeps track of time, handles castling and en passant moves, and is programmed to display appropriate statements at disconcerting moments. It may pop up with a comment like, IS THIS A TRAP? or I EXPECTED THAT. CONGRATULATIONS is displayed if you win; CHECKMATE if you lose.

Several other features make BORIS an excellent way to play Chess. For example, if you're just learning the game, and are un-

sure of your next move, you can ask BORIS to suggest the best move for you. If BORIS is winning, and you can't stand to lose, you can exchange places, and let the machine have a taste of its own medicine. Furthermore, you can stop a game in the middle, rearrange the pieces as you like (both on the board and in BORIS's memory), and resume the game.

In short, you can do things in computer Chess that you'd never be able to get away with when playing with another person. And when you're alone, but feeling in need of some keen competition, the computerized Chess player is always ready for you.

## PROGRAMMABLE COMPUTER GAMES

*One or more players, depending on the game*

*Home computer, or access to a computer terminal*

*OBJECT: The object differs with each game*

If you have your own programmable home computer (available now for under $400), or if you can get access to a larger computer through a local school or business, you can play any of the dozens of computer games that programmers delight in inventing during their free time. These games are typically conversational, talking (or rather writing) to you in plain English. They can simulate everything from a space war to a danger-fraught hunt through a series of caves. Some of these games are extremely complicated, while others are so simple any child who can read can deal with them. In addition, once you are used to the computer, you can program your own games—limited only by your time, abilities and imagination.

The small home computer itself is a plain box, sometimes studded with a few flashing lights, and a typewriter-like terminal through which the computer sends messages and you type responses. The terminals used in schools and offices usually produce many yards of typed printout after a long game. Home terminals generally produce no printed output. Instead, the messages you type to the computer, and the results the computer sends back to you, appear on the screen of a television tube. Your communications with the computer continue until your "conversation" reaches the bottom of the screen. Then, when the screen is filled, the computer clears it, and you can continue the dialogue. Whatever is on the screen disappears when you turn the machine off.

How you get access to the games described below depends on the kind of computer you are using. If you are using a school or office terminal, the computer itself is usually remotely located and accessed by several users simultaneously via telephone connection. To get in touch with the computer, you will have to be shown how to dial the computer, link the phone up with the terminal, and "log on" by typing a string of code numbers. Once you're hooked up, there are various commands to give the computer in order to gain access to game programs it has stored in its memory, and have it ready those programs for play. After you understand which commands to give (they are usually brief and simple), you can play any game you want to. If you don't know the rules the computer will explain them.

If you have a home computer, you can purchase game programs you want inexpensively from the manufacturer, or from

*Some computers are programmed to draw pictures.*

his local distributor. Programs are the coded instructions that allow the computer to play the game. Ready-to-play programs come punched on paper tape for computers equipped with a tape reader, or on magnetic tape for those equipped with a cassette recorder. Several computer magazines also regularly publish programs for new games, and if you have the patience to do it, these can be typed into your own computer by hand, and stored in its memory unit just as games programs are stored in larger commercial computers.

After a game is loaded into your home computer, just start the program up (according to the instructions in your manual), and play the game. If you find the names of the games below confusing, it is because each is stored under a title no longer than six letters or digits.

## HNGMAN

This game is good for young children, and as a general introduction to computer games. It is a form of the time-tested pencil and paper game of Hangman. When you start the program, the computer first retrieves a word stored in its memory, and types something like EIGHT LETTERS _ _ _ _ _ _ _ _. WHAT IS YOUR GUESS?

Your job is to guess letters, one by one, by pressing the appropriate typewriter keys. After each guess, the computer tells you if you were right or wrong. If right, the computer prints out the dashes again, with the letters you guessed correctly filled in. If wrong, the computer types out the wrong letter to one side, and begins "hanging" you by drawing part of the little man in typewriter symbols. When you think you have the correct word, type it all in. If you beat the computer, it prints, DRAT. YOU BEAT ME. WANT TO PLAY AGAIN (YES OR NO)? When you lose, the computer prints out the correct word, hangs you completely, and writes, HA. HA. I WIN. DO YOU WANT TO PLAY AGAIN (YES OR NO)?

## WUMPUS

The next game you might try is "Hunt the Wumpus." In this game, you are put in an imaginary cave divided into a series of rooms connected to one another by tunnels. You are also given a quiver of arrows. By giving the computer certain commands (explained by the machine before the game begins), you can move into another room, or shoot an arrow. After you move from one room to another, the computer tells you where you are in this manner: YOU ARE IN ROOM 12. THERE ARE TUNNELS TO 9 14 20.

The purpose of the game is to wander through the cave complex in an attempt to track down and kill dangerous monsters called Wumpuses. Hazards lurk in the dark: pits to fall into, and giant bats that snatch you up and drop you in some unexplored portion of the caves. The computer lets you know the trouble you're in. When you are getting near your goal, the computer alerts you with I SMELL A WUMPUS! You may then fire an arrow into the room in which you suspect a Wumpus is lurking. If you are wrong, you may be gobbled up.

## LUNAR

Lunar Landing puts you in the pilot's seat of a spaceship landing on the moon. After giving you instructions, and wishing you luck, the computer sets up a landing situation. It tells you how many miles above the surface of the moon your ship is, gives your velocity, and prints the amount of rocket fuel you have left. Then the machine types THRUST?, waiting for you to tell it how many pounds of thrust to pour into the retro-rockets. After each response, the computer gives you a revised status report: your new altitude, velocity, and the quantity of fuel remaining.

The trick is to slow your craft down to zero miles per second just as it touches the lunar surface. This isn't easy. If you play cautiously, using your retro-rockets to slow you down for an easy descent, you'll run out of fuel long before you reach the surface, and go into a crash dive. If you try to conserve fuel, chances are that you won't reduce your speed in time. When you hit the surface at high velocity the computer prints out SPLAT! CONDOLENCES WILL BE SENT TO YOUR NEXT OF KIN.

After a few tries, this game becomes an obsession. Keep trying, it can be done!

*When you look closely at computer pictures, you can see that they are made of typewriter symbols.*

## TREK (TREK2, TREK3, STRTRK...)

This game and its variations come under many names. Many computer enthusiasts consider it to be the cream of computer games. It has spread so widely that few computers (even business computers usually used to handle billing) are without some version or other. Many versions of the game are so long that a home computer needs an extra-large memory to handle them. Be sure you get a version that is within your system's capabilities.

The rules of the game (they run about three feet) are very involved, but the game is well worth a little confusion in the beginning. Basically, you're given a simulated starship based on Star Trek's "Enterprise," which is placed in a broad galaxy of sixty-four quadrants. Scattered among those starry quadrants are enemy Klingons out to destroy the Enterprise and conquer the Federation. Your mission is to seek out and destroy the Klingons within a set number of Stardates, and before they destroy you.

The "command option" codes you're given include commands for short- and long-range sensor scans, commands which move the Enterprise within and between quadrants, and com-

mands which fire your two weapons—photon torpedoes and phasers.

When you encounter Klingons, fire your weapons, If you are lucky, the Klingon ships will all be destroyed. If not, the Klingons will fire back at the Enterprise, draining its shield energy, and possibly destroying it. In some versions of TREK, the Klingons move around and hide behind stars when they're at a disadvantage, or surround the Enterprise and try to destroy it when they've got the lead. In other versions, the Klingons are fixed in space.

When the Enterprise is low on energy, or some of its systems are damaged after an unusually hard fight with Klingons, try to locate one of the few Starbases scattered around the galaxy. When you locate one, limp to it, and try to dock. Once docked, the Enterprise is rejuvenated, and again in shape for battle; but if the Klingons catch the Enterprise in a weakened condition, things look bad for the Federation.

Other options allow you to use the Enterprise's "battle computer" to get damage reports, and to initiate the Enterprise's self-destruct sequence.

*A game of Trek can stretch out considerably. These children are playing at a local computer facility that serves several school districts.*

## THE GAME ROOM

*For those who don't have a game room, don't want one, or can't afford the extravagance, here is an alternative. Go out for games. Commercial game rooms are springing up in many areas. They tend to be small, lively, and not at all tinged with the hustling atmosphere of an amusement park. Game rooms offer a variety of Pinballs, Pachinko, Bumper Pool, Air Hockey, Electric Target Games, and others. A jaunt to a game room goes well with a stop for hamburgers, pizza or ice cream cones, and the cost for an hour or so of family play is reasonable.*

# Index